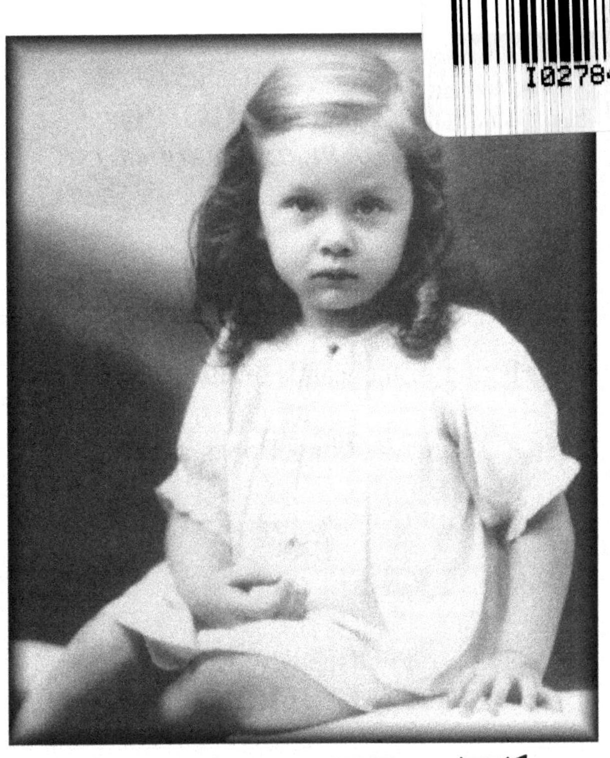

Growing Up The First Time

by

Mary Smith

HERITAGE BOOKS
2011

HERITAGE BOOKS
AN IMPRINT OF HERITAGE BOOKS, INC.

Books, CDs, and more—Worldwide

For our listing of thousands of titles see our website
at
www.HeritageBooks.com

Published 2011 by
HERITAGE BOOKS, INC.
Publishing Division
100 Railroad Ave. #104
Westminster, Maryland 21157

International Standard Book Numbers
Paperbound: 978-0-7884-5347-2
Clothbound: 978-0-7884-8857-3

This book is dedicated to Marilyn Serna Lyons.
Porterville, California *June 4, 2011*

Marilyn is the Dedicatee of *Growing Up The First Time*. She made friends with me twenty-two years ago, when her two small sons played in the park with my youngest granddaughter. It wasn't long before her sharp eye found The Big Red Book on my bookshelf, and when she saw it on the shelf she asked to take it home to read. I said: "Oh, I just wrote that book for my kids and grandchildren, so they'll know how our family came to be."

For the next twenty-two years Marilyn and I remained close friends, but she never missed a chance to try and get me to sell this book. In June of 2010, Marilyn and her husband, Stanley, both on summer break, stopped to see me. They are both very dear to me and after lunch, Marilyn said: "We've come to take your Big Red Book. I'll be your agent and I'll find a publisher for you." The "B.R.B" must have shivered when she looked at it in my bookcase. Pondering this bold announcement, it came to me that since it covered only the first fifteen years of my life, and that all of the people I'd written about were now quite dead and gone, it would not hurt any feelings if the "B.R.B" made an appearance. So, I said "Okay, but I only have my original manuscript, and I–um-ah-don't-want-um-eek-to lose it!"

Chapter 1

Pounding down the long darkened hallway, I dashed into the gloomy kitchen slamming the door behind me, and in the same motion tore open the refrigerator door and stood there, out of breath, in the pale illumination of that small frosty shine. It was quiet, the servants had left, and I sat on the wooden chair near the cook's work table and tried to wait patiently

The smell of dinner still lingered around the stove and I thought quickly about the anise pork with chestnuts the cook had made that night. It was one of my Grandpa's favorite dishes, and mine as well.

Earlier that day, I had gone into the kitchen and had told the amahs about an incident at school. When I'd arrived at the convent gate I found that someone had left a baby, all bundled up, on the path and I'd had to call the gardener to come and take it away. The amahs said,

"People think that where there are nuns, it must be an orphanage, and that's why poor people leave babies there."

I suppose I had been talking excitedly about abandoned babies to the servants, waving my arms around indignantly and clucking very melodramatically, when a face I had not seen before peeked around the door in surprise. The face belonged to a friend of cook's and she said,

"I did not know who was speaking and telling this story, and I am surprised that it is you, little Missy! It sounded like a Chinese girl talking."

The remark was enormously flattering to me and pleased me greatly because I knew that the Chinese were always astonished to find a foreigner, especially a child, speaking their language with ease and fluency, even though, in my case, when I had learned to speak it had been in the Shanghai dialect together with English and I was quite comfortable in both tongues, which was not particularly surprising for someone growing up in a Eurasian family.

Woolgathering made the time pass but not as quickly as I wished it would. Why didn't my Grandma call me? She'd said "only five minutes" but I knew she would stretch it out if she could and make it six minutes or more. There wasn't a clock in the kitchen, but the allotted time surely must have gone by since I'd thundered down the hall. When my Grandmother finally called out I thought perhaps I'd just stay in the kitchen and lie on the floor and pretend to be unconscious and give her a fright instead; but there were ants there sometimes and the darkness was not friendly, and I didn't want to stay a moment longer than I'd bargained for.

She called.

"Mary! Come out! Come out now!"

With one hand on the door knob and one foot stretched towards the refrigerator door, I simultaneously opened the one and slammed the other shut, and streaked back into the sitting room where Grandma sat on a large cretonne covered chair with my two brothers and sister piled all over her with their knees pulled up to their chins and their eyes wide with fear. At the door, I slowed down to a petulant saunter, gave my Grandmother what I considered a haughty look, and collected my fifty cent piece. The children studied me in awe.

I was eleven years old, and it was 1939 in Shanghai, China. It wasn't the first time that I felt that a large part of the reason for my existence, and that of my brothers and sister as well, was for my Grandmother's amusement. She had gathered us in the sitting room turned off the lights and told us the story of her supernatural experiences and visions which had converted her from a staunch member of the Church of England to a fanatical follower of the Roman Catholic faith. The performance was always given in the same quivery notes when it came to the parts where she'd seen the various apparitions and even though I'd heard these stories dozens of times I still couldn't help glancing over my shoulder and shuddering slightly. There was no such thing as not listening once she got started, and it only made one all the more frightened to try to stay in another room, out of earshot, because you'd know quite well what was going on and you almost knew exactly where she'd be in her account at that precise moment since Grandma had her story down by heart and could tell it without the tiniest variation, word for word, time after time.

Once, when we were all gathered around, huddling in delicious fear, I felt suddenly brave and bored, and just as she came to an especially ghastly point in the tale I put my fingers in my ears and made a loud growling howl to drown out what she was going to say. It never occurred to me that my action would have such a startling effect upon my brothers and my little sister, Annie, but this riveted captive audience sprang up shrieking and gibbering as though they had become one body in their terror, convinced that the primal sounds coming from me meant only one thing; that I was, at that moment, having my own metaphysical experience. Their unearthly screams in turn frightened me, and well gave our Grandmother such a start that she joined in the general confusion and panic.

Both my brother, Vincent, who was nine, and Jordie, who was seven, momentarily lost control of their bladders whilst trying to find a place on Grandma's ample bosom in which to hide their faces so as not to see the horror they were certain was now in the room, and Annie took a bite out of Grandma's left ear lobe. My sister was known to have closed her teeth around parts of whomever was near at hand whenever she was frightened, and, indeed, had inflicted a bite upon me at one time which had surely retarded the development of my meager breasts, or so I thought, when only one little nub appeared instead of the usual two as I reached my twelfth birthday. After several anxious weeks, during which I cast many suspicious and accusing looks at the small villainess, the other nub made itself known and I was overjoyed not to have to go through life as a uni-mammary oddity.

On the night of this latest story-telling session, I had not done anything untoward, and our Grandmother seemed disappointed that the performance was going to come to a lackluster end with the children yawning and snuggling over her. I don't believe we could ever have reached such a pinnacle of success again as that time before when her story had ended to the accompaniment of satanic shrieks and frantic scramblings, she keenly aware of a sharp pain in her ear lobe and a sense of warmly spreading dampness seeping through her stiff corset.

So, she had dared me. She dared me to go down the long dark hall and stay for five minutes in the kitchen with the light off. Grandma said that if I could do that she would give me fifty cents.

Fifty cents was her top bribe and was usually reserved for coercing any one of us into saying a rosary. She thought, mistakenly, that when she went out of the apartment she could keep us from doing mischief for at least as long as it took to say the rosary, which, if one does reverently and properly, would take approximately fifteen minutes.

"Grandma will give you fifty cents if you'll say a rosary when she leaves," Grandma would tell us, and we'd all whoop and jump up and down and say gleefully that we would. As soon as she'd gone we'd stand holding hands in a small circle and say,

"A ROSARY," and snap our heads down and laugh madly, running off to do whatever dreadful things we might have had in mind.

She would come back after a bit and ask each one of us if we'd said a rosary, and we'd have no difficulty whatsoever in looking her straight in the eye and lying.

"Yes!" we'd say emphatically, and there'd be fifty cents all around, Grandma perhaps none the wiser, but sometimes I think she knew of the deception and might have even enjoyed the game. To this day I wonder if she had been aware of my duplicity and known how I'd tried to outsmart her at having sat in the dark kitchen with the fridge door open. If nothing else, living with that lady proved to be a course in survival tinged with the flavor of the utter absurdity of so much on the human scene.

My Grandmother referred to us, my brothers and Annie and me, as "My Four Little Orphaned American Grandchildren." She would speak of us in this way with total strangers, in our presence, and we would stand there in front of them listening to their patronizing clucks and feeling like so many freaks in a side show. It always angered me to be pitied, and I did not want to have attention drawn to us for any reason. Almost everyone in Shanghai must know of our story, I thought, although I am sure that in that great wicked city where so many thousands of incredible lives were unfolding every minute, few would actually have paid much notice to the likes of us. However, for a number of years, if strangers glanced at me in even a mildly interested manner, I was certain that they knew who I was and had heard of how I had come to be.

In truth, we were not entirely orphans. My father, George C. Smith, had committed suicide, choosing to die by hurling himself from a high building in Hong Kong when I was eight years old. His death had made the headlines in the newspapers and my Grandmother had saved the clippings of the gory and explicit reportage and would read the account to me whenever she'd spend the day rummaging through her papers and files. I often wondered how they'd scooped up what was left of my father to bury properly, but when I asked her that she would look shocked and admonish me for my tasteless questions.

When I was ten, my mother, who was not quite thirty, delivered the Four of Us children to her parents and went away. I loved my mother with a combination of idolatry and intense passion and grieved constantly that we did not live with her. She had a wistful childlike charm and needed looking after as much as we did. Secure in the knowledge that the children would be fed and housed, she sailed off to Manila to seek her fortune, make a new marriage, have a little fun and perhaps someday be able to have us all together again. I don't believe that my mother intended to abandon us, but the effect was, nonetheless, quite the same.

My maternal Grandfather, Vincent Vizenzinovich, had been born in Ningpo in 1866 to an Austrian seaman and a Chinese lady from Soochow whose name was Mary (Song) Zih. Matteo Vizenzinovich had come from Ragusa Meleda near the town of Dubrovnik in what is now Yugoslavia. Matteo and Mary were married in the Catholic Church and had one son, Vincent who lived with his parents until his father's death sometime in the early 1880's, and had then lived with this mother in the Chinese sector of Shanghai until he married for the first time. Matteo and Mary

Vizenzinovich are buried in the old Pah Hsien Jao Cemetery in the former French Concession of Shanghai.

Vincent had been well educated in the finest schools in Shanghai and learned five languages quickly. He could speak, read and write English, French, Spanish, German and Mandarin, as well as several Chinese dialects. During the first years of his long career, Vincent retained his Austrian nationality even though he was in the diplomatic service of the Spanish Consulate General in Shanghai as Chancellor-Interpreter. He also sat as a Judge (or Assessor) in the International Mixed Court of Shanghai, sharing the bench with the Chinese judges who tried Dutch, Spanish and Chinese cases. As I remember my Grandmother's account of it, at the outbreak of World War I, Vincent was urged to seek and claim the protection of the government of Spain at the behest of the Spanish Ambassador in Peking who cabled Vincent that he would otherwise not be allowed to sit in a Chinese court as the Spanish Assessor unless he were a Spanish subject, China having declared herself at war with Austria in the general conflict. From then on, Vincent Vizenzinovich and his family held Spanish papers and travelled on Spanish passports. He retired in 1948, after having served for fifty years as the Chancellor in the Spanish Consulate in Shanghai.

When I came to know him, Grandpa had had a distinguished career, having been knighted by King Alfonso of Spain and by Queen Wilhelmina of Holland, and he held the titles of "Caballero de la Real Orden de Isabel la Catolica" and Knight (Ridder) of the Orange Nassau Order. He had also been decorated by President Yuan Shih Kai of China on October 16, 1915 with the Fifth Class of the Chia Ho Order. There were framed photographs of him in formal dress, wearing his medals and looking very proud and important. My Grandma, in her hey-day, liked to be addressed as "Lady Georgina" and had a dressing table set with this name emblazoned on the mirrors and brushes. Grandpa was a modest man and preferred to be called Mr. Vincent, which was easier to pronounce than Vizenzinovich.

Our Grandfather was of medium height, soft-spoken and had impeccable manners. He wore his silver hair neatly trimmed, kept a small brush of a mustache, and carried himself with a quiet dignity. His skin had become mottled and there were brown patches all over his face and hands, and I used to sit in his lap and trace the markings with my finger and pretend that there were maps on his face and make up names for all the places, and he would laugh and call me his "Chick-a-biddy-chum" and rub his whiskers against my cheek which he called giving me a "cock-a-doodle-do."

Vincent had built several mansions in his lifetime and I lived for a time in the last two of them. When the war broke out in 1937 in Shanghai he had been forced to leave the Moorish manor he'd built on Hungjao Road in the countryside and he and my Grandmother moved to the apartment in the I.S.S. Building on Avenue Joffre where we now made our home with them.

The house on Hungjao Road had been filled with elegant and expensive furnishings, most of the beautiful things having been sold or given away, and only the essentials were brought to the small apartment. Crammed into the two main rooms were the dining room set, the cretonne-covered sofa and arm chairs, the piano, several beds, bureaus, boxes of books and papers, a life-sized statue of Christ the King in plaster of Paris holding a scepter, the Infant Jesus of Prague with silken robes which were sent regularly to the cleaners, a bronze figure of Our Lady of Lourdes with Saint Bernadette, an uncannily life-like bust of Jesus Christ entitled "ecce Homo" showing Him with a crown of thorns, Eyes raised to Heaven in agony and with His Blood dripping in rivulets down His Face; a very large painting in a heavy gilt frame of Saint Michael the Archangel on a stamping horse, spearing an ugly demon; another painting of Saint Paul with a book in one hand and a wicked looking sword in the other. St. Paul, with his piercing, avenging gaze, was the first thing I would see upon waking in the morning, and long after we'd left my Grandpa's home and awoke in so many different rooms in strange places, the image of that angry face of St. Paul was still the first vision my mind's eye had upon coming back into consciousness.

The apartment, on the third floor, had three main rooms, a box-room, a bath and the kitchen, a floor plan which included many angles and the long dark hallway I mentioned. The three main rooms were built side by side; the first one was occupied by my Auntie Ida, my mother's only sister who had not married at that time; the middle room served as living and dining room for our family, and the third room, connected to the bath which also opened to the hall by a second door, was the largest and held a bed for my brothers, a bed for Annie and me, and a double bed for Grandma. Our Grandpa slept in the sitting room on a couch which was made up each night with his high stiff horse-hair pillows and many blankets because he got so cold. Sometimes one of us kids would sleep with him to keep him warm and he would lie so still, sedate even in his sleep.

It was not always easy to sleep when Grandma felt compelled to play the piano which she would do far into the night. She used the piano as an instrument with which to exorcise the demons who possessed her every so often and she would play with a ferocity and an exquisite savagery disregarding the hour and oblivious to those around her who tried to rest.

"Go to sleep Jordie," Grandpa would moan periodically, but she would play on with increasing frenzy, filling the night air with crashing crescendos and splintering chords. Quite early on we learned to sleep through the screams of sirens as fire trucks and ambulances roared around the city during the war.

On very hot nights when the Shanghai summers were oppressive with humidity and the hum of giant mosquitoes buzzed relentlessly my Grandmother would run cold water in the bath tub and soak herself for hours. I'd lie in bed with my sister beside me, thinking of how Grandma would be turning into a great wrinkled prune, and wondering what she would do when she emerged from the water. There were several hobbies she pursued when all of us had gone to bed. Sometimes she went into the kitchen and made terrible slapping sounds with her slipper in one hand, killing ants with a vengeance, her clatter punctuated by my Grandpa's plaintive cry of,

"Go to sleep, Georgina!"

But she knew they were in there, a constant enemy, silent, busy and voracious, and she'd follow tidy columns of "Pharoah's Gifts" as she called the species who visited our apartment on their nocturnal wanderings, through the cupboards, up the walls, into the floorboards, behind the stove, everywhere, slapping and stamping, toppling the stacks of pots and pans, sweeping aside the plates and bowls until she was satisfied that she had stopped the ant parade for that night. Grandma thought of the ants as her own personal tormentors put on earth for the sole purpose of driving her mad. We had a Flit gun somewhere but it did not give the same satisfaction as the killing-by-hand method she preferred. (I went to visit her grave a while ago and had some flowers to put in to the container by her headstone only to find that when I picked the container out of the grass, a flurry of ants was building a nest in it. The horror of seeing them was unequalled in my memory of things that had caused my flesh to creep and I ran to the caretaker and asked him to look to it at once. I am certain that he thought I was unduly concerned over a few ants and I did not stop to tell him about my Grandmother and the red ants in Shanghai over thirty years ago.)

Turning over in my sleep, I'd become aware that the covers were stuck and that someone was sitting on the edge of my bed. I'd look up over the sheet and say,

"Oh, Grandma. What is it?"

She'd be sitting there, searching my face, with her hand in my long hair and her eyes full of tears. She would slip her arm under my shoulders and bring my face up to her warm neck and rock me back and forth.

"You look just like him."

You could have been mine.

You could have been mine.

You know, you should have been mine.

You know that, don't you, Mary my little darling?"

"Yes," I'd say. "Yes, Grandma, I know." Sleepily.

"Wouldn't you rather be mine?

My very own?

Look, your mother went off and left you.

Didn't even want you.

I want you.

You couldn't have had a better mother than I."

I'd put my arms around her and pat her with my small hands and say, "Yes, I know. I'm as good as yours now."

"It's not the same! You could have been MINE!

I loved him and he belonged to me, but Louise took him away, and now look she doesn't even want you.

And you look just like him."

And I thought dreamily of Louise in Manila and wondered if she would ever make her fortune, or marry again, or have any fun, or remember me.

"You have to make allowances for her," Grandpa said quietly.

He'd put on his hat and taken me for a walk in the smoky Autumn evening and I kicked at the leaves in our path to show him that I was still angry.

"She threw a cup at my head this morning and it would have smashed in my face if the amah had not pulled my braid to get me out of the way!" I told him furiously. He smiled and tucked my hand into his arm. I knew she had thrown things at him too and that he was remembering some of the precious objects she had broken in her fits of temper.

"Why did you ever marry her? Why?" I cried.

"She was very beautiful, you know. Very."

I knew that. I'd seen hundreds of pictures of Grandma as a young woman and she'd told me often enough of how everyone in Shanghai had considered her a "great beauty." She kept a large framed photograph of herself, taken in Paris, wearing a long flowing rose-colored silk dress and all the jewelry my Grandfather had given her. She had had many dozens of copies of this photo made so that there would never be a shortage of that bye gone view of herself taken on the European trip she had made with Grandpa in 1911. They had made the grand tour, leaving their two small daughters in the keeping of her parents and had seen the sights of the continent together as a second honeymoon. Vincent had prospered beyond all his expectations and wanted to enjoy the world he'd only read about until then. His wife, young and restless, needed a diversion and a little extra time to recover from a sad affair of the heart she had recently suffered. Georgina had not been the soul of discretion and had fallen in love with her German doctor shortly after the birth of her second child. Vincent, with his characteristic uxoriousness, had ridden out the scandal, said little, and then had proposed the trip both as a consolation prize to this wife and a celebration at having her to himself again.

The Paris portrait stood on our piano in an ornate silver frame and it showed a cool self-possessed and lovely personage in the full summer of her days.

"Well, she isn't beautiful to me," I grumbled to my Grandfather, "and she is just a cruel old witch who has to have her own way about everything, and I hate her."

"You only hurt yourself when you hate," he said. "Learn to make allowances. Others are not as strong as you, and allowances must be made or you will find life too hard."

It was hard enough as it was, I thought sulkily. And all over a pair of bloomers. The convent I attended required that the girls wear blue serge skirts, white blouses, blue ties, long black stockings and black shoes. There was not one word about bloomers! My Grandmother insisted that I wear them over my regular pants and each morning that she got out of bed before I could sneak off to school she would inspect me, roughly flinging up my skirt to see that the bloomers were on and that the long legged part of this hated garment came well over my knees. When I was younger I had borne this indignity with a resigned air, but as I grew older I became increasingly irritated until I finally showed a rebellious face about her arbitrary rule and put up a fight.

"Why?" I asked in my whining voice, a tone reserved for when I wanted to especially annoy her.

"Don't whine," she snapped. "Just wear them!"

"But they're ugly and I hate myself in them."

"It's cold," she said.

"But I've got long black woolen stockings on and they keep me warm enough. And besides, I'm wearing a woolen singlet, a red hug-me-tight and a belly band!" whining. "The nuns don't ask me to wear black bloomers."

"Well, I do."

"But WHY?" You've never given me a good reason," I squeaked.

She was sitting at the dining table having a cup of tea; Cambric Tea she called it because it was very sweet and had cream in it. My Grandmother held the cup daintily and pursed her mouth as she addressed the rim and sipped it just a bit too noisily to be lady-like. I could see her mind working like a pot of water on the stove, coming to a boil, just before the bubbles start. She set the cup down with a small determined gesture and said,

"If you happen to be going up a flight of stairs and a man happens to be on the lower landing, I don't want him to be able to look up and see anything."

I was appalled at the prospect of such a disgusting encounter, but for the first time I realized that perhaps I was about to become something or someone who might attract that kind of lewd attention and that my Grandma had noticed that I might turn into a butterfly after all. The bloomer-cocoon was meant to put off the inevitable for as long as was humanly possible.

Dropping the whine from my voice, I said acidly, "Well, if a man does look up and sees under my skirt, if he's never seen it before maybe he won't know what it is!"

And that is when she had thrown the cup at my head. Grandpa had not laughed when she'd told him what a truly revolting remark I'd made, but I think we went for a walk because he was having a hard time trying not to laugh in front of her.

"Let's ride the tram for a bit," he said.

We lived at the end of the line so there was always an empty seat at the beginning of the ride. The tram had two long benches below the windows on either side and when the seats were filled new passengers had to stand in the center aisle and hang on the straps. My Grandfather was a courtly gentleman and would rise to give a lady passenger his seat when there were none left. Then, as other ladies got on he would give me a special look and an almost imperceptible squeeze of his eye-lids and I would also rise and give a lady my seat. He said I need not tip my hat as he did because I was, after all, a girl. Once I asked him,

"When will I be able to stay in my seat and not have to get up and let another lady sit down? How old do I have to be, Grandpa?"

"You may keep your seat, Mary, when you can sit on the tram bench with your back against the window and with both of your feet on the floor. As long as you have two feet dangling there to kick other people in their shins as they stand in front of you, it is only right that you get up, put your feet on the floor and let the lady have your place," he told me.

The absolute logic and fairness of his reasoning made a lasting impression on me and there have been many landmarks along the way which told me that in this or that fashion I had finally passed from childhood, but none so soul-satisfying as that memorable morning when I got on the tram, sat with my back to the window and felt both of my feet touch the floor. There were chairs at home and at school in which I could sit and accomplish this but none of them was the measure of the bench on the tram in the first-class section, and I knew my place, at least there, and I kept it until it was time for me to get off at my stop.

Chapter 2

My favorite books were those written by Mazo de la Roche, Author of that sudsy saga The Whiteoaks of Jalna. The thing I loved the best about these books was that in the front of most of them I would find a diagram of the family tree with the names and dates of each character making all the relationships quite clear. I considered genealogy, pedigree, lineage and circumstance of birth to be of the utmost importance, and one day I made a diagram of my own.

It settled the matter for me and even made sense in its own peculiar way.

There was never a time when I did not know my Grandmother's story about her marriage to my Grandpa Vincent. She liked to tell me about "the olden days" and how he had come to court her when she was but a girl of nineteen and he a middle-aged man of forty. Vincent had been married before to a woman named Louisa Rego, of Chinese and Portuguese parentage, who had died. They had had a daughter whose name was Mary Catherine, and I know this because I found her name in Grandpa's prayer book listed among others who had died and in his fine hand he had written her age as "one and a half years old." All I ever heard about Louisa Rego was that she had been an avid collector of Chinese objets d'art and their home overflowed in pieces of carved ivory, embroidered silk scrolls and screens, jade lamps, cloisonné plates and bowls, and many exquisite and priceless antiquities.

It intrigued me so very much to think of my dear old Grandpa having a wife before he'd married our Grandma, and the thought of it lent him an air of mystery. I asked him about Louisa Rego once, but he just smiled and said,

"That was so long ago," and he looked bemused and sad.

A widower at forty, at the height of his career, the owner of a spacious Victorian-cum-Oriental mansion he had built on Kiangwan Road, Vincent had great need of a wife to entertain for him; a woman who was gracious, hospitable and charming, lively and beauteous to look upon as well. A friend had introduced him to Georgina, the eldest daughter of an erstwhile publisher named

Frank Ferris who had been the founder of the largest Chinese circulating newspaper in the whole of China. It was called the Sing Wan Pao, but due to inept management, Mr. Ferris had lost this business to a scurrilous partner and had a difficult time providing for his large family. The Ferris family was also Eurasian, being a mixture of English and Chinese, and their many children were very handsome and spirited.

Georgina took great pride in her English heritage and played down the Chinese ancestry while never really denying it. Each of her parents had had a full-blooded English father and a "pure" Chinese mother. Her father, Frank Ferris, born in Shanghai in 1862, was the only son of Captain William Ferris, an English-Welsh Master Mariner, and a Chinese woman named Rose (no last name is known for her), who came from Ningpo as it is shown on Frank Ferris' birth certificate. William Ferris is buried in the Pootung Cemetery in Shanghai. Frank Ferris was sent to school in London from 1877 to about 1882, at which time he returned to Shanghai.

Georgina's mother, Nellie Hooper, born in Shanghai in 1861, was the sole issue of one James Hooper, an English merchant and a Chinese mother from Chusan Island whom Nellie never knew. In those early days, children of mixed parentage were often abandoned to the care of missionaries, and Nellie, with her fair hair and light eyes, was considered a bit of an oddity. Mr. Hooper had recognized her as his own and she eventually bore his name. In 1875 she was sent by her missionary foster parents to the Western Female Seminary in Boston, Massachusetts, where she studied for five years. In 1880 she returned to Shanghai, and on March 16, 1885 she was married to Frank Ferris. Frank and Nellie Ferris died in the 1930's and are both buried in the Hungjao Cemetery. James Hooper, Nellie's father died in Hong Kong on March 7, 1868 at age sixty-five. This information is written on the back of his photograph, and in Nellie's handwriting one can read the words, "Darling Papa." She had not known her father well, but he had acknowledged her and she loved him for that.

There was a great to-do made about the fractions of the admixtures of European and Asian blood in our veins and the importance given to it interested me although I did not understand why I was admonished not to mention the fact that I was Eurasian, especially to strangers and foreigners. I was told there was no need to let on about that "since you are fair and can pass." It is a great loss to me that neither my Grandparents nor my mother ever were able to sit down and write a short family history so that we who come after will have a broader knowledge of our origins, and a clear picture of what life was in the early bustling days of old Shanghai. My mother started to write about her young life at one time, but she never finished it, and I have often wished that she had.

Mr. Vincent pressed on with his courtship of Georgina Ferris, giving her a number of beautiful jewels which she still had when I came to know them; but she protested throughout the length of his pursuit that she did not love him. She would tell me, with a pout,

"I didn't like it when he kissed me. His ways were so Chinese, and I am an English woman."

In her words, "I resisted. He persisted."

This line was always delivered with one fist clenched upon her breast and the other hand stretched out in a pleading attitude, head cocked slightly to one side and eyes lowered in typical Bernhardt character. And then, the punch line!

"Love me little, but love me long!" Vincent had said.

And that is precisely what Georgina Ferris did for well over fifty years.

There is a picture of their wedding which I still have showing Vincent and Georgina seated in the front row surrounded by her family, and some of her father's friends. Her father sits on her right wearing a bewildered expression, his curly hair combed from the middle of his fine forehead and his blond mustache drooping over slightly parted lips. Her mother, sitting to the left of Vincent, is impassive and vaguely uninterested. Georgina's six younger sisters and two brothers are grouped around, all dressed in carefully tailored finery, the girls wearing large flouncy decorated hats in the latest fashion of 1906. I heard once, from an aunt, that all of their dresses had been made from bolts of silk which

Vincent's first wife had hoarded in his attic, and Louisa Rego's acquisitive presence is felt in this stiffly posed photograph.

Vincent sits with his gloved hands held in his lap, looking very much at home in formal clothes cut in the post-Victorian style. He has an unmistakably Oriental face and wears a confident, anticipatory air. He had chosen Georgina Ferris, and had stubbornly refused to take "No" for an answer; and for all that happened in their years together, he had meant it when he promised to take her for better or for worse.

And she, sitting there beside him, holding a bouquet of white carnations and fern, in the lovely traditional white bridal gown with its flowing veil, what might she have been thinking? The face she showed in her wedding picture was grave and joyless, resigned and wondering, and she leans away from her new husband ever so deftly. Perhaps their knees are touching beneath her long skirt as they sit beside one another. I never saw them hug or give each other even the lightest loving pat while I lived under their roof, but I often saw a wanting look in my Grandfather's eyes when he spoke to her, although it was never mirrored in her own.

"How could you marry him if you didn't love him?"

And she would say with a sigh, "Mary, when a man wants you there is really nothing you can do about it."

I believed her, and I knew what a high price some men paid for getting what they wanted. Her tolerant husband paid willingly, and dearly, and the price rose steadily as the years came and went.

Georgina had two miscarriages and then gave birth in 1908 to a daughter whom they named Louise. She had soft brown hair and a creamy complexion and Georgina rejoiced that she had not had a child with coarse black hair and Chinese features. Louise was pampered and lovingly cosseted and shown off and dressed up and photographed endlessly, but nevertheless developed into a shy, quiet little girl with a gentle voice and liquid movements.

Her father doted on her and there are pictures of the lovely baby posing prettily among her French dolls with porcelain heads and hands, dressed in delicate costumes, some even with necklaces and earrings, and unless you look closely it might be difficult to tell which one is the little human being in the group. It is possible Louise may have grown up thinking that she was indeed a doll, a plaything, an ornament, a prized possession. A self-concept such as this is an insurmountable burden carried into one's middle age when the ravages of time and the force of gravity exact their inevitable toll.

A second daughter and last child, Ida Vizenzinovich was born in 1910. She idolized her older sister and although she was possessed of a much more aggressive nature, she grew up mainly in the reflected light of Louise's glory and beauty. In the long run, Fate was kinder to Ida than she was to Louise, but the two little girls played together, learned to dance and gave recitals on the violin and the cello. They went for rides in their Papa's carriage sitting next to their resplendent mother, they summered at fashionable spas on the China coast, and they helped each other define themselves.

Georgina's life in the house on Kiangwan Road, known as number One Park Villa, was glamorous and stimulating in a superficial way. Afforded every luxury, surrounded by comforts and a battalion of servants, she held court in the highest Shanghai society, giving the most sumptuous feasts with entertainments, garden parties under awnings in the park-like atmosphere of their spacious grounds, hosting teas for ladies of similar consequence and organizing charity fund-raising soirees which were reported in the North China Daily News in every detail.

Grandma had saved each scrap of newsprint which carried her name and she and I would sift through the mounds of old clippings on rainy days when I didn't mind, and on lots of sunny days when I did. One account dated May 18, 1915, told of a charity fete at Park Villa and its "unqualified success." It went on to say that "The grounds were transformed into a miniature fairyland of green bowers, and at night by the glow of hundreds of colored lights under the direction of Mr. C.E. Mencarini of the International Banking Corp." The Carlton Orchestra and the Philharmonica Portugueza provided the music for the entertainments and Ida and

Louise came down and danced for the guests. Their specialty was the Hesitation Waltz. "These young ladies, pupils of Professor Montes, performed the tango and one-step, the fox trot and the hesitation waltz, one (Louise) wearing male costume and acting the part of the man most becomingly." So vividly did my Grandmother describe these occasions to me that I almost felt I could breathe the air of that rarefied atmosphere and see the colored buntings and flags, the twinkling lanterns strung all over the garden, the outdoor dance floor, and Louise doing the tango with Ida, both smiling shyly, on display for a good cause.

Of all the past glories of my grandparents' lives, I knew very little at first hand. When I was six years old Louise brought us children back to Shanghai for a prolonged visit. We had been living in Hong Kong with her and our father in a weak facsimile of family life, and she having no way to support us on her own had taken us to her parents while she was in the process of divorcing Smith.

The divorce was violently opposed by my Grandmother who had developed religious scruples about the sanctity of marriage in the past few years, and she and Louise had countless bloodlettings over the subject. This must have been when I first became conscious of the tension between my mother and grandmother as the awareness of their rivalry over Smith dawned upon me.

They would go from room to room, up and down the stairs, shouting accusations and curses at one another, oftentimes coming to blows, Louise returning a slap in the face by her mother at one point, the performance climaxing in anguished screams and storms of scalding tears. They banged doors and threw things at each other and mother called daughter vile names, listing each of the transgressions Louise had committed, underscoring her recital with words such as "depraved" and "corrupt" and "degenerate." I heard those words a great many times and had an inkling of what they meant long before I ever searched them out in the dictionary.

Georgina attacked. Louise defended. But my mother was no match for her mother, even though Louise had married George Smith who had been Georgina's lover for several years before he had spirited Louise away. There doesn't seem to have been a reasonable explanation of how that wedding had actually come about, and I was to hear conflicting versions of the story. When I came to understand the situation, it might have occurred to me, cynical child that I probably was, that Smith, seeing his lucrative affair with the Lady Georgina guttering out, and knowing that their liaison was not going to end in her divorcing Mr. Vincent and attaining a sizable settlement of property, had turned his attentions to Georgina's daughter, Louise, with no appreciable difficulty. The fortune hunter found the ladies from Shanghai easy prey, but perhaps it was they who had ensnared him, and the hunter became the quarry, as often happens in life.

The garden parties and galas had palled on Lady Georgina, and soon after Louise turned nine years old her Mama went to Whiteaway Laidlaw's, a ladies clothing shop in Shanghai (which would have made I. Magnin's look like Filene's basement on bargain day), and bought herself a marvelously dramatic wardrobe, complete with veiled hats, tasseled gowns, jet-embroidered jackets, capes and several kinds of furs. She then had the bulk of the curio collection my Grandfather owned meticulously crated, and with her small daughter, Louise in tow, sailed to America on a luxurious ocean liner, the object of this voyage being to lecture on the Chinese art she had, in large part, inherited from Vincent's first wife, and Louise was to be a most important cog in the machinery of her mother's demonstrations. As Georgina would come to each individual piece of silk embroidery, it was to be Louise's job to unroll the lovely work in front of the audience, and then later to roll it up again. Louise found it boring.

The tour proved to be highly successful in terms of the numbers of ladies' clubs who wished to be entertained by Georgina and her Chinese collection, but there was no money to be made in such an endeavor, and instead the project cost Vincent Vizenzinovich a staggering sum to finance the travelling costs and the hotel bills that his wife and daughter incurred. Vincent might have thought it was all a harmless, if expensive, adventure which kept Georgina absorbed and occupied, and since he could not leave his work for so extended a period of time, saw in it nothing more than a beneficial change of scene and an amusement for his wife who had become increasingly bored and irritable at home in Shanghai with what she thought to be a stultifying life.

It was more than a change of scenery that Georgina craved, and she found it in the dazzling person of one Mr. George Channing Smith, an American born in Baltimore, Md. of a middle-class family. Smith was eight years Georgina's junior; tall, blue-eyed and with a mass of curly blond hair, he had a high forehead and a direct gaze, a showy manner, and a disarming smile. He dressed in the style of a matinee idol, affecting spats and gray doe-skin gloves, and carried a walking stick which sported a gold knob on the handle. They met in San Francisco shortly after Louise and Georgina had arrived in America, and if Smith had been studiedly waiting for his ship to come in, he waited no longer when he set eyes on the fascinating Eurasian lady who swept into the hotel lobby with sixteen steamer trunks in her wake, and a small silent girl by the hand.

Vincent Vizenzinovich knew of Mr. Channing-Smith, as Georgina liked to introduce him. Shanghai was a city which battened on gossip, and this was gossip of the most delectable variety; but Vincent kept his head, said nothing and paid the bills flooding across his desk from America.

The only time I ever spoke of my father's entanglement with my Grandmother to my Grandpa was when, in a rage over yet another of her unreasonable demands, I'd asked him why he hadn't rid himself of Georgina when he discovered how much she had shamed him and disgraced herself. His only reply was,

"I thought she would get over it."

His answer to me was said in such a way that I was truly ashamed of myself for having asked such a question, and I could see that I had overstepped the perimeters of my friendship with my Grandfather and ever again was silent o that wretched subject as far as he was concerned, the both of us knowing that if Georgina had "gotten over it" I would not have been born.

Grandpa knew that Grandma trotted the whole story out and regaled me with the particulars whenever she was overcome with that inexorable urge to re-live the past, and for all its mawkish self- indulgence she somehow would make it a dazzling romance, replete with remembrances of dancing until dawn, moonlight in Miami, the Barrel of Fun at Coney Island and candlelit dinners in the Garden Court of the Palace Hotel in San Francisco.

The small silent girl child grew up into a lithesome pliable maiden with a gossamer soul and no sturdy education. Having her along gave a certain sanctioned appearance to the threesome, especially when registering in hotels across the United States. Georgina, Louise and Smith covered almost every major city in the country and three years later they boarded a ship and sailed back to Shanghai together. The Chatawqua tour was over.

Vincent welcomed them home and was courteous and hospitable to Smith whom he invited to stay at their house on Kiangwan Road, and I am certain that his guest had been overwhelmed with the opulence and grandeur which surrounded him at Number One Park Villa.

I heard very little about her next few years, except that Smith returned to the States only to be followed in great haste by Georgina, again with Louise in tow. Louise's schooling was less than adequate but she had learned to read and whiled away the months with her nose in a book. Her younger sister, Ida, stayed at home with her Papa and was a bright and apt pupil in school which resulted in her being far better equipped than her peripatetic sister in her ability to grace the work-a-day world in the years that were to come.

Circa 1926 Georgina bought a house in Miami, Florida for herself and Louise. The Gerritt Smith family had settled at that time, and although Smith did not actually live with her he was a constant visitor and they saw much of each other and thought less than they had of each other too, perhaps.

The Roman Church, with all its pomp and panoply, appeals to every part of our temporal selves; incense wafting from a golden censer to titillate the nostrils, Gregorian chants enrapturing the ears, soaring Gothic architecture and stained glass windows for the eyes to feast upon, litanies to roll deliciously off the tongue and Himself in the form of a fragile wafer to hold in the mouth for a splendid melting moment.

Lady Georgina had made a friend of and charmed the famous Cardinal Spellman in New York City when she was on tour there, and her conversion to Catholicism was the logical conclusion to her ultra- romanticism. At the age of thirty-five she turned towards the Church and away from the vanities in which she had wallowed for so long. She had visions and signs from Heaven; hot blasts of air had engulfed her once when she visited a church in New York City and had approached the altar; streaks of blinding light had encircled her throat on one occasion and the Blessed Virgin Mary had appeared to her looking, oh, so sad and downcast, she would tell me. (When I learned about the menopause it crossed my mind that the supernatural phenomena she described so graphically could have sprung from the early on-set of my Grandmother's "change of life" and she was horrified at my suggestion of such a "devilish" explanation.)

Channing-Smith waned and Jesus Christ waxed.

How could a man compete with a rival who never grew older, who had no annoying habits, who gave no argument, made no carnal demands and never needed a drink? She had done with dancing and sighing and being amused by Smith and he knew that he no longer held Lady Georgina's attention nor her romantic heart in his crude hands.

Georgina was totally preoccupied with the arrangements for her baptism in the Catholic Church and planned to be confirmed in that faith and to receive her First Holy Communion on the First Feast of Christ the King. It was as though she were preparing for her wedding day, only this time it would be a joyous celebration for she was surrendering willingly and passionately as she had never before done to any man on earth, she told me.

She had heard a Heavenly voice speaking to her, "in perfect English" as she would say, and the voice told her that "the end of the world is coming." Georgina Vizenzinovich would make ready for that day but the voice also said,

"The end of the world will not come until you have done your mission."

As she interpreted those words to mean that her mission was to convert the rest of humanity to Catholicism the stage was set and no one who ever crossed her path again was to escape hearing of her miraculous conversion, everyone being exhorted to renounce the Devil and offer himself to Christ the King. She would laugh and tell me,

"I became a Holy Terror!!"

She also became a bore on the subject of religion, and she let herself get fat.

Vincent and his younger daughter, Ida, came for the Christmas holidays, and the family was reunited in the house Georgina and Louise occupied in Miami. It was December, 1926.

Louise told me that on New Year's Eve that year, while her father, mother and sister were attending an evening Benediction service at church, a friend of Smith's appeared at the house in a very agitated condition, saying that Smith was in trouble and would Louise come with him at once. She got into the friend's car, and they met Smith, who did not seem to be in any difficulty whatever. He greeted Louise with a luminous smile and outstretched arms, and I never heard what they actually said to one another, but Louise told me she did not have much choice in the matter and agreed to marry Smith because it would clear Georgina's name, forcing the old gossips in Shanghai to see that there had been nothing scandalous in her mother's relationship with Smith. It is an acceptable story since Louise was young and impressionable, but in retrospect the story seems apocryphal. Years later, Ida told me that she had been dumbfounded by her sister's action, and when she'd questioned Louise, asking her, "How could you have married that man?" my mother, crying bitterly, had answered,

"Oh, but I want him so much."

God often punishes by answering our prayers, and getting what one wants is sometimes the very worst thing that happens.

Louise, Smith and his friend drove through the night until they came to the small town of Dothan, Alabama where they were married by a Justice of the Peace. The friend had brought a ring for the wedding and Smith had held Louise's hand reassuringly and said "I do" in a firm loud voice, and the thing was done. The bride and groom were then driven to a dusty hotel and after a few desultory hours there Smith had pushed Louise away from him in the bed and said,

"Who wants little green apples anyway."

What is known to be true is not always fit to announce, but few of the principals in this drama had learned that particular courtesy. Louise told me this story of her first wedding day herself.

"What did Grandma do when you both came back?" I'd asked my mother, knowing so well the effect my Grandma's unleashed fury could have on me; but I never heard the details of that encounter from Louise, and I never knew what her father thought or felt about the marriage. There was no doubt that Georgina had been outraged and greeted the news of the elopement in low spirits and high dudgeon. Louise, in one fell stroke, had raised adolescent rebellion to a high art form by taking her mother's lover as her own husband. (I knew what the word 'revenge' meant by then).

An annulment was discussed and offered to Louise by her parents. She steadfastly rejected the proposal, and it is quite understandable that she saw in her marriage to Smith the escape route from which she could now avoid being subjected to her mother's domineering and arbitrary ways. Louise held her ground and refused any further consideration of an annulment of her marriage. Smith, in the meanwhile, seems to have been remarkably silent. He had played his strongest hand and appeared to have won the match.

Somehow, Vincent convinced Louise that she should accompany him, together with Georgina and Ida, on a trip to Europe, saying that if she would not agree to dissolve the unfortunate marriage she could at least go with him to Rome and have it legalized by proxy. He was an ardent Catholic and said that a wedding by a Justice of the Peace was not sufficient in the eyes of the Church. Louise agreed, and sailed on "La Bourdonnaise" with her father, mother and Ida. Smith remained in Miami, promising to get a job and prepare a home for Louise for when she returned to him in a couple of months from the European trip.

To my Grandmother's credit, she did have the good grace not to lapse into hackneyed phrases when telling me about these bizarre happenings and never said, "Where did I go wrong with Louise?" However, she did admit once that "the joke had been on me," and she'd made the remark without rancor or resentment as though it had indeed been the slyest joke ever played on anyone.

Grandma loved jokes and the first one I was to hear from her was the riddle of why the chicken crossed the road. I still don't "get it" but I smile whenever it comes to mind, which, luckily, is not very often these days.

During the period when Louise was waiting for her divorce and we lived with her parents in the house on Hungjao Road, the turbulent clashes between my mother and grandmother were not an every day occurrence. They often spoke quietly to one another and I would see Georgina put her arm around her daughter and say,

"Poor little one."

They gave dinner parties then in the formal dining room with all the tinkling crystal and polished silver gleaming under the chandeliers, the Number One Boy in his finest starched white serving uniform; and if I wheedled them enough I'd be allowed to come downstairs wearing my nightgown just before everyone was seated where I'd curl up on a chair placed near my Grandpa at the head of the table and put my head in Louise's lap as she sat next to her father. I was not visible to the guests and from where I had positioned myself enjoyed an excellent view of everyone's knees, skirts and shoes if I lifted the linen tablecloth over my face. I'd listen to their conversation, most of it baffling, and be ever so still for fear of being sent away as my Grandmother had threatened to do if I made a sound.

One night the talk had turned to the King of England and his affair with Wallis Simpson and every tidbit of the scandal was discussed and analyzed. The King had just abdicated his throne and there was not one person in the entire city who had not glued an ear to the short-wave set to hear His Majesty deliver the famous "Woman I Love" speech.

My Grandfather's dinner guests were too polite to venture into the more squalid aspects of this bit of history and the conversation was held on a fairly high plane.

I'd heard a new riddle at school which I didn't comprehend any more than I had the chicken-crossing-the-road question, and an overpowering desire to get into the act had the better of me. To everyone's surprise, I sat up in my chair and said chirpily,

"I have a riddle about that!"

Seeing my little head bob up from under the table took them all aback, and before my mother could stop me I swept the company with a feverish look and asked,

"What is the difference between Mae West and Mrs. Simpson?"

A thundering silence greeted the question.

It was too late. I had to go on with it.

"The answer is, Mae West only charges half a crown."

Louise scooped me up and ran from the room shaking with laughter but making no sound, and I was banished forever from my secret place at every other dinner party given in that room.

Right:
Sir Vincent Vizenzinovich
Shanghai, China, 1915

Below:
His official calling card, showing both sides.

魏聖取

佩帶日斯巴尼亞國依撒伯爾加特利加勳章
嗬蘭國勳賜奥郎那齒勳章
中華五等嘉禾章
日斯巴尼亞國駐上海領事署總科長兼會審官

VINCENT VIZENZINOVICH.

Caballero de la Real Orden de Isabel la Catolica
Ridder in de Orde van Oranje-Nassau
Retired Chancellor

Spanish Consulate — *Shanghai*

Vincent Vizenzinovich with his mother and father

Right: 1876 Mary Zih and son Vincent
Below: 1884 Matteo and son Vincent

GEORGINA FERRIS VIZENZINOVICH

Paris 1913

William and Rose Ferris
circa 1862
Parents of Frank Ferris
Frank Ferris 1882
(Georgina's father)
Below: James Hooper 1861
Father of Nellie Hooper Ferris
Below: Nellie
Hooper Ferris
1880 (Georgina's
mother)

Wedding picture of Georgina Ferris to Vincent Vizenzinovich with the Ferris family and friends in attendance, on May 4, 1907, Shanghai, China.

Newly married couple

Left: Louise with her Amah in 1909.

Right: Louise in her English Pram.

Below: Louise in her finery age four.

Louise at 3 yrs. above in studio. Below with her Paris dolls age 4.

Above Left: Louise, dressed as a boy, dancing with Ida at a fundraiser for starving children at Park Villa. Above Right: Louise at age 6.

Article about Lady Georgina's Grand Tour of Embroideries 1922

Your Newspaper — Published Daily except Sundays and Holidays for Guests

HOTEL PENNSYLVANIA NEW YORK

Volume XIII — Monday, July 24, 1922

RARE EMBROIDERIES OWNED BY EURASIAN CONNOISSEUR

Collection of Panels Unsurpassed by Those in London Museums Are Owned by Lady Georgina Vizenzinovich

"When I discovered the eight Pah Hsein embroidered panels which are the finest pieces of Chinese embroidery I have, I was transformed into a collector," declared Lady Georgina Vizenzinovich, wife of Sir Vincent Vizenzinovich, Senior Judge of the International Court, at Shanghi, China. Both Lady Georgina and Sir Vincent are guests of HOTEL PENNSYLVANIA.

Lady Georgina has probably the choicest collection of Chinese embroidery of anyone in the world. The eight pieces she speaks of are panels representing the eight Chinese immortals and were made sometime during the Ming dynasty over four hundred years ago. White panels of silk, yellowed with age, these wonderful small and priceless museum pieces are said to be the only set of the kind in the world today. They were discovered by their owner in Shanghi, China, and are finer than anything in the Natural History Museum in London, which heretofore it has been conceded has had the best examples of that form of Chinese art.

"Collecting is great fun" declared Lady Georgina. You have great sport poking around in the quaint old curio shops in the dirty side streets in the big Chinese cities. If you hear that one of your friends has come into possession of a rare specimen, you are nearly in a frenzy until you secure a finer one.

"I think the reason I took to collecting Chinese embroideries was because, being a woman, delicate needlework appealed to me very strongly. The embroideries on the famous panels are exquisitely fine. The smallest needle ever made in modern times is in the Smithonian Institute at Washington, but a needle small enough to have made the Pah Hsein panels could have been put through the eye of the one in Washington.

"The panels," continued Lady Georgina, "depict the eight immortals down to the very finest detail of features. The fine hair in the beards, the minutely worked long pointed fingernails, the muscles in the legs of the mule, ridden by one of the immortals, and the decorations of the saddle-bags are all so perfect that to be appreciated they must be seen through a powerful microscope."

Lady Georgina who is an Eurasian, is a great linguist and speaks besides five modern languages, a number of Chinese dialects. She spent six months in Pekin during the reign of the old dowager empress of China and was entertained by that famous personage. Her husband Sir Vincent Vizenzinovich is also quite famous and has been decorated by King Alphonso of Spain, by the Queen of Holland, and the former President of the Chinese Republic.

Lady Georgina Vizenzinovich, Connoisseur of Embroideries

(Harris & Ewing, Washington, D. C.)

Probably the largest and finest collection of marvelous old Chinese embroideries is in the possession of Lady Georgina, who is the wife of the Senior Judge at the International Court at Shanghi, China.

Left: Georgina 1908

Below: Georgina is modeling Chinese Robe Collection

George Channing Smith 1922

Chapter 3

Vincent and his wife and daughters made a pilgrimage. They sailed to Europe with Rome and Lourdes first on their itinerary. The continent braced itself and welcomed the embattled foursome to its shores. I am sure they argued all the way across the Atlantic about Louise's situation, but she was adamant and would hear no more of an annulment.

My Grandmother held me in thrall with stories of the dried blood of a saint which turned into a viscous bubbling mass on certain feast days (which would invariably be many months off at the time of her visits there), the catacombs with piles of skulls and skeletons heaped against the clammy walls in underground Rome, the Coliseum in the dark where hundreds of valiant Christian martyrs had let themselves be mauled to death by Roman lions rather than deny that they were followers of Our Lord Jesus Christ. It is a certainty that Georgina saw each and every item on the list of tourist attractions in the Eternal City from Veronica's veil to pieces of the true cross, and each marvel made an indelible mark on her sensation hungering spirit. Lourdes, with its boardwalk atmosphere of hawkers pushing their tawdry souvenirs and miraculous water in cheap little bottles, was not even in the least way a disappointment to my Grandmother. She saw the hundreds of crutches hanging on the ceiling of the church in the little town, silent testimony of countless cures granted by the grace of Our Lady Herself, and she believed, oh, yes, with all her heart.

Georgina loved it all and the Bernhardt in her had a new script, a new role and a new Leading Man.

Louise's father and mother petitioned the Holy Father, Pope Pius XI, for official Church sanction of her "illegal" marriage. There is a letter written in Latin on stationery headed "Vicariato di Roma-Ufficio III-Sezione Atti Amministrativi-Piazza della Pigna, 12" and not being a Latin scholar I cannot translate it here. There is, however, a phrase which reads "...curetque insimul removere scandalum..." which speaks volumes. There is also a photograph of the Pope on an illuminated card and in Georgina's handwriting

"Mr. and Mrs. George Channing Smith" is carefully penned over the following:

"...humbly prostrate at the feet of your Holiness, beg the Apostolic Benediction and a Plenary Indulgence to be gained at the hour of death, on condition that, being truly sorry for our sins, even though unable to confess them and to receive the holy Viaticum, shall at least invoke with our lips or heart the Holy Name of Jesus." It is a most impressive document, a fitting receipt for what surely must have been a costly exercise in legitimacy for Vincent. One Raphael Huber, O.M. procured the "Sanatum est in Radice" for Louise and Smith and they were then "married in the eyes of God," as Grandma used to tell me with great relief. Grandpa Vincent paid the Pope 10,000 gold United States dollars for this dispensation.

Before Vincent and his family returned to America, they stopped for a short time in London. He had taken his wife there once before and Grandma's description of that ancient City was the very best part of all her adventures abroad, in my opinion, and the postcards and mementoes of those visits remain as fresh in my memory today as when I first saw them.

London was the only place in my own experience which far exceeded its advance notices, and when I spent three weeks in that city a few years ago, I was astonished to find that most of it was just as Grandma had said it would be. She would say,

"When you go to London (never 'If you go to London'), you must get up early in the morning and go down to the Billingsgate Fish Market and watch the fish mongers display the day's catch. And you must buy a big salmon and take it somewhere and have it poached. I could never do that because we were staying in a hotel and I didn't know anyone with a stove to cook a fish for me."

It was as though her not being able to do that one thing had been the most crucial disappointment in her life, and when I was in London I did the very deed she had been denied. On a misty July morning at daybreak, a friend and I carried off a large handsome salmon from the bustling market of Billingsgate Hall and brought it back to the flat we had rented in Hampstead overlooking the beautiful Heath. We made a proper court bouillon and did as I had been instructed by my Grandmother; and that dinner closed a circle in the past that had gaped open far too long. Georgina had died before I'd had the poached salmon for her, and I am truly sorry that she shall never know of the Lucullan feast she missed.

After the trip to Europe in 1927, Vincent and Ida returned to Shanghai with Georgina, and Louise joined Smith in Florida. They lived for several months in Miami and Smith's mother, Mary, was very accepting of Louise. I think old Mrs. Smith taught her new daughter-in-law a few homely arts and from what little I heard about those few months, the family was kind to Louise and I think she flourished among them. They must have all been relieved at Georgina's departure, especially when Smith, for the first time in years, had found gainful employment.

Louise became pregnant in January of 1928 and the Smith family seemed to be genuinely pleased that Smith was to become a father. He was thirty-five years old at the time and Louise was nineteen.

The young wife was inexperienced in the ways of home-making, having had servants all of her life to do the cooking and cleaning, but it seems that Louise and George managed to get along well enough. He had learned to cook from his mother and from what I gathered, George Smith did most of what was necessary in the kitchen.

It is difficult to know what went through Louise's mind during these months, but whenever speaking about that time with me she would say that she and Smith had been happy together before she became pregnant with me, and that she had felt he truly loved her. After all, they had known one another for many years when they ran off to Alabama together that New Year's Eve in 1926.

Louise told me that she felt Smith made an honest effort to be a good husband and that they had become very loving towards one another in the time they live in sunny Florida.

"He could be terribly sweet, you know," she'd said. But the man was ill prepared for any proper work and each thing he tried ended in dismal failure and angry surprise. Perhaps it was because

Smith was unwilling to start at the bottom of the ladder, wanting always to be a general before putting in time as a foot soldier. He appeared to have an inflated opinion of himself and his talents, but the evidence shows that he was riddled with self-doubt and overwhelming insecurities. He did have an abundance of charm, however, and he'd travelled a long way on the strength of it. He would show Louise an inordinately optimistic attitude and would assure her that "Good luck was just around the corner" and Louise, the perennial victim, having placed her life in his hands, believed him.

The little green apple turned into a honey-dew melon and Smith and his parents fussed over Louise a great deal. She was thoroughly convinced that pre-natal influences had a decided effect on babes "in utero" and listened to pretty music on the Victrola, read only books with happy endings, and averted her eyes whenever she was in danger of having to look at a deformed person. Of course, the most dangerous pre-natal influence of all was safely back in Shanghai, totally involved in a new-found and passionate commitment, and news of the impending birth of Louise and Smith's child was received with glacial indifference by Lady Georgina, now the self-styled "Ambassador of God" and scourge of heretics everywhere.

Vincent, on the other hand, wrote Louise affectionate and encouraging letters, and rarely neglected to enclose a draft for a goodly sum of money in the envelopes. He was invariably the most practical of men and it was against his nature to condemn or banish anyone, or even to think that a situation was beyond all hope. He lived his own life and would never allow the actions of others to govern his course, nor did he behave in the embarrassing manner one might expect him to have, suffering, as he did, the sharp-tongued comments made by the professional gossips of his home town about the strange activities of his adored wife and beloved daughter. Vincent was calm dignity personified. He laid no blame, cast no aspersions, put a "hard heart against a hard sorrow" and made allowances.

Smith took Louise to New York City, saying that jobs were easier to find there, but in June of 1928 the Great American

Depression was taking shape and the next ship he was certain would come in for him sank before Smith ever so much as had it in his sights. He saw to it that Louise wrote to her father at regular intervals, and Vincent's replies were looked forward to an anxious anticipation. He did not disappoint them. As Louise's day drew ever closer, Georgina came to seize upon a valid excuse for making a trip to New York. It was not so much to help her daughter with a new baby that stirred her to action, but the firm conviction that this child would have to be baptized in the Catholic Church, and unless Georgina herself saw to it there was no telling what would befall the soul of the poor little mite about to be born. What if it died in its infancy without ever having been consecrated? The thought of that innocent babe writhing forever in Limbo, that gray cheerless vacuum somewhere between Heaven and Hell, filled Georgina with an unholy dread while she packed her trunks once more and sailed to New York in August of 1928. Ida stayed at home with her Papa.

Louise's mother arrived three weeks before the baby was due and all the good offices she had performed throughout her pregnancy to ward off evil spirits and insure the birth of a whole and healthy child went to naught. The moment Georgina and Smith faced each other they had squared off and launched into a battle which was to be a never-ending conflict until he died, and even then she was never to let it rest. Recriminations and accusations were hurled back and forth, charges and counter-charges rolled between them constantly, all at the top of the decibel scale. The only quiet was Louise's silent terrified weeping and she tried bravely to keep herself under control and not upset her baby.

Smith smashed two of the Della Robbia religious statues from Rome which Georgina had brought with her, climaxing one especially odious exchange, and had then slammed out of the hotel suite and come back, many hours later, murderously intoxicated. It was the first time Louise had seen him in such a condition, but it was not to be the last in the next six years while she was married to that bedeviled man.

Upon her arrival in New York, Georgina had moved her daughter and Smith out of a gloomy little flat which they had been renting, and installed them in a better hotel near Saint Anne's Hospital on Lexington Avenue where Louise was to be delivered. They did not buy anything but baby clothes for the child who was coming, and Louise made a snug little bed in one of the bureau drawers for her baby when she brought it back from the hospital.

When I grew up and was a young mother with children of my own, my eldest daughter asked me once to tell them all about when I had been a baby; and I started the story off by telling them of how my mama and papa had taken me back from the hospital and brought me to a hotel room where they'd made me a bed out of one of the drawers in the bureau. My children laughed uproariously over this piece of information, and indeed had laughed so hard that it was as far as I ever got in telling them anything else about my life and times. I suppose that they, who had never lived anywhere else but in our own sunny and spacious home, who had only known one Mummy and one Daddy, who flourished untrammeled by incomprehensible familial whirlpools, would have found it foreign and amusingly transient. What a stranger I felt to them that day, having almost a kind of pity for their wholesome safe and uneventful lives, and the uncomplicated emotional landscape into which picture they were then painted.

My children were very small then but their lives and mine were changed wrenchingly later on, and for all what may have seemed to me safe and uneventful about their childhood they showed a remarkable endurance and an admirable gallantry when their turn came to stand with me in a gale that threatened to lay waste to our spirit and devastate our family; and they, like their Great-Grandfather, whom they had never met, went about their business and got on with their lives with an equanimity and a self-containment I had not fathomed in them. Vincent Vizenzinovich would have acknowledged their valor, and I salute them in his name.

"Mary was the only love baby I ever had," Louise used to tell us, and when I learned the true nature of how my arrival had come about it never ceased to amaze me that my mother's entire family in Shanghai had heralded my birth and welcomed my addition to the clan. I was the first great grandchild to be born in Frank and Nellie Ferris' large brood, and there is a photograph of Louise flanked by at least twenty of her cousins with Grandpa and Grandma Ferris seated in front, and Grandma Ferris is shown holding me on her comfy lap. Legend has it that the crowds of relatives who came to see The Baby Mary fingered my blond hair, gazed into my green eyes and would ask, "What is it?"

Vincent wrote a letter as soon as he heard the news and I set it forth here because it gives an accurate picture of the sort of gentleman my Grandfather was.

"My dear Smith:
Congratulations and best of wishes to you and Louise and Little Mary. I received your telegram conveying the glad tidings that Louise gave birth to a girl safely on Tuesday, September 18th at 3:45 a.m. This telegram was delivered this morning at 6:30 so I went to Father Cueva's chapel for Mass to thank God for His generous gift to you and Louise, and prayed that He will always protect you both and your baby, and give her a long and happy, prosperous life, that she will be a blessing to her parents and to the Catholic Church. And that God will give you the strength to bear the responsibility as the head of your family. I was somewhat disappointed at first that the baby was not a boy, but I am sure he is reserved for the next, so let us rejoice; a daughter will always be a daughter, and much more loving and tender to her parents, especially to her father, as she is usually his pet. Like Louise is to me, and I hope that baby will be like her mother, sweet and patient in nature and will grow up pretty and graceful in body and in mind and heart. Of course the news was broadcasted amongst the family and everyone has been happy to hear the good news.
Kiss Louise and baby for me, and my love to Georgina and all of you. Now I am waiting for your letter giving further details of the happy event.

Grandpa Vincent
Shanghai, 21st September 1928"

Georgina kept that letter from Vincent to my father, and after her death I found it among her papers and I wept for them.

It seems that "being in love" is a trick Nature plays on human beings so that the race will be propagated. There is neither rhyme nor reason why certain men and women suddenly find themselves parents. It matters not at all that they are totally unsuited to one another. There is a deep and abiding force which arranges these things, and one day, we are here. Louise, as she had said many times, had only one ambition in life.

"I want to have four children," she'd said.

And that is exactly what she did, even though only the first was a "love child."

Chapter 4

Georgina had convinced Smith that the best move for him to make at that point was to return to Shanghai with Louise and their new baby, and the financial scene being so tenuous in America at the moment lent added weight to Georgina's argument. Besides, the Vizenzinovich family had a large home on Yu Yuen Road at that time, and there seemed to be no shortage of money from Vincent's lucrative career. He had recently sold the old place on Kiangwan Road, as well as the Park Dairy and Hopkins Butcher Shop which he also owned, and the new house on Yu Yuen Road had been built in a modern style and was equipped with many conveniences and innovations. He had let it be known that he would welcome Smith there and looked forward to seeing Louise once more, to say nothing of his eager anticipation of holding her baby in his arms. Ida had written her sister a letter when I had been born and it too indicated that my presence was happy news to the newly-made Auntie.

As soon as Louise was well enough to travel, Georgina booked passage on the "Empress of France" and the Group plus One set sail for China. During the voyage Louise nursed her babe contentedly while her mother fussed mightily with the diapers and infant laundry, and would ever afterwards mention the fact that she had gone thousands of miles just to see to it that I'd had clean nappies, as though she expected a special award for this noble endeavor, or at least a trophy inscribed to "Number One Grandmother." Smith amused himself by scribbling poetry and having long conversations with "a lot of rummy people" in the assorted saloons on board.

Once I asked my Grandmother what sort of poetry Smith had written, and she'd answered by saying,

"Oh, he was a very good writer and his poetry was most amazing." She'd burrowed around in her old trunk and produced a poem of two stanzas which she told me he had penned on the "Empress of France" during what was to prove his last trip from his "good ole U.S.A."

To my dismay, found myself reading the following:

"Get Up and Git"
Right where you are, if you'll get up and git
And hustle and rustle and do,
And put your heart in it, and never say "quit"
There's plenty of good things for you!
The prizes are waiting right there to be got;
You'll find them wherever you are,
By proving if you're a "go-getter" or not
A "flash in the pan" or a "star"!
It's always hard times, if you're thinking that way
And prospects are gloomy and blue,
But while the sun's shining if you will "make hay"
You'll get what is coming to you!
Don't let hard times floor you and steal your good "rep"
Don't dream about "green fields afar"
We know you're a winner-now show us some "pep"
Make good on the job where you are!
***By** George Channing-Smith*

At the time of this startling revelation of my late father's attempts at poetry writing, the English assignments I had been given at the Sacred Heart Convent by Mother Lewis, a most fastidious and ardent Anglophile, included readings from John Milton's Paradise Lost, passages from Chaucer and the sonnets of Mr. Shakespeare. It is needless for me to enlarge upon the absolute horror I felt upon reading "Get Up and Git"; suffice it to say that the song which was first on the American Hit Parade that year, which blared relentlessly over the shortwave radio, caused me sufficient pain and embarrassment to the degree that for the first time I felt ashamed of being an American person among my friends of English, French, Italian, Russian and German nationality. At least <u>they</u> need not be constantly humiliated about those damned "Fwee Widdie Fitties" we heard so much bleating about, and my father's "poem" fell into this disgusting category of artistic attempts. I recoiled, weltering in my snobbery, only to emerge some time later with yards of my own doggerel of which I was terribly vain, and became insufferable in wanting everyone in the family to listen to me reading the deadly stuff.

The only comfort afforded me over those ghastly couple of stanzas purported to be from my father's fertile brain was when I came across the word "plagiarize" and looking it up preferred to think that Smith owed an apology to some minor light in the Edgar Guest School of Poetry for having purloined the offending lines.

Louise, it is certain, was overjoyed to be home again, safe in her father's house and surrounded by his staff of accommodating servants, all of whom had been in his employ for many years. The amahs were delighted with the baby and since there were enough willing hands on call round the clock, it is very doubtful that I was ever put down except to sleep and was probably never left to cry alone.

Rearing children in Shanghai in those days was not the burdensome task that it appears to be for so many young people nowadays. If all one has to do is sit quietly several times a day and suckle one's infant, it leaves large blocks of time for reading, shopping and taking long naps, while as if by magic the hundreds of mundane aspects of infant care are attended to without one's even having to ask. There is always someone to hold the baby and sing to it, or cuddle it, to make funny faces and otherwise stimulate a tiny brain.

Much of the time amahs were left unsupervised, greatly trusted as they were, and left to their own devices would perform such delicate ministrations as chewing a water chestnut for a toothless charge. Of course, I cannot remember having anything chewed for me by my amah, but I can still see one of them with a mouthful of some savory goodie giving one of my baby brothers little bits straight from their mouths into his; and have concluded that I must have been accorded the same special service before I had cut my own teeth.

Woe betide any amah caught in such an act by our Grandma who had created a horrid scene at discovering baby Vincent's amah kissing the little darling right on his lips. Grandma had snatched my brother away from the hapless woman, berated her violently, pulled her hair and sacked her on the spot.

Both my brothers were born in Shanghai, Vincent in 1930 and Jordie, in 1932. Louise nursed them as she had done with me, and the amahs did the rest. We were photographed a great deal during these years and my Grandmother left stacks of pictures of us in various stages of our development, clear evidence that we were healthy, happy and extremely well taken care of children. We'd turned out to be attractive little people with winning smiles and dimpled knees and my Grandmother was satisfied to have our three tiny scalps all properly baptized hanging from her Ambassadorial Belt. Grandpa appeared to have been inordinately proud of having two grandsons and gave not the shadow of a hint at being resentful of Smith's children in his house. My Grandfather took care of the entire brood and was responsible for us all.

It is difficult sometimes to draw the line between that which I truly remember and that which I was told had happened, and being only four years old when my father and mother decided to try living on their own in Hong Kong it is more than likely that the latter holds true. Nonetheless, I do remember many things about our life in the Yu Yuen Road house and a memory of Smith bringing me down to the kitchen in the middle of the night is still vivid to me. He'd carried me downstairs very quietly so as not to wake the others I suppose, and had put me on the table saying things I did not understand. He got out some crackers and broke them into a glass of milk and I remember that we shared this soggy snack together while he told me that his "dear sweet angel mother" died. My father cried and held me close to him.

He showed me a snapshot of old Mrs. Mary Smith and said,

"I'll never see my mother again. She was a wonderful woman and I shall miss her so much."

Perhaps his mother's death gave Smith the excuse he needed and he rarely drew a sober breath after that time. My Grandfather tried to get him involved in one business after another, but each arrangement turned into an abortive attempt at getting a foothold in the commerce and industry of Shanghai, and Smith had yet another excuse to seek the solace of a bottle.

One morning while my Grandmother was having her breakfast late, my father showed up after having been out all night. They engaged one another in a screaming row over Smith's profligate ways and Grandma stood up and threw a cup of hot coffee in his face. Smith leaped to his feet and returned the compliment, dousing Grandma in a shower of his own coffee and then stormed up the stairs, pausing momentarily on the landing to ram his fist through the wall. That hole in the wall was never repaired, remaining as silent testimony to his enraged outburst and his unspeakable manners. I don't remember the fight, but I do remember the hole at the landing, and I used to stand in front of it, too short to reach the jagged plaster, and wonder what everything was all about.

My brother Vincent did not have a haircut until he was almost five years old, and while we lived in the house on Yu Yuen Road he looked very much like the prettiest little girl one could hope to meet. He had large liquid brown eyes and a shy sweet smile and said very little as he did not really speak in sentences until he had his hair cut. Vincent looked like Louise and had her slow quiet manner and gentle nature. I'm afraid he followed my lead more often than not, seeming to be satisfied with staying in the background and allowing his cheeky noisy sister to monopolize the limelight.

Smith had taught me to reel off the names of all the presidents of the United States and I could also recite the names of each State in the Union, had committed fifty nursery rhymes to memory and did a mean shimmy upon request. I'm sure that my father had a hand in my early education, so he must have spent a certain amount of time with me and taken some pride in the fact that I was such a clever being, considerably more fun to train than a seal, and I understand that I was called upon frequently to entertain visitors to our house with my various intellectual feats and my one talent for Terpsichore, the shimmy, which by then was well on the way out of fashion.

All children want to think well of their parents, and there being so little to admire in Smith, I had for many years cherished a particular memory of him keeping a sort of zoo in the attic of my Grandpa's house on Yu Yuen Road. I remember clearly that he used to take me up the steep stairs to the attic and the difficulty I had getting my short legs up each step. I'd have my arms full of lettuce and carrots and we'd spend hours there while he fussed with several small hutches he had built from light wood slats and chicken wire. My father kept a colony of white bunnies, a few guinea pigs and a sleepy hedge-hog which would roll itself up into a prickly ball when we poked a carrot at him through the wire. It wasn't dark in the attic since lots of light came in through the dormer windows, and it wasn't full of spooky things like dress forms or indefinable lumps of God-knew –what covered over with dust cloths. It was not a bit like that. Just a clean wooden floor with the small light-weight cages on some saw horses was all there was up there, and my father and I spent many a happy time together looking into the rabbits' pink eyes and watching their noses twitch as they munched on the greens we brought them.

Once I'd seen an albino boy begging on the streets as I waited for the tram to come and I'd told my Grandma about how strange he'd looked to me and how much he reminded me of those rabbits my father had kept in his little zoo in the attic of the Yu Yuen Road house.

"What little zoo?" Grandma asked.

"You know those little cages he had with the guinea pigs and rabbits. Even had a hedge-hog. And I used to go up there to the attic and help him feed them. Don't you remember?"

"Never!" she snorted. "There was no menagerie in that house. I wouldn't have allowed such a thing. The very idea! Where did you get such a notion? Zoo!"

"But Smith and I used to go up a lot! I remember it so well and sometimes he'd take one of the bunnies out of the cage and let me pet it and I'd bring carrots for them to eat. I know we did!" I said, baffled.

"What a lot of rot. Never heard of such a thing," she said giving me one of her sidelong squint-eyed looks that told me plainly she had her doubts about me at times.

Many years later, never satisfied with my Grandma's denial of the presence of any livestock in the attic, I had occasion to be with Louise, and I asked her,

"Do you remember the time we lived in the Yu Yuen Road house?"

"Of course I do," she answered.

"Do you remember if Smith ever kept any small animals like rabbits or guinea pigs in the attic there? I asked, not really wanting to hear the answer, not knowing what she might say.

"Oh, those, yes." She wrinkled her nose quickly in distaste and shrugged. "Kept them in cages and starved them to death slowly. Gave them a bit less to eat every day to see how long it would take for them to die of starvation. Terrible man." Louise flicked me an uneasy look and said, "How could you remember a thing like that? You were only three or four then."

I can't say if I vomited at the thought of that sadistic tableau or if it was because the one and only memory of my father which I had cherished now came to light as a warped game played by a pathetically disturbed man. His death in 1938 was decidedly not an untimely one and I am relieved for my brothers and my sister that he did not live longer and cause them any irreparable harm. He could not have been totally devoid of any redeeming qualities' no one is, and perhaps some people in his life saw a gentle side to his nature and could enjoy his rough charm and take him as he was without trying to make a silk purse out of the sow's ear that he appeared to be. It was sad for Smith that he never quite measured up to all the expectations the women in my family (not including our Auntie Ida,) seemed to have for him. It was sad, I used to think, that he "got what was coming" to him when the sun rarely shone for Smith, and he never really got to "make hay." His death saved us from him, and, more importantly, his death saved him from himself.

Smith may not have been good for much, but he certainly sired healthy children. Louise, for all her ephemeral loveliness proved to be a sturdy bovine creature when it came to feeding those children with her own milk. I was only two when Vincent was born in the Country Hospital, and can't recall Louise nursing him, but I used to spend a great deal of time watching her with my younger brother. I remember one afternoon following my Grandmother downstairs; she had tiny Jordie bundled up in her arms and was saying,

"Hungry, are you? Time for tea, is it?" and we'd gone into the sun room to find Louise sitting on Smith's lap. When she heard us come in, Louise sprang up at once, looking rather guilty and embarrassed, and Smith had turned his bored gaze out the window. Grandma, in a cold voice, said,

"Here's the baby. I think you ought to feed him."

"But I just did about an hour ago," Louise answered.

"Well, he got hungry again. Here." Her mother thrust the infant towards my mama, turned on her heel and abruptly left the small room.

Louise sat on the couch and unbuttoned her dress.

The baby was old enough to know who she was by now and he squealed in happy anticipation and squirmed toward her full breast, snapping his rosy little mouth and rooting about in her clothes with his fat tiny hands. He jounced around for a spell, his voracious and eager body against hers, gave several rapid heaves and got down to business. Jordie was a most professional baby. He held the breast of the moment in both his greedy hands and pumped while he sucked. I would try to get his attention sometimes and poke one of his dumpling cheeks with my finger and he would wrench his head away from his mother's nipple and bestow a wide open-mouthed grin on me, the milk running out between his toothless gums for a second, and then he'd remember the task at hand and return to it, doubling his attack. Louise would flinch and say,

"Mary, don't make baby do that. It hurts Mummy."

So, I'd go around the back of the couch where I could watch him without causing him to turn his head, and the total absorption and complete enjoyment of that precious time became mine as well. Sometimes I would sit close to my mother and lean over the baby while he fed and he would dig one of his wriggling feet into the inside of Louise's thigh, twisting it around and trying to stand up in her lap. He was the very embodiment of sensual pleasure and it is difficult for me to believe that there are women who will give birth to a child and then choose to dry up their milk, never to know the experience of having that lusciously extravagant contact between themselves and a tiny creature of their own bodies, never in any other quarter to be so avidly sought, so ardently embraced or so strenuously desired, except, one would hope, in the creation of yet another to take its place.

The four years Louise and Smith and their three children lived with her parents and Ida in the house on Yu Yuen Road came to an end shortly after Jordie cut his first teeth and Louise had weaned him. As I came to hear the story, Grandpa realized that his household was fraught with tension, but the dynamics of his family militated against there ever being a peaceful solution to the situation. Ida, with good cause, grew increasingly resentful of Smith's presence and she was painfully aware of the anti-social behavior he constantly exhibited to her great embarrassment and dismay. My Grandfather was well acquainted by this time with Smith's dependence upon him and it broke his heart to admit that his daughter's husband had a proclivity for self-destruction, drinking as he did. (Whenever I went into the Palace Hotel on the Shanghai Bund with my Grandma she would point to the enormous chandelier in the Baroque lobby and tell me of how my father had gotten drunk one night and swung from that twinkling crystal mass, causing a minor riot with his Tarzan-like bellowing, finally to be subdued by the police.)

For several months Grandpa had been forced to have his son-in-law committed to a sanitarium for acute alcoholism, and he hoped that the man would learn to overcome his severely debilitating weakness. My Grandfather would not have turned anyone out into the street and perhaps he carried his overprotectiveness to a dangerous extreme. Nonetheless, he offered Louise and Smith the sum of $400 U.S. Gold Dollars each month, which in 1932 was a considerable amount of money, and urged them to take the children and move to Hong Kong to try starting life anew. Grandma opposed the move, saying,

"Those two can't even look after themselves; how do you expect them to look after three children as well?!"

In the end, the tickets were bought and passage booked for Hong Kong, and two amahs that were good with the babies were dispatched along with us, and we sailed to that teeming island city to try our wings as a separate unit, Louise having high hope that Smith would "straighten out." He had been despondent after the stay in the sanitarium but brightened up at the prospect of Hong Kong, and had promised that given this new chance he was going to "make something of himself" and give Louise a husband of whom she could be proud. He was going to "turn over a new leaf" and "get up and git" I suppose, but he was forty years old then, and, after so long a time spent in indolence and dependence, what an unrealistic expectation trusting Louise held of George Smith, and what a luxury of deluded optimism he afforded himself.

The Shanghai amahs had been sent along with us because my Grandmother had a deep distrust of Cantonese people in general and of Hong Kong people in particular. There existed a natural rivalry between folks from the north and "those others" from the south of China, and like the English who refer to certain social diseases as having originated in France, when one was afflicted with a case of athlete's foot in Shanghai it was to have been cursed with the "Hong Kong Itch." (I would venture to guess that the so-called Hong Kong Flu which invaded our shores some years ago got its name in Shanghai, the present political situation in China not being conducive to the healing of this ancient rift between these two cities.)

My Grandmother would tell the story that just as the boat we were on docked in the Hong Kong harbor "Mary threw one of her shoes into the bay and had to land in her socks," Louise said. I was frequently asked why in the world I had ever done such a silly thing and I am at as much of a loss for an answer now as I was then, except of course that no one puts this query to me any longer. It must have been an omen, or perhaps I was trying to warn my parents of a sense of impending doom I might have had about the new adventure that faced us. In all candor, I probably wanted to watch my shoe float out to sea, but because I knew the end of the story I might have felt constrained to give some dramatic explanation to my Grandmother of that mysterious action.

Chapter 5

My parents rented a large flat on the second floor of a very acceptable apartment building in an area called Happy Valley in Hong Kong. The place had southern exposure (very high on the list of criteria upon which Grandma had insisted,) a deep veranda with a fairly spectacular view, and lots of room for us and our two loyal Shanghai amahs, both of whom spoke not one word of Cantonese which caused them a great deal of trouble in the market places and shops. We lived in this flat for about two years and eventually were all chattering like magpies in the Hong Kong dialect.

Louise and Smith sometimes took the three of us children to swim at the Repulse Bay beach and there is a snapshot of Vinnie and me in our bathing suits that had little skirts with tank tops. We are standing on the sand with our arms akimbo wearing very cheeky expressions and a trace of defiance to our small bodies as we stand there together, he slightly behind me. There have been times in our life when I strongly felt that he and I were really two halves of one whole person and that whoever saw only one of us was missing something; but then after Annie was born I always thought of The Four Of Us as a completed set and have cherished the symmetry of our number.

We looked happy enough, there on the beach at Repulse Bay, and I remember Smith making ice cream in a hand freezer and putting bits of carrot into the mixture. I've never had carrot ice cream anywhere else. We loved being at the seashore and played in the waves, made sand castles and did all the things that children everywhere do at beaches. At home in the flat, Louise knitted sweaters for us and told the amahs what to cook for tiffin and dinner. She had weaned the new baby, and he grew to be a delightfully cuddlesome small fellow with a tangle of golden curls and large innocent eyes which belied his mischievous nature. My father was fond of taking naps, and he would usually lie down on the counterpane with the baby on his chest and they'd fall asleep in that fashion. Sometimes, when Smith couldn't take his nap with the baby he would come and carry me off saying, "Let's have a little nap." I hated that, much as I liked Smith's attention, because I had too many things to do and did not want to lie down in the middle of the afternoon and miss all the fun I was sure would take place as soon as I left the room where Louise sat with my brothers. Something always happened around them, and I did not want to sleep through any of their adventures.

But I would go off with my father, unwillingly but having no choice, and we would lie down with the top of me being completely enfolded in his arms, and the rest of me pinned under one of his legs. We'd lie together, I wide-eyed and longing to be set free, for what seemed an eternity, and sometimes I would move ever so slightly and then again, hoping to wrest myself from his vice-like grip as he fell asleep and escape that detestable occupation of Assistant Napper. But Smith could sense the faintest almost imperceptible movement and would redouble his grip around my stringy frame, undoing all my stealthy plans for slipping away from his grasp. Sometimes I think I must have fallen asleep too, only to wake up in a very disagreeable temper at having allowed it to happen. It was especially confusing to me when the nap was started during the daylight and we would come back into the Land of the Living after the sun had set, which threw me off balance in a most disturbing way, since shortly after dinner I would be put to bed for the night, and I remember feeling terribly cheated out of the day that was my due.

It seems to me that we spent a long time living in a hitherto unknown peace and tranquility, my parents rarely out of sight and my father doing quiet things like reading or holding the skeins of wool while my mother rolled the yarn up into loose balls for her knitting. One morning as he sat in front of Louise with his hands out in front of him holding her skein of wool, Smith said,

"Why do I have to do this when all you need is the back of a chair for this job?"

He got up and draped the wool over the upper part of one of the dining room chairs and looked as though he had made a momentous discovery. Louise said,

"Well, it's not as much fun that way." My father just laughed and replied,

"Women either want a man tied to their apron strings or all tangled up in their wool."

Grandma came, uninvited. She was also unannounced. She burst on the scene laden down with presents wrapped up with fancy paper and ribbons and found us at home, in good health and even tempers. Louise was relaxed, and Smith was affable, and Grandma clucked over us three children saying,

"My, how you've grown."

This is the one sentence I consider the most inane of remarks made to children by their elders. It must have been a long time since she had seen us as I hardly remembered who she was.

Without warning, Georgina and Smith detonated the emotional bomb they held between them, and the flat became a battleground mined from one end to the other, shrapnel bursting around our heads as they leveled their heavy artillery at one another, yelling and cursing, not stopping to reload. Louise was crying and running around the room as though she was looking for a way out and the two amahs rushed in and whisked my brothers and me to the kitchen. I wrenched myself from their arms and ran back into the front room in time to see Smith take hold of Grandma in both his hands and run her down the stairs in a style he later referred to as "the bum's rush." He had laughed as he said it to Louise and she had put her hand up to her mouth trying to stifle a laugh of her own, I suppose.

Grandma left us alone after that and I did not see her again until after Annie was born, but the spell was broken and those languorous tranquil days we'd enjoyed were over. Smith went in search of an ocean of whiskey hoping to change his interior environment, and in Hong Kong one does not have to look too far for a drink. My father did not have the responsibility of providing for his family because his father-in-law was as good as his word, and the $400 arrived on time every month, only now Louise had to hide the "chow money" sometimes for fear that Smith would spend it all in the cabarets in that wicked city, second only to old Shanghai in notoriety. He would come home sodden and taunt my mother with lurid tales of having spent the day with "a Samoan princess who was tattooed from her neck to her navel" and Louise would cry and tear up the newspaper as Smith laughed mockingly.

Repulse Bay beach seemed to have been forgotten, and I took no more naps with my father. He was not around the flat much now and we learned to live in fear of the moment when he would appear. He'd wait until it was dark and then he would lurch in while we were at dinner, looking disheveled and unkempt and he'd snarl at the amahs and say ugly things to Louise who tried to ignore him with a pained expression on her face. His voice would rise and he would stand up and bang on the table with his fist, throwing dishes on the floor, saying words I couldn't understand except that it was clear he was winding himself up into an ungovernable rage.

Smith would stumble wildly over the furniture and snatch Louise up by her dress and slap her with his free hand, blow upon blow, anywhere, everywhere, and she'd try frantically in terror to tear away from him and run, but he'd hold fast and double his fist and strike her again. Louise screamed for the amahs but they were too frightened to be of much help to her, the best they could do being to carry the boys and me out of sight. The servants would peek out the door and I'd try to look from between their legs, and I could see my father dragging my mother by her hair across the floor of the dining room while she shrieked and begged to be let go.

"Ruin my life, will you, you Eurasian bitch!"

"Smith, I'm Louise!! It's me!" she'd scream.

"I'll show you who's not good enough!" he'd shout, baring his teeth, shaking his unruly head of hair from his reddened eyes. Darkly and threateningly, my father would look at my mother and suddenly he'd yank Louise up against the wall and with his hands full of her soft brown hair he'd beat her head on the door jamb and on the door to the bedroom, and then let her drop to the floor in a pitiful heap. She'd stay there whimpering and Smith had gone in and filled the bath tub full of cold water once and had thrown Louise into it with all of her clothes on after one such assault.

I know I cried during these marathons, and perhaps I even wanted to help Louise, but the amahs held me fast and were so impotent in their fear that I must have realized the futility of my circumstances, small as I was, and fear is the worst of the communicable diseases. There were other times when I showed a more courageous spirit during my father's excesses. Abusing Louise was his main intent when he came home blinded with whiskey, but he soon found a second distraction. He would rush into the flat and look wildly around saying,

"Where is that little bastard?"

And spying Vincent sitting on the amah's knee, or wherever, my father would crash towards him, pick him up roughly and weave toward the veranda with Vincent held over his head to throw the child over the railing down into the street far below. I, being short, dived for Smith's legs, sinking my teeth into his calf and holding on for dear life, while the amahs and Louise would scream and push their bodies against him trying to turn the maddened man away from the open balcony. Vincent would grasp his father's hair in both hands and clamp his teeth wherever he could, shrieking as loudly as the amahs and Louise were, and somehow it would be enough to stop Smith and he would give up in sheer exhaustion and maybe even relief at having been prevented from maiming or killing his innocent little boy whose only fault was his face, so like his mother's.

When he was sober, my father would spend the day apologizing to Louise in remorseful tones and being very quiet around the amahs who did not look him in the eyes. He'd sit on the veranda and brood, shaking his head in disbelief at what Louise told him he had done to us all the night before.

"You must think I am Mama when you get like that," she'd say to Smith.

How could he forget the chaos of the previous night? How could he not know what he had done to us? Why did he hate us so much?

What was it all about anyway?

In April of 1934, Louise became pregnant for the fourth and last time. In July of that year she made a trip to Shanghai to see her father, hoping that he would give her the money she needed. She had decided, she told me years later, that she did not want to have another child belonging to "that drunkard." She was only twenty-five hardly more than a baby herself. Grandpa argued very convincingly against abortion and promised Louise that he would give her a much larger amount of cash than the operation would cost if she'd abandon her plans to interrupt her pregnancy and go ahead and have the child. My Grandfather was a skillful advocate, and I am grateful to him for helping to spare Annie's life.

Louise's stay in Shanghai lasted two weeks and she left thinking we would be safe with the faithful amahs in her absence.

While Louise conferred with her father, my brothers and I were safe enough. The two amahs fed us and saw to our needs, and I have no special memories of that time, except one night I heard people talking in my parents' bedroom and thinking that my mother had returned home I got of bed and padded in to greet her.

The light was on in their room and on their bed I saw my father lying on top of someone with long black hair who was speaking Cantonese. He was complaining about something that he could not do. They were both naked. I stood in the doorway gazing at the soles of their feet. In English, he said,

"I can't seem to….damn you, damn you."

The woman laughed, twisted about in the bed and I saw her face. She and I looked at each other for a brief moment. I saw she was a very young Chinese girl. I turned and went back to my room. I heard the two amahs moving around in the kitchen whispering to one another in hushed panic. They must have known; they must have seen me going in there. Why else would my Mama have interrogated me? Why else did she pull me into the store-room and shake me so hard, asking wildly if there was anything I wanted to tell her? No! Nothing! You're lying! Tell me! What happened while I was gone? What did you see? I know you saw something! What was it? No! Nothing! Truly! Nothing! Nothing happened! No! You're lying! I know! Screaming. Shaking me.

She slapped me. My mother did not slap me in the normal course of our days. She rarely raised her voice to me. I rushed towards her and threw my arms around her waist and cried loudly and told her what I'd seen while she'd been gone and wailed that I'd thought it had been Mummy in the bed with Daddy that time. I said,

"I heard the water running into the rubber bag." Louise groaned, ran into the bathroom, grabbed the rubber bag and hose and threw them out over the rooftops, wailing.

In the early evening of a sultry day, my father was sitting in a wicker chair on the veranda with his feet up on the railing. I went and stood near him, looking out over the tiled roofs and listening to the street vendors calling their wares. Louise stepped onto the open balcony for a breath of air and rubbed her hands over her rounding belly. I heard her say sharply,

"Oh, Smith, put it away. Not in front of…."

And I turned around, curious, but she came between my father and me, blocking my view. In an instant he was on his feet raining blows on her and then he lunged at her pushing her into the room where she fell to the floor. He drew one of his legs back and kicked her viciously in the stomach and she cried out in agony.

Annie floated serenely away in the amnion, unaware, undisturbed, oblivious and undamaged.

The amahs were crying and packing our clothes in a great hurry. Louise said to them,

"Quickly! Quickly! I must leave before the Master comes back. When I go, you go too. Go back to Shanghai. My Papa will take care of you," and she gave the two weeping frantic women a handful of money. I know that they got back safely because the older one, Nee-Doo, was promoted to Number One Amah when I went to live in my Grandfather's house after Annie was born.

We took only our clothes and I helped carry a small valise and kept hold of Vincent's hand so he would not get lost while Louise carried my baby brother and a large suitcase. We went to Kowloon. Louise took us to a dilapidated rooming house and I have sharp memories of the smell of boiled cabbage and rancid oil that pervaded every corner of that establishment. We stayed there for a few weeks I think because it was where Vincent had his fourth birthday on the 13th of August. I had prudently packed a miniature Japanese tea set and I put the tiny cups and saucers out on the table and told my brothers to sit down. Louise was lying on the bed with one arm over her face. I found a box of Sun Maid Raisins on a shelf; the red wrapping was attractive and the smiling girl on the label was fittingly cheerful and suited my purpose. I couldn't read then, but that red box fixed itself in my mind, and the hot sunny place where it had originated came to be of great moment later in my life.

Louise had looked at Vincent that morning and said,

"Poor little fellow. You are four years old today."

If it was his birthday, then he'd have to have a party, I thought, and I portioned out the raisins putting a few in each cup and plate, and mounding up a handful of them on the largest plate in the set.

"That will be the birthday cake," I told Vincent.

It took us a long time to eat all the raisins because we wanted to make that lovely party last as long as we could, putting them in our mouths one at a time until they were gone. I got the baby to stand up in front of me and we sang, or rather, I sang while he burbled along "Happy Birthday dear Vincent, Happy Birthday to You." Vincent clapped his hands and was satisfied with the recognition of the fourth year that he had stayed alive in this beautiful world. He and I have a quiet laugh over the first birthday he remembers and it remains a pungent experience shared between us even now that we have come so far from those days of our childhood.

Louise had to go out on an errand, but the baby was asleep, so she said to me, "You stay here and watch the baby and Mummy will take Vincent. We'll be back very soon. I have to go to the bank and see if our money has come. Don't let anyone in this room. Keep the door locked, now."

I looked out the window into the alley below and watched two girls with blondined hair standing in the doorway laughing and talking to a group of American sailors in white suits. The girls wore flimsy kimonos and smoked black cigarettes. Russians smoked black cigarettes I'd heard my father say.

The key turned in the lock. My mother had hardly had time to get to the corner. Maybe she'd forgotten something; maybe...

Smith had the key in his hand and he let himself into the room. The landlady must have given it to him. The baby was sleeping peacefully on Louise's bed and I was relieved that it was not Vincent who lay there. My father was wearing a straw boater and his spats, looking neat, clean-and sober. He spoke gently to me as he sat down on one of the rickety chairs.

"Come to Daddy and give him a hug," and he stretched out his arms. I stood there frightened and couldn't decide if giving him a hug would be a good move to make. But he seemed calm and friendly, chastened perhaps, so I went slowly but not unwillingly and standing between his knees I put my arms around his neck and gave a perfunctory squeeze. He placed his hands on my shoulders, looked straight in my eyes and said,

"Mary, when your Mama comes back tell her that what you saw in the Happy Valley flat was only a dream you had."

I shook my head.

"Tell her you were only dreaming and then we can all go home and be together again."

I looked in his eyes, glittering hopelessly, and shook my head. Smith drew his knees together against my legs, pinning me between his thighs and gave me a rough shake so that my head snapped back and my hair flicked around my face.

"It'll be your fault then. I'll lose everything."

I wondered why I wasn't crying. I was so afraid.

He got up and left the way he had come and locked the door behind him.

The baby stirred and smiled in his sleep, dreaming his baby dreams, his curls damp with sweat and a small bright trickle of drool puddling on the milky pillow.

I was helping my mother pack the suitcases again.

"We're going to Canton," she told me, and said that it was not far away. I wrapped my precious tea set in its wooden box and reached for a ragged fur muff I loved to put on top of it in the valise when my mother grabbed my hand and looking intently into my face, said,

"What happened during those three days when you and Smith disappeared?"

"Disappeared? What three days? I said.

"Those three days he took you somewhere while I was away seeing my Papa in Shanghai," she said softly. "Smith kept you alive on bubble gum, I heard."

"Bubble gum? What three days?" I asked. "What three days?"

Chapter 6

Dr. Todd's Hospital in Canton became home for us as we waited for Annie to be born. Dr. Todd was an American missionary and he had taken Louise and her three children in with much kindness and fatherly concern. Louise, in return for his care during her confinement, gave English lessons to his staff of Cantonese nurses.

Annie arrived on the 7th of December, 1934. Smith came to have a look at her, telling Louise that unless she returned to him after Annie's birth, he would refuse to register my new sister in the American Consulate as an American citizen. Louise led him to believe that she would reconcile with him, and he seemed to think she was as good as her word.

Smith and I sat waiting outside the door where Louise was in labor. We sat side by side as I dangled my feet from the hard, straight-backed wooden bench and spent the time choosing a name for the baby who was coming. I already had two brothers, and thought it was only fair for the next child to be a girl, so I would not consider thinking about boys' names. Smith said to me,

"What if it turns out to be a boy?"

"That is not going to happen," I said.

I was determined to have a sister and I was going to name her Annie. Smith paced up and down in front of Louise's room, looking at his watch nervously.

"Do you have to be somewhere?" I asked my father.

"No, I have nowhere else to go right now," he said.

We talked about the baby and Smith said he thought Dorothea was a nice name. How about Dorothea? It sounded like a name for an old maid aunt with a warty nose, I told him and he laughed and looked fondly at me. He and I went in together when Dr. Todd called us into the room, saying,

"You are in luck, Miss Mary. Here's a baby sister for you."

I was overjoyed, and so pleased with my mother for not disappointing me. The nurse had Annie bundled tightly with only her fat, purple face peeking out of the swaddling, and Smith picked me up beside the high hospital bed so I could get a proper look at the baby lying in the crook of Louise's arm. Annie kept her eyes screwed shut and was frowning. She yawned and squeaked, and Smith touched her chin with his finger and smiled sadly.

We never saw him again, and Annie never knew him, but each year on her birthday I would tell her the story of the day she was born and how Daddy and I had sat outside the maternity ward and chosen her name. Even now, she and I remember more than Pearl Harbor on the 7th of December.

When Louise was satisfied that Smith had registered Annie's birth at the American Consulate, and had the certificate in her hand, she went ahead with her plans for separation, showing a side of herself which few people knew she possessed. She gathered us up once more, and a short time after Annie presented herself, we five moved to a suburb of Canton called Shameen, and Louise instituted divorce proceedings against Smith. She also took a job with a life insurance company and we lived in a courtyard apartment in the downtown area so that she could come home during tiffin time at noon to nurse the baby. We were left in the care of an old amah named Bah-ta-po who had an evil visage and a temper to match. She smoked cigarettes, a dirty habit my Grandmother would never have countenanced in an amah, and she cooked a variety of marvelous things for us to eat. My brothers played in the courtyard, and Annie lay in her pram in the weak winter sunshine, and I was sent to school for the first time in my life. I was six now.

Sister Rosary's School for Children was where I learned to read, and a painful process it was. I cried a good deal while having the English alphabet drummed into my hard, stubborn head, and I was convinced that I would never learn how to read all those impossible books stacked on Sister Rosary's shelf waiting for me. I remember nothing of that lady's methods. I only recall the pain of it, but I learned to decipher the written word and when it got easier and I discovered that I could indeed read words on billboards and signs, it thrilled me beyond description. I learned only how to read and write at this time, and can't remember doing any sums, or any other kind of school work. I read everything I could find, and gobbled books like a starveling urchin.

Master Billy Hoskins was eight; he fell in love with me and after school he'd take me for rides on his bicycle, I perching precariously on the handle bars while Bah-ta-po cursed us loudly in her shrill Cantonese. Billy Hoskins told my mother that he would marry me when we grew up and that he'd search the world over for me until he found me if we lost track of one another. That little boy from England and I never met again after my family left for Shanghai; but I dreamed of him once when I was twelve and saw him dying on a smoking field with armored tanks rolling over the ground, and I cried in my sleep and hoped that the dream was not true when I woke.

A young Russian woman would look out of her window and see me coming from Sister Rosary's school, and one day she followed me home and waited until my mother came back to ask her for permission to keep me for a weekend because she was lonely and promised to take good care of me. I did not want to go with her but the young woman, whose name I can't remember (It might have been Shura), smiled so invitingly and said she did not have a little girl of her own and would be so happy for my company for a day or two. She lived in a luxurious house with plants growing everywhere in pots and she slept in a huge bed with frills around it and a pink satin coverlet beneath a pink organdie canopy. Large fluffy pillows were piled high on the bed and her dressing table spilled over with a prodigious number of jars and bottles of perfume with long stoppers in them. She had several servants at her beck and call, and someone invariably brought a silver tray with tea things on it, plates of buttered toast with the crusts cut off, smeared with strawberry jam, for us to nibble. The lady appeared to live alone in that big house, but she kept a picture of an elderly looking gentleman in a British military uniform on the mantelpiece, and she told me that he was her friend who came to see her whenever he could. I suppose I substituted for the gentleman when he was unavailable, as she would come for me every other week or so to spend a day and a night at her house.

On my visits I would sleep in her bed with her, and she'd cuddle up against me and stroke my hair and sing sad Russian songs to me until I fell asleep. There was something rueful and melancholy about the young woman.

She called me her "malinkaya dyevetchka" which meant "little girl" in Russian and ordered her cook to make "piroshki" for us to eat. I loved those deep fried yeast rolls filled with meat and cabbage, and we'd drink tea with jam in it with the hot, freshly made savories.

She used to tell me stories about her family who still lived in Harbin as I sat on a polar bear rug in her parlor, patting the head of the great beast that had been stuffed so that its teeth showed in a fierce open-mawed red-tongued mouth. She was quite different from my mother in that she did not seem to have any hair except on her head, and I was unaware at that time that women shaved their legs and under their arms. One morning I woke early and slipped out of that high bed and sat in front of her vanity table to look at the powder puffs, mirrors and silver boxes scattered over the glass top. The sleeping lady rustled in the tangle of bedclothes, and shifting her weight she raised one knee in her sleep. I turned around to see that the covers had fallen away and slipped to the floor. It was then I noticed that not only was she devoid of hair in her armpits and on her legs but everywhere else as well. She looked the way I did to myself, only she was taller and shaped like my mother; it was many years before I realized that women give themselves the appearance of being glabrous by design with the help of a razor blade, hoping, oddly, to improve upon nature.

Shura came to see Louise one day, wearing a big flowered hat and white gloves. I think she wanted to give the impression of being a proper lady and she asked my mother if she could adopt me. The request struck terror in my heart and I burst into tears, creating a most frightful scene at the conclusion of which my mother told her kindly that it would not be possible and she left crying. I felt sorry for Shura; she had always been very kind and solicitous, but the thought of never seeing my brothers or Annie again was entirely out of the question, and I was shocked that the subject had even been discussed, much less in my presence. But at least I had the opportunity of stating my position, and I did so in no uncertain terms. Louise backed me up.

The courtyard apartment did not have an inside kitchen. Bah-ta-po cooked our meals in a small shed in which someone had installed a primitive cement stove, and I used to watch the amah make a fire in it and fan the flames with a bamboo fan. She would grumble the whole time and hold her cigarette between her wrinkled old lips, only taking it out to shout warnings to my brothers of the grisly fate in store for them if they caused her any kind of trouble. She merely tolerated me, but she seemed quite fond of Annie, and was able to summon up a dram of tenderness from her arid and acerbic depths for that sweet babe of mine; and mine she was as I had developed a fierce proprietary interest in Annie which, even now, in our middle age, still sometimes rears its head to make sure that no harm comes to our little sister. I learned in later years from Louise that Bah-ta-po, the wretch, had offered to drown Annie for my mother if it proved that the responsibility for another baby became too great for her. The awful woman had drowned four infants of her own, and had no compunctions about doing a similar favor for her beleaguered Mistress, should the necessity arise. Bah-ta-po must have taken us on for a pittance in wages, and I am sure that my mother did not engage her services through the Registry for Domestic Assistance.

Louise did not have as much time to spend with us as she once did, but she nursed Annie for several months, and I had many opportunities to sit with them as when Louise had nursed Jordie, and I vicariously enjoyed the closeness of those moments. Babies who are sustained on their mother's milk (a wet-nurse will do just as well), have an indescribably sweet breath, vastly different from those fed on formulas. Louise would let the task of getting the baby's bubble to come up fall to me, and I was so proud to be given the warm bundle to hold against my own shoulder and pat vigorously until we were all rewarded with a resounding belch.

The way the world around me smelled and all the hundreds of aromas that filled my childhood remain stored in my bank of scents, and any one of them can evoke a host of scenes, happenings, faces, voices, emotions and memories, so many of which surprise me with their tenacious longevity; and the loveliest thing I can remember is Annie's sweet baby breath, and the way my mother always smelled so cleanly delicious and real.

Sister Mary Rosary painstakingly prepared me for my First Holy Communion. She drilled me in the catechism I had to know by heart before being allowed to partake of that most holy of sacraments. My religious training had been purposefully neglected during the time we lived with Smith, and Louise was too busy tending to our bodily needs to take much trouble with our immortal souls. So, Sister Rosary taught me all the answers in the book that I needed to know and explained in great detail the sublime significance of what was about to befall me. She instructed me in the etiquette of the confessional box, and I dutifully read the Examination of Conscience in my prayer book, searching it assiduously for any transgressions of which I might be guilty. The good nun ticked off the Seven Deadly Sins, only two of which were familiar to me; Anger, the first deadly sin, because I had seen a lot of that during my few years on earth, and Gluttony because I had two small brothers who gorged themselves whenever they were offered the chance. My teacher explained Covetousness and Envy, but I was not overly impressed. She skipped over Lust. I asked what "lust" meant and was told that I would find out in good time, and soon enough, at which point Sister Rosary stammered on towards Pride and Sloth, neither of which caught my imagination or curiosity.

My mother, in the meantime, did her part in having a dress made for me by a clever seamstress who always had a mouthful of pins sticking out towards me as she scurried around on her knee-pads. It was a white, tiered dress made of very fine Indian lawn material and it had long sleeves with a ruffle at the wrist and round covered buttons down the back. A filmy veil, part of the traditional costume, was secured to my head by a hand-made wreath of tiny flowers from the same material. I had several fittings before it was pronounced perfect, and we brought it home wrapped in yards of tissue paper in a large brown box. I was terribly excited over the dress and would beg to wear it around the house to practice walking decorously up to the altar with my hands clasped piously on my bosom and my eyes cast downwards in a contemplative attitude. My mother said, "Stop being so silly."

The Big Day was to be on a Sunday, and the Saturday afternoon prior to that I made my first confession under the watchful eye of Sister Rosary. All was well and I went home in a state of grace, my soul as unblemished as it had been on the day of my baptism. We were to meet at church for the 8 o'clock Mass, and since I was the only child receiving her First Holy Communion that morning, my sponsor in Christ promised that she would personally escort me to the altar and stand beside me during the sacred moment.

That night I hardly slept. Visions of myself in that gorgeous bride-like gown, with its diaphanous veil floating behind me, and the exquisite hand-wrought circlet of miniature roses clasped about my brow, oh, heavenly spectacle! Kept me awake long after my mother had bid the amah good-night and turned out the lights in the house.

The day, which was to have been the Greatest Day of My Life, broke to dark ominous clouds and the distant rumble of foreboding thunder. I flew to the window and the sky was rent by shards of brilliant lightning which streaked through the torrents of rain that poured unremittingly into the courtyard, churning the gutters into rivers and the street beyond into a raging sea.

The church was only a block away from where we lived and my mother and I had planned to walk the short distance, I being especially pleased at the prospect of showing off my white tiered dress to all and sundry; but the rain had changed our plans. Oh, cruel fate! Oh, ill-starred First Communion Day!

"Oh, damn the rain!" my mother growled and called Bah-ta-po to help me into my bridal finery. We now had a surly truce. They dressed me in a hurry saying we'd be late and Bah-ta-po to help me into my bridal finery. They dressed me in a hurry saying we'd be late and Bah-ta-po cursed me when she saw she had buttoned the dress in front and had to do it over again down the back, roughing me up in the process of getting it on properly again. In the frantic scramble they'd put my right shoe on my left foot and that had to be done over again as well, and the amah, who was not Catholic and had little knowledge of veils, stuck it on my head sideways giving the rosebud wreath a cockeyed angle. I surveyed myself in the mirror, completely undone, not wanting to go to my First Holy Communion looking jaunty! My mouth dried to dust with anxiety and forgetting that fasting was mandatory, I drank some water, but Louise saw me and yelped sharply,

"Don't drink that! You know you're not supposed to eat or drink a drop before communion! Well, never mind. It couldn't have been much."

I choked on the mouthful I'd had when she called out about the water, and what I didn't swallow exploded from my throat, spattering the bodice of my immaculate costume. I grabbed a towel and was trying to sponge off the front of the dress while my mother and the amah were engaged in a loud conversation in which Louise shouted instructions to Bah-ta-po who seemed to be truculent about following the orders.

The next thing I knew, my mother rushed toward me with her raincoat into which she wrapped me from head to toe, and I was then carried out to the courtyard and dumped unceremoniously into Annie's baby buggy, where the amah angrily buttoned the rain-flaps onto the hood, and before I could bray in protest, she was galloping into the street, cursing and fuming in choice obscenities in her Cantonese tongue. I could look out at Bah-ta-po through a slit in the rain-flap and saw her drenched and sodden in the downpour, her clothes heavy with water, the flimsy black trousers she wore clinging to her old-crone legs and her hair streaming in rivulets, furiously pushing the rain out of her eyes and face with one free hand while she held the pram handle with the other as she clattered arthritically onto the portico of the church.

If the amah was enraged, my state of mind and being defied description and Reason abandoned me. Logic was my enemy. My gorge had risen so far and so high as to have engulfed me. When the amah unbuttoned the rain-flap and unwrapped me, I grabbed her hand and bit it in my fury, and the next few minutes found us in a tangle of baby blankets, Louise's raincoat and partially dry layers of Indian lawn. Bah-ta-po, righteously indignant at being bitten for all her trouble in seeing me through the deluge, seized one of Annie's rattles which lay in the pram and cracked me over the head with a celluloid pig! I was rescued from any further indignities by the appearance of Sister Rosary who had been waiting in the vestibule. She came out to investigate the ruckus and I shall never forget her face and the dainty manner in which that religious personage recoiled upon seeing me emerge in all my bedraggled array from that baby buggy. She waved the irate and wounded servant away, hurried me inside the church, rearranged my dress and coif and walked majestically by my side to the front row.

During the Mass, I had ample opportunity to regroup, and marshaling my scattered ranks managed to make it through to the Kyrie when it struck me with the full force of its horror.

I had committed one of the Seven Deadly Sins! I was guilty of the Sin of Anger on my very way to my First Holy Communion! No time for atonement! No time for absolution before the profound moment which was at hand!

I looked up through the spiritual quagmire that had caught me to see Sister Rosary smiling confidently down at her star pupil and knew that even she could not save me. I accepted my doom as she nudged me softly. We rose in unison and walked towards the communion rail. I knelt down and ceased to think. Sometimes it was as though that other Mary stepped out of me and stood by watching, and she did it then, sniggering and pointing, wearing her mocking face.

The priest stood before me. I closed my eyes and thrust my tongue forward and he placed the host on it softly. I swallowed hard, trying not to cry, and Sister Rosary told my mother later that she had never seen a child receive her First Holy Communion who had been moved to tears by that beatific experience, and that Mary was "truly a little saint."

George Channing Smith's Family

George Channing Smith
1922

Smith

Smith and a friend

Smith's brother Dale, mother Mary and father Gerritt Smith, Miami, 1921

Sister Margaret with Mother Mary

Margaret, Gerritt and Mary Smith

Louise Vizenzinovich's family

Above: Louise and her father at "Park Villa" in 1923.

Above: Vincent and his family Shanghai, China, 1924.

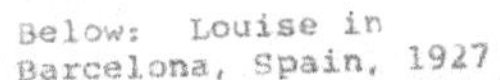

Below: Louise in Barcelona, Spain, 1927

Below: Louise at the Miami house in 1926.

Louise 1926

Above: Georgina, Louise and Smith at the Miami house in 1926

Left: Louise and Smith on the board-walk at Coney Island after their marriage in 1927.

Louise 1927

Louise and Smith on "La Bourdonnais" April 8, 1927 as she left for Europe with her parents.

Louise and Vincent in Lourdes, 1927.

Baby Mary arrives

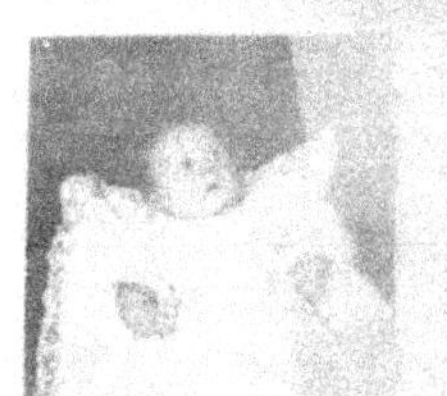

Above: Mary Smith, born 1926
in New York City

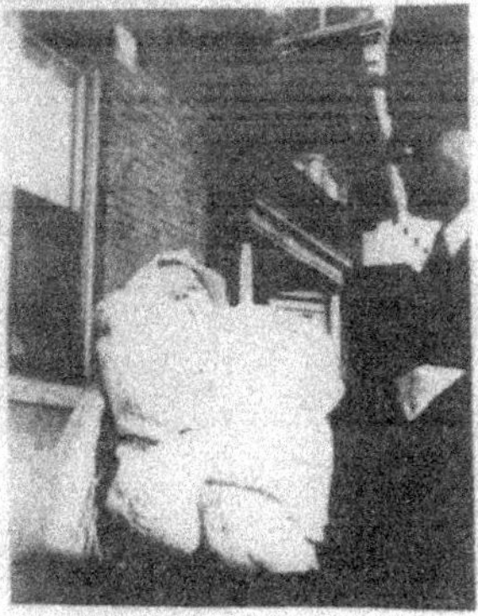

Above: Smith holding Mary

Above: Georgina holding Mary

Above: House on Yu Yuen
Road. Grandpa in front.

Above: Louise and Mary
Yu Yuen Road

Above: Smith and Mary
Yu Yuen Road

Mary in Chinese pram
Yu Yuen Road, 1929

Frank and Nellie Ferris
with first great grand-
child Mary on her lap, 1929

Louise in sedan chair with
her father walking beside her

Smith holding Mary on
sedan chair trip, 1929

Smith holding Vincent and Mary, 1930

Georgina, 1931

Life in China 1929-1931.

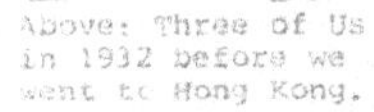

Above: Three of Us in 1932 before we went to Hong Kong.

Louise, our beautiful mother in 1933.

Left: At Repulse Bay Beach, Hong Kong, 1932. Smith told Vincent and Mary to "pose" and they did.

Right: Vincent and Jordie in Shameen, 1934.

Below: Jordie and Vincent with Louise in background. (Bah-ta-poh lurking somewhere nearby.)

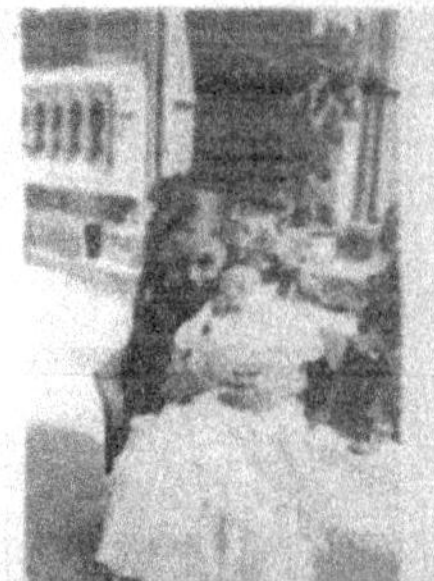

Mary and Anne, Shameen
1934

Mary's First Communion
Shameen, Canton, China
1935

The Four of Us, Shameen,
1934

Going back to Grandpa's, 1936

The Four of Us on our
way to Manila in 1937.

Grandpa's house on Hungjao Road.

Back to Shanghai 1938

Left: Annie, Jordie, Vincent, Louise and Mary in the front garden of the Santa Scolastica School, Manila, 1938.

Above: Mary and Vincent, Manila, 1938, before he and Jordie returned to Grandpa's in Shanghai.

Right: Passport picture of Mary and Anne taken with Louise for the trip back to Shanghai after Smith died in 1938.

Chapter 7

Old Bah-ta-po amah helped Louise pack our trunks, showing no sign that she was sorry to see the last of us. She shuffled around gathering our clothes and muttering to herself, pushing me out of the way with a snarl when I got underfoot. We were planning to sail on the President Lines back to Shanghai where we would make our home in my Grandpa's house on Hungjao Road. Louise had found it extremely difficult to support her brood and had asked if she could return home.

Her father said he would welcome her and the children, and the house he had at that time was large and commodious; but she knew that her mother was vehemently opposed to the divorce action Louise had brought against Smith in spite of the shambles they had made of their lives together. Georgina's main objection was on the ground that after the Alabama elopement the negotiations for a special dispensation from the Catholic Church having been granted bound Louise to Smith in an irrevocable bond of matrimony, and in the eyes of the Church divorce was an unpardonable sin. Louise was, by now, something less than a lukewarm Catholic and cared nothing for the Papal indulgence. It had been bought and paid for by her father at her mother's insistence and no longer concerned Louise who was determined to make her life apart from Smith regardless of the consequences.

The ecclesiastical legalization of that union by proxy in Rome had cost Vincent Vizenzinovich several pretty pennies, and my Grandmother thought of Louise's divorce, only six years later, as an unconscionable waste of money.

Before we left Canton, right after my First Holy Communion, my mother had taken me to a photographer to have my picture taken in the white dress and veil. The portrait of Saintly Little Mary was mounted in a hard paper casing (there were two poses of me in that dress,) and I was told to present this to my Grandmother the moment we disembarked on the Bund at Shanghai. The ship docked, my brothers and I scampered down the gang-plank into our Grandparents' welcoming arms and I solemnly proffered my pious likeness to Georgina. So overcome was she at the sight of Louise's child surrounded by a heavenly aura (the Canton photographer had known what he was about,) with her ivory hands clasped in prayer and her eyes raised skywards shining with the hint of blessed visions only she could see, that when Louise came ashore holding Annie, my Grandmother enfolded her daughter in an all-forgiving embrace, which forgiveness was not to be of an enduring nature, but which was long-lasting enough to gain us the entrée that was necessary at the time.

It turned out to be a happy year for The Four of Us. Louise got a job and went into town with her father every day, and Grandma had her hands full with my two hyperactive brothers, my adorable baby sister, and me. We were glad to see Nee-Doo amah once again who had been taken back into service in my Grandfather's household and were not surprised to learn that she now ruled the roost in the servants' quarters.

One evening while she gave me a bath, Nee-Doo amah scrubbed my toes and said, "Can you remember where you went during those three days you were with your papa in Hong Kong?"

I looked into the woman's questioning eyes and, feeling a wisp of uneasiness and discomfiture, I said,

"Three days? What three days? When was I with him?"

"While your Mama was gone for a short trip," she said, "Don't you remember? I was so worried about you."

"Worried?" I said. "What about?"

"I don't know, but I was relieved when he brought you back. Can't you remember?" she said, soaping my neck.

"No. I remember that you let me stay up late while Mummy was gone and you showed me how to fold paper birds."

"And that's all?" she asked.

"That's all," I said, and we spoke no more of it.

The house on Hungjao Road had a red-tiled roof and a large veranda or roof garden on the third floor. The four of us children occupied one enormous room which was the top floor, and Louise and Ida had their own bedrooms next to their parents' on the floor beneath us. There was a passage-way from the second floor hallway into an Annie over the garage, and it was here that the servants slept. The downstairs was furnished in formal style and from the sitting room one could walk through French doors into a glassed-in conservatory filled with potted palms and other indoor plants which grew luxuriantly in the bright Shanghai sunshine. My Grandmother had two gardeners who kept up the grounds, and she had planted numerous trees, bushes and flowering vines. There was a tennis court and a sweeping driveway where we rode our tricycles. One day a friend brought us several pairs of stilts. I loved walking on the stout shafts and will never forget one evening when my Grandpa, who must have been about sixty-six years of age at that time, came out to join us and hoisted himself up on a pair that fit his size and clopped all over the driveway. Another time, my Grandma took the cook's new bicycle and pedaled around us as we wheeled about on our trikes, my Grandpa watching in great amusement, cheering her on.

"Riding a bicycle is one thing you never forget how to do," he said, giving her a round of applause, and she looked girlish and a trifle smug as she took her hands off the handlebars and rode toward the gate without holding on. It gave me a glimpse of what they must have been like as children themselves and I sensed a kinship in this older generation of mine.

Right before bedtime in our big room upstairs the amah would make us a drink of hot Horlicks's milk in a glass container that had a metal plunger in it which she would pump up and down to mix the sweet powdered milk with hot water. I loved the sound of that plunger and the comforting taste of the malted drink. I rarely have it now, but for years I have kept a jar of this compound handy and it pleases me just to know it is in the cupboard, even if it isn't the Horlicks's brand, which I have not found in America.

We ate our meals in a breakfast nook off the kitchen earlier than the adults were served, and on certain special occasions it was a great treat to be allowed to sit at the carved dining room table for a festive dinner. It was at this table that I popped up to tell my Wallis Simpson riddle, and it was under this table where, finding the floor button near my Grandpa's chair which summoned the manservant to serve the next course, I drove the kitchen crew to utter distraction by pressing it whenever I passed by.

Vincent and I went to the Asbury Academy, an American mission school which we hated energetically. In the main hall there hung a large painting of Martin Luther, my Grandmother's arch-heretic, and it remains a puzzle to me how my younger brother and I ever came to attend that iniquitous milieu, Grandma had told me that Luther repudiated the Catholic Church, abandoned his holy priesthood and entered into a pact with the Devil to "divide and conquer the One True Church of Jesus Christ" all for the love of a nun whom he wanted to marry, and did. I had never heard such a shocking tale in my entire life, and there he was, hanging on that wall, with his stern Teutonic face staring down shamelessly on us. My Grandma detested King Henry the VIII almost as much as she did the Honorable Mr. Luther and would gossip with me about their ignominious "doings" as though they still trod the earth creating havoc within the orthodoxy. I am sure she resented bitterly, the success these two gentlemen enjoyed in making the world "go topsy-turvy" and in their ability to govern their own marital circumstances, an effort which, in her case, had come to naught, giving rise to my Grandmother's feelings of professional jealousy towards these historical characters.

In 1927 she published a book she'd written entitled "What is Heresy?" There was a devastating report on the book by a critic for the New York Times, and the most charitable thing I can say for the work, having read it, is that the ponderous question was never answered.

On one side of the garden at 251 Hungjao Road there was a wild marshy section which was to eventually be planted in flower beds and ornamental trees. Vincent and I went hunting in that tangle of vines and bracken with a deep cylindrical Chinese fruit basket into which we would stuff as many frogs as we could find. Then, putting the bamboo cover over the squirming jumble of amphibians trying to escape from us, we would drag the basket up the back stairs to the roof garden and with a mighty pulling and tugging we'd hoist the heavy burden to the ledge and push it off so that it hit the driveway with a sickening thud. We'd race downstairs again and repeat this gory exercise until we were satisfied that the frogs had become "Frog Jam", at which point we'd heave the basket to the kitchen door and bang loudly. The cook's helper would come to the door and open the bamboo container and scream in horror at the sight of the curdled carnage within it, acting as if he were swooning. Vinnie and I, hiding behind a post in the garage, could watch the servants' reactions and it gave us the utmost pleasure to witness the hullabaloo our back door offering had caused. One could hazard a guess that the hysterical act the servants put on was solely for our benefit because they never told on us and we went unpunished for being so cruel to the frogs. It must have been a fine charade since no self-respecting Chinese would allow the sight of a basketful of squashed frogs upset his insouciant aplomb, surrounded as they were with scenes of incredible human suffering in the streets of Shanghai which were crowded with beggars and refugees from the ever-present war. In the conflict with the Japanese in 1932 legions of ragged peasants flooded into the city, most of whom had never recovered themselves, and hordes upon hordes of Chinese people lived in appalling squalor and poverty in the gutters of that labyrinthine metropolis which was Shanghai.

The house sat on several acres of land and my Grandpa had built a high bamboo fence around the entire property. The front gate faced the main road, but the back gate opened onto a wide expanse of countryside in which one could see workers laboring in the bean fields and cabbage patches. Along our fence was a narrow path, and one morning I heard someone going by the back fence making guttural noises and moaning. The bamboo was so closely woven that it was impossible to see through it, but I could tell from the light that came through the tiny holes in the weave that a person in great pain was inching down that pathway and leaning against the fence every few steps. I ran inside and called one of the amahs to come quickly and open the gate so we could see what was happening. She hurried out with me, unlocked the back gate, poked her head out for a brief moment and then slammed the gate shut, saying,

"It is only a "shang-wo-ning" (country bumpkin) having a baby."

I forced her to re-open the gate and ordered her to fetch my Grandmother, and I must have been an imperious seven-year old because the amah did as she was told immediately.

I stepped outside the gate onto the narrow dirt path and saw the woman who in reality was only a girl of about eighteen squatting on her haunches against our fence.

She was totally absorbed in what she was doing to pay much attention to me as I watched her holding her knees in her elbows, her feet slightly apart and her head down on her hands which were gripped in front of her. She had ripped the seams of the crotch of her baggy black trousers and every so often the girl would lean her head back against the fence and let her hands drop to her sides and I could see sweat pouring from her brow as she put her face up to the sun, breathing hoarsely. The girl would rouse herself from the short respite and grunt vigorously, screwing her face into a tight scowl, straining her body down towards the earth in what did not seem like pain but strenuous work. "Labor" is an apt word to describe what women do in the giving of birth.

The country girl gave a sharp cry, and then again, and saw a dark little head slip out from between her legs. Her body whipped in short convulsive movements and a pair of wet shoulders squeezed out. She put her hands down near its head and her baby slithered out of her womb like a swimmer from a murky lake. The young mother caught her breath and, still on her haunches, she looked at the infant and examined its hands, feet and genitals. It was a boy and she seemed pleased.

My Grandmother flapped onto the scene holding a gold crucifix in one hand and a bottle of holy water in the other. The amah had brought a towel, some newspapers and a pair of scissors and she set about to help the girl with the baby's cord. My Grandma busied herself making the sign of the cross with the crucifix over the mother and baby and then in English said,

"I baptize thee in the name of the Father, the Son and the Holy Ghost," while sprinkling the holy water on the newborn's forehead. His young mother was suspicious of the incantation and disapproved of the water being sprayed on her son's head and taking the towel wiped the offending droplets away with a firm gesture. My Grandma was quite annoyed with the woman and proceeded to baptize the child over again, only to have the mother spit on his forehead and wipe it a second time. My Grandma, peeved but persistent, gave her a brittle lecture which did not sound any too kind, and started once more to save the poor babe from the fires of eternal damnation; but the woman won all three rounds and walked off with her tiny son wrapped in the newspapers, muttering and looking over her shoulder as she went down the path with an expression that said unequivocally that she thought Lady Georgina to be a white foreign devil woman who had tried to bewitch her baby with foul water and evil recitations, and my Grandma was cheated out of another anointed head to add to her collection.

"That ungrateful wretch!" my Grandmother said as the girl moved out of sight.

We had many adventures that year. Vincent was bitten by a savage Alsatian dog and underwent Pasteur treatment for rabies which seemed to me worse than going mad from dog bite. As my Grandmother, that font of all wisdom, had told me that victims of this dread affliction went about frothing at the mouth, barking like a dog and biting other people, we scrutinized Vincent with extreme caution until we were assured he had escaped unharmed, and he innocently passed up a golden opportunity by behaving with characteristic docility. Think of the fun he missed by not running madly around barking like a dog and biting his sisters and brother; think of the panic he might have caused his Grandmother, who loved nothing more than a bit of excitement. I had accompanied Vincent to the doctor's office for the injections he was given in his abdomen and his screams chilled my marrow. Vincent was the only one of us four I can remember being taken to see a doctor during our childhood.

One day, while running through a bean field in back of the house, Vincent fell waist deep into a "kong" (an earthenware barrel sunk into the ground), whose cover had been left off. Night soil was stored in these containers and he was lucky that it was only half-filled or my brother might have met his end by drowning in a very ugly fashion. The two gardeners hosed him off and we had to throw his new shoes and all his clothes away; the amahs were unanimously in favor of throwing Vincent away as well, but Grandma said,

"When a boy has a dirty face we wash his face; we don't dynamite the boy!" and ordered the amahs to give him several baths in rapid succession, which they did with much nose wrinkling and exclamations of "Aiee-yah" and many admonitions against playing in the fields when the farmers were fertilizing their crops.

I think I had a bout of malaria during this time, and can still taste the bitter and acrid quinine in my mouth. The malaria brought dreams out of delirium fever and I remember shivering and sweating simultaneously while my Grandmother dosed me with anisette and Benedictine. I didn't know what these liqueurs were at that time, but I recognized the licorice taste of the anisette when I grew up, and laughed to think that it had been used to counteract such a serious illness as malaria. Benedictine became familiar to us because my Grandma used it as a universal placebo, and it has the same comforting effect upon me as does the powdered Horlicks's when I think of it.

A handsome fellow on a motorcycle came to the house one afternoon to take Louise for a ride, and while he waited for her to get a scarf, I sat in the living room glaring at him and sighing in loud, aggravated "whooshes." My mother came in just as I was asking him:

"What are your intentions towards Louise?"

He laughed disarmingly and replied: "I'm going to take her for a spin in the country." My mother ushered me out of the room, frowning and throwing the gentleman (which I doubt he was,) anxious, apologetic glances. I can't say that it was at this or that time in my life when I know I lost my innocence. I never lost my innocence because I have no memory of being an innocent. Perhaps I shall have an ingenuous old age.

The finest thing I can recall about our days at the Hungjao Road house was when the Monkey Shows appeared. The Chinese are fabulous entertainers and there were bands of strolling musicians, acrobats, jugglers and magicians who would stop at our gate and ring the bell. The gardener ran to the house to tell my Grandmother that they had arrived and would put on a show for our pleasure. The Mistress of the house ordered the servants to close all the windows and lock the doors, a necessary precaution, my Grandma said, because,

"Some of those rascals are human flies and can scale a wall in a jiffy, and while we're all out here with our mouths hanging open they're inside looting the place."

We'd trample each other in our rush to get to the lawn and sit at the edge of the circle which formed and watched the colorful troupe enter the grounds. They came in beating their drums and clanging their cymbals, somersaulting and leaping over one another, weaving their brilliantly dyed silken scarves around in the warm air. People from other houses on the road came into our garden and sat on the grass to enjoy the show, masters and servants alike creating an appreciative audience, drawn by the lively carnival atmosphere of the high stepping performers.

There was a nervous bright-eyed monkey bedecked in a cunning uniform, climbing excitedly on his trainer's head and shoulders. The monkey waved at the crowd and had also been taught to hold his hands together and make the Chinese greeting gesture of "kung-shi kung-shi" to which everyone responded in great glee. After the show our simian star ran through the crowd collecting money in his hat and my Grandmother gave me a silver dollar to pay him for his trouble.

First the tumblers did their turn, bouncing in a series of body twists that defied gravity and made one think they surely had "ziang-be" (rubber) bones. Then a group of them would do the chair balancing act, piling many wooden chairs one on top of the other to form a wavering tower while one of their number remained on the uppermost chair; and at the end of the act, when all the chairs were up in the air, he did a handstand on the topmost one to wild applause and rousing cheers.

An acrobat came forth looking as though there were in reality two men, having a dummy that resembled a man attached to his own hands and feet. The real man then proceeded to wrestle with his "opponent" and there followed a gracefully disciplined ballet-like routine that was wild and vigorous as the man simulated a fierce wrestling match to the stirring sounds made by the drums and whistles of the company. Of course, the real man always won and the audience cheered the over-dog strenuously. The plate-twirlers, a dozen or more of them, stepped forth with long bamboo sticks of great resilience and china plates balanced at the tip of each stick, and the players giving each plate a sharp turn kept them twirling overhead in perpetual motion, the expert of them all adding a stick and plate to his handful of whirling crockery until he had at least six in each hand; then the grand finale in which the champion twirler, keeping his plates aloft and spinning, did a series of intricate back-bends and leg-over-leg tricks which brought down the house.

There were small children in the troupe and they did the same sorts of tumbling and balancing acts on the sidelines, learning the tricks of the trade from their elders and keeping a sharp eye on what was happening in the center ring. Sometimes I would turn away from the main show to watch these little ones going through their paces knowing that they would someday be the stars of the Monkey Show. I looked closely at their intent faces and knew that they took this business very seriously, and I wondered what their lives were really like; roaming through the Chinese countryside as they did, sleeping in different places every night and starving when it rained and folks were reluctant to come out to see their performance.

Last year I watched a television production of a team of acrobats from the Peoples' Republic of China and I wondered then, marveling at the beauty of their classical movements, how many of them I might have witnessed as neophytes in the travelling circuses of Shanghai so long ago. The show I saw on the electronic box was exactly the same as I remembered it, except that the clever creatures had added several new flips to their old routines, making the tricks vastly more intricate and mind-boggling. There they were, once again, hurtling through the hoops and barrels, flying around the stage like playful dolphins leaping and curling high in a silver sea. They did my favorite tricks in which two of them would rush at each other and each grasping their partner's ankles would in one swift bound then be circling the floor like a large human wheel. Two others also twined themselves in a big ball and rolled easily around the stage.

The Chinese love a good boisterous show and I have yet to see anyone present himself in as professional a way as did those fascinating Oriental Gypsies on our green lawn. The tumblers and acrobats and jugglers of the Peoples' Republic of China were far and away more sophisticated than the ones who used to parade into our garden, but their bright eager faces and sparkling eyes, their supple bodies and exquisitely graceful maneuvers had not changed, and I rejoiced that their celebration of life remained undiminished down through the grinding years of regimentation and uniformity and I found myself cheering them on over the air waves, feeling a surge of pride in that noble breed to whom I can lay a partial and affectionate claim.

Chapter 8

"The China Incident" erupted in 1937 and, in order that we escape the bombing, my Grandfather had Louise take us children to Manila where he thought we would be safe. We sailed on the "President McKinley" on Tuesday, the 17th of August, and I saw Black people for the first time in my life, all the stewards and waiters in the dining room being Americans of African origin.

We landed in Manila harbor and were greeted by a serious earthquake which splintered the dock in front of our very eyes, frightening us greatly. My mother took rooms in an inexpensive hostelry (a former Army barracks, I think) and I remember that we had a lot of canned milk and corn flakes to eat, and not much else for several days. We loved riding in the horse-drawn caramettas and Louise took us to see the famous walled city. I did not like Filipino food, and was especially put off by the way the natives of those islands ate with their hands, using their thumbs to push the food into their mouths, unlike the civilized Chinese who could pick up a stray noodle in a pair of chopsticks.

Louise took us to a mountain town called Baguio and parked us in a Maryknoll convent boarding school. The unfamiliar weather in that high altitude was clear, crisp and very cold, but the scenic beauty was awesome. We stayed in that place for about two months, or so, and I can't remember being taught anything except deportment. When any one of us was guilty of the slightest infraction of a single of the endless rules the nuns had made, all four of us would be sent to the cellar to ponder our bad behavior. The basement was a dark and ominous place where statues of the saints were stored, and these plaster figures, some of them larger than we were, loomed around us in the blackening shadows. The boys and Annie (she was only two years old then) would huddle close to me and I'd try to circle my arms around them, pretending not to care that we were in that dreadful cavern, and we'd lay intricate plans for escape, none of which were ever put into operation.

Our mother appeared suddenly and took us back to Manila. Somewhere along the way during the next few weeks my brother Jordie and I were invited to go to a place called Ilo Ilo by a rich Filipino family named Zamora who thought we might be amusing playmates for their only child, an obnoxious girl of seven, who was the most spoiled brat it had ever been my misfortune to meet. Jordie loved her. Louise said it would be a lot of fun for us, and paid no attention to all my tearful entreaties not to let us go. In the back of my mind I was convinced that we were being sold to this wealthy family, and I wept in my terror at being separated from Vincent and Annie; but they came and took us away one evening and we said lachrymose farewells to each other as they carried us off like prizes.

Louise had said it would only be for a month or two, but it seemed like an eternity. I suppose I did not fare too well in Ilo Ilo because I was sullen and morose, but they loved my brother with his charming smile and bouncing, golden curls, and he became quite a pet among the clan. I resented my little brother's easy way with these strangers, and thought that if only he would behave in as recalcitrant a manner as I affected the family would soon tire of us and send us back where we'd come from. I wanted to be with Vincent and Annie again, who were our own, and besides, I had a rigid concept of The Four of Us being an unbreakable set, and was bitter about this enforced separation.

We did not see my mother or Vincent and Annie all the while we stayed on that island, and it was like doing time in prison for me. The parents of Nasty Girl fought constantly, reminiscent of the bloody battles I'd witnessed between Louise and Smith, and listening to them my stomach would contract into a leaden knot as I lay in the musty dark wondering what that was all about.

Grown-ups are an insane lot, I thought, and children should be protected from them at any cost.

Nasty Girl so obviously favored Jordie over me which only increased my churlishness, and no wonder, since I did not smile once in her direction, nor would I play any games with her, or even deign to speak to the little baggage, and her parents, when they held short periods of noisy armistice, came to realize that they had made a mistake about what fun it was going to be , and wrote to Louise saying we were too homesick to be much good to them in their scheme of things.

While we were in Ilo Ilo, my brother Vincent had been put into the La Salle School for Boys as a boarder, and when we returned to Manila, Jordie joined him there. Annie had been taken in by a friendly American couple whom she called Mummy and Daddy Darling. Louise worked for a time in a florist shop, and, when faced with me once more, arranged for both Annie and me to be enrolled in the Santa Scolastica Catholic School on Pennsylvania Avenue also as boarders.

Annie was allowed in as a boarder under the condition that eight-yr. old Mary would be in full charge of her care. The nuns had said, "But she is only two and a half years old!" and started to refuse her admission. Annie came to my rescue by stating firmly that "I won't always be two!" and upon my promise that she would be no trouble to anyone in the convent, they accepted her, the youngest person ever to have been on their official roster of students. We were together, and it did not disturb me as much to be apart from the boys. because I knew they were also together and not far from where their sisters would be living.

The convent was a dank and medieval building, reeking of boiled turnips, parsnips and rutabagas which were served, or so it seemed, at every meal. A rotund postulant read to the girls sitting at long tables in the stone-walled refectory, and I think the readings were in Latin as I never understood a word of what was said. Everyone kept silence during the mealtime and to insure this custom there was always a monitor-nun who glided around the hall slowly, with her finger to her lips, shushing the assemblage in a constant hiss.

We were required to take a bath once a week, and when it came my turn I was issued a voluminous blue cotton gown which I could now describe as being a Mother Hubbard. I was instructed to wear this bulky garment into the bathtub where it would fill up with air, ballooning out, and I'd be forced to punch it down only to have it mushroom up in another place behind me. I was ordered to get the stubborn gown thoroughly wet and then to soap it, thereby washing what there was of me underneath the rough cloth. I thought this a peculiar way in which to get properly clean, but the Sister-in-Charge-of-Lavabo carefully explained that the bathing-dress was to be used so that I did not have to touch my naked little body with my hands, thereby eliminating any chance for exciting myself and falling prey to such abominable sins as "concupiscence of the eye" and worse. That big word came back later as my Grandmother was fond of using it and I was to hear it from her many times in the future.

I read, long after my sojourn in that gloomy place, that Saint Augustine held the opinion that infants and children were the most sinful, iniquitous, unregenerate and lustful of all God's creatures, so the Benedictine nuns in charge of us had no choice but to issue naked, frail, eight-year old girls in need of a weekly bath the means with which to avoid further contamination of the mind and body in the year of Our Lord, 1937.

In June of 1938, my two brothers had been sent back to Shanghai on a steamer to live once more in our Grandparents' care. Grandpa's big house on Hungjao Road had been confiscated by the Japanese and other financial misfortunes had befallen him. My Grandparents salvaged what they could and had taken an apartment in the I.S.S. Building on Avenue Joffre in the French Concession of Shanghai. Louise came to see me and said that when the ship with my brothers on board had docked in Hong Kong on an overnight stop, she had already paid the stewardess to lock both boys in their cabin so that Smith, who might have heard they were in the harbor, could not come aboard and kidnap them. My heart leaped into my mouth and stayed there until I had news that the boys were safe with Grandpa on the mainland. They might have remained locked in their cabin for the entire trip because I also heard that they kept the whole crew busy with their bad behavior and had jumped onto a table and from thence up to the creaky arms of a slowly-turning ceiling fan, all of which caused a disturbance among the stewards and passengers on board, who were not amused at being informed that my brothers merely wanted "to go for a ride".

In the middle of August, 1938, Louise again visited me at the convent school. She said I was to get ready and that within a few days Annie and I would follow the two boys and return to Shanghai. I was overjoyed at the thought of leaving that morbid and depressing cloister, and beside myself with happiness at the prospect of seeing my brothers again; but then I said,

"What will happen when the boat gets to Hong Kong? Can you have the crew lock Annie and me in the cabin so that Smith won't be able to take us away?"

Louise, in an off-hand manner, brushing the air with an agitated wave of her hand, said,

"Don't worry about that…Smith is dead."

I reeled in shocked disbelief, stunned at the electrifying relief I was experiencing, and she went on, saying,

"Jumped out of a high building. They found his body on a roof-top without any clothes on. What he'd had on was folded neatly on a chair in his room. Even had the carnation in the lapel of his coat turned to the outside. Maybe someone pushed him. Stupid man."

It ran in my brain like a movie, playing over and over, and I watched him falling, falling, naked and white.

My mother looked out of the casement window and said,

"If only he'd done that two years ago. I could have saved the divorce money. I wouldn't have had all that awful trouble."

I looked at her face and saw someone lurking within who was a stranger to me.

"Well," she said brightly, "don't worry about any of it. You'll be all right, and Grandpa will take care of you."

On the boat going back to China, I was very cautious and never took my eyes off my tiny sister for a moment. We spoke to no one and held ourselves apart from the rest of the passengers. I was paranoid in my suspicions that Smith was, in fact, not dead at all, but would suddenly appear on the gangway or in the cabin and take us with him when the boat got to Hong Kong.

When we arrived in the British protectorate, friends of my mother came on board inquiring about me, and when the stewardess took me to them I felt sick with alarm, certain that they were only there to kidnap Annie and me for Smith, and were just pretending to be friendly. However, they seemed very earnest and reassuring and said that they were there at Louise's request to see if Annie and I had gotten that far without incident. I relaxed a bit and slowly recognized the couple as people who had lived near us in Happy Valley, or I thought I did. They said they were sorry to hear that our father had died. I didn't believe they were any sorrier than I was, and I asked: "Is he really dead?"

"Yes. He died on August the 8th and is buried in the Happy Valley Cemetery."

We went with them to see the grave. There was no marker, simply a wooden plaque with his name and dates. Annie skipped to the mound and stood where his head probably was under the soft earth and studied her new, shiny, black patent-leather shoes. The woman friend called to her not to walk on her Daddy's grave. Annie smiled and danced away, not knowing why we were there.

The apartment in the I.S.S. Building looked pokey and crowded to me after remembering the Hungjao Road house, but I was so happy to be back with my good Grandpa that anything would have been acceptable. The boys, who preceded Annie and me by several months, knew their way around the stairwells and corridors of our new home, and took me into every nook and cranny they had discovered. They briefed me on the other children in the big complex and told me all their new secrets and scary adventures.

I found that I had an urgent need to sit on my Grandfather's lap and tell him about the terrible things that happened to us in Manila, and I complained about the skittering lizards that shot up and down the walls of places where we had stayed. I made him laugh when I told him about a time when someone had thrown a cat into the sea off a pier near a house where we'd stayed for a short time, and the animal had come back through the septic tank to perch on a ledge right beneath the wooden commode. No one could save it and it yowled for days before it probably died from hunger, making it very unpleasant for whoever was sitting on the toilet seat up above the wretched beast.

We talked about a theatre which everyone called the "Iddy-All" and when I finally went there to see a movie I noticed that its real name was the "Ideal." He said that was probably the Spanish pronunciation of that word in English. I could speak a little Tagalog and compared notes with my Grandpa about our own Shanghai dialect which we both agreed was a far superior language, all told. (My ethnocentricity is still alive and well today.) I had forgotten much of that masculine sounding patois I'd learned to speak as a baby, but it soon revived itself since the amahs spoke almost no English, and there was no other way to communicate with them in spite of the eloquence of Chinese hand signs and the wide-spread use of Pidgin English.

In recent years I learned that the present Government of China did much to unify that sprawling country by having the people speak Mandarin as the official language, so that if I were to return to Shanghai I would be hard pressed to find anyone under thirty who spoke the dialect of my childhood. The uniformity of the Chinese language is, in my view, an excellent idea because I can remember that there were so many hundreds of versions of that complicated tongue that oftentimes one could not converse with people who lived only across the street, so different was one dialect from another.

I loved the food in my Grandfather's house and I felt safe and secure among the familiar objects and comforting smells. He, especially, always smelled of crisp linen handkerchieves, and fragrant tobacco (he smoke Craven A's from England,) and shoe polish and soap. Grandpa took a cold bath with Life Buoy soap every morning and walked the two miles to his office in the Hanray Mansions in Frenchtown. He had several rituals upon returning home, and his utter reliability and meticulous behavior steadied my life and gave shape to my days.

With unwavering regularity Grandpa would come into the apartment and stop at the kitchen to see what the cook had planned for dinner and give him instructions for the following evening's meal. Grandpa would then go to his chest-of-drawers in our bedroom and put on a rose-colored felt skull cap after pegging his Homburg on the hat rack. He would remove his suit and hang it carefully in the closet, and step into his padded Chinese gown of wine-red silk if the weather were cold. During the summers Grandpa had the warm "ss-mee" gown put away in moth balls to guard against the moldy season and wore a lighter cotton garment in the Chinese style. I would sometimes help him button the frogs under the arm and up the neck of the robe and help him out of his Western style shoes into cloth slippers. Then he would fit a cigarette into an ivory holder that had a lion standing fiercely on all fours carved on top toward the tip. Grandpa smoked only one cigarette each day and he looked as though it gave him the greatest enjoyment. He would then get the evening newspaper and sit in his chair and smoke and read. When he was done, it was time for me to come and sit on his lap and tell him about my day and listen to him tell me of what had happened to him.

The routine rarely varied, and the certainty of my Grandfather's patterns, in counterpoint to my Grandma's unpredictability and capriciousness, gave meaning and substance to a deep longing I had for continuity and a never-ending need for reassurance which he rarely denied me.

Louise had been right. Grandpa did take care of us and we were safe with him from everything except the impending war over which he had no control.

Chapter 9

My ninth birthday arrived on the 18th of September, 1937. Grandma had given me a rosary made from blue glass beads strung on a silver chain with a heavy crucifix which had been blessed by the Pope. She set about to make up for the inconsistencies in my religious education in spite of the months I'd spent in the company of nuns in Manila. I was enrolled at the Loretto School at #10 Route Poittier which was administered by a group of American nuns who had tricky names like Sister Mary Josella, and who wore outdated habits. Rumor had it that they did not shave their heads as did the others belonging to French and Spanish orders, and it was the one resentment my Grandmother harbored against them. For some forgotten reason, I did not do too well at this school and my Auntie Ida had me transferred to the Convent of the Sacred Heart where I fit in more comfortably and whose uniform I especially liked.

We addressed the nuns there by the title of "Mother" and the atmosphere was one of formal gentility and elegance. The women of this school were highly educated and were compared to the Jesuits as to the degree of their classical erudition. In the years that followed, my classmates and I were to study ancient Greek and Roman history, and the history and geography of England, India and Australia. French was mandatory and I became fairly proficient in that most lovely language, and regret that after many years of disuse I am now reduced to reading menus with a smidgeon of confidence when in a fancy restaurant and catching a shade more meaning that is given to the audience in the sub-titles of French movies. My brothers went to the Saint Jeanne d'Arc School at 18 Route Doumer and were taught by the Brothers of a French teaching order who were noted for their strictness and who brooked no nonsense. My Grandma left behind her several of our old report cards which indicate that, while we were able to hold our own, we were in no danger of being touted as child prodigies.

Until Annie was old enough to go to school with me, I either rode the tram or went on my bicycle in the company of my friend, Nina Pagani. I've lost track of Nina and would love to find her again because we shared so many experiences of growing up together. I developed a protective feeling for this little girl, which was almost as intense as it was for my brothers and Annie, and I often think of her, hoping that she survived the war which separated us and that most of the dreams we shared as children have come true for her.

Every Friday the nuns held a ceremony which was called "Exemptions." White gloves were "de rigueur" and we would troop into the big reception hall in the order of our classes. At the Sacred Heart Convent one started in the Twelfth Class (first grade) and progressed to the First Class which was the equivalent of the senior year of high school in America. We sat in a semi-circle on wooden chairs, rising in respect when Reverend Mother Nourry entered, curtseying to her and remaining standing until she had seated herself in a throne-like chair on the dais. This August Presence was treated with the utmost courtesy and esteem and I have yet to meet anyone who could command the respect of her "subjects" as did our Reverend Mother. She was a European lady who spoke heavily accented English, moved with a ponderous grace and had whiskers on her chin.

The object of "Exemptions" was to have each teacher read a list of her pupils' performance for that week; every good piece of work and stellar behavior was mentioned, and each incidence of disobedience or inappropriate conduct was aired. The best girl of the week was then called to the dais to kneel in front of Reverend Mother who spoke a few words of praise and encouragement; she then bestowed upon the lucky student the Blue Ribbon of Excellence. If one received the Blue Ribbon of Excellence one could wear it for the entire week, and it was a great honor and privilege to have it draped over the shoulder and hip every morning before classes began. It looked rather like the Order of the Garter and had an emblem embroidered in silver thread near the top. I tried so hard to be the Best Girl, but invariably managed to queer my chances by getting caught sliding on the slippery corridor floors, or smudging a paper that had to be turned in, or looking too scruffy to pass daily inspection. We were severely reprimanded for crossing our legs and gum chewing simply was "not done." One Friday afternoon a miracle occurred. My name was called as Blue Ribbon recipient of the week, and dizzy with pride I approached the throne, passing among my friends who clapped and smiled in surprise, racking my brain to see how it was that this honor had fallen to me since I had abandoned all hope of ever winning the sash, and had not even been making the feeblest attempt at putting in a faultless week.

One Saturday morning I went to school to get a copy book I had forgotten. The sexton-nun admitted me to the vestibule and I waited in front of the chapel as she left to do my errand. I was quite alone and stole around to make sure no one else was about. The bike ride to the convent had made me very thirsty but there was no drinking fountain downstairs. I looked at the holy water fonts on either side of the chapel doors. They were large marble shells held forth by smiling cherubim and I knew it would be a sacrilege, but my need for water was desperate; so, I stood on my tip-toes and sucked in a long draught of holy water, swallowing a big mouthful before I realized that the ratio of water to salt must have been about two-to-one. I did not know at the time that part of the purification method was to add salt to water before the priests blessed it, and I took this briny gulp to mean that God was punishing me for committing such a mortally sinful act. I was choking and sputtering when the nun returned with my copy book, and grabbing it from her dainty hand, I raced out of the building and leaped onto my bike, hardly stopping to say "Thank you."

The next time I went to confession, I told the priest what I had done and begged forgiveness, promising never to drink from a sacred font again. Behind the dark grille, the man was silent for a long time and finally he gave me a novena to do in penance. As I left the box, he opened his door and peered out to see who I was, and I felt certain that he wanted to mark down in The Book who it had been guilty of such an unspeakable crime as the defilement of the house of the Lord, and I scurried off in shame, imploring the heavens that Father would forget my face.

When Annie started school she and I would ride the five miles to the convent on my bicycle, and with my little sister clutching tightly behind me, I pedaled through the treacherous traffic twice a day, dodging rickshaws, taxis, Pedi cabs, other bikes, cars, trucks, wheelbarrows, trams, trolleys, buses, delivery vans, mounted police, wheeled vending carts and men on foot carrying long poles with heavily laden baskets suspended from either end. These carriers sang a special work song and chanted out their "Eh-hoh-Ah-hoh" over and over as they hoisted their backbreaking burdens down the snarled thoroughfares. Chinese customarily sang rhythmic songs while they worked in unison, and I suppose they must have known for centuries that it helped to bring oxygen into their bloodstreams, making the weight of their efforts easier to bear. Amongst ourselves, if someone we knew came in carrying a heavy parcel, we'd say, "Did you 'eh-hoh-ah-hoh' that all over town?" and laugh at each other.

Annie and I set off for home after school and rode under the mulberry trees lining Avenue Joffre. We had silkworms one season and fed them with the leaves from those trees; we kept them in shoe boxes but they cleverly escaped and my Grandmother found them inching along in the drapes and screamed crazily, smacking us all when we blamed one another for the tragedy. Sometimes I stopped if I saw a street vendor with some tasty snack for sale and would buy a bag of hot chestnuts which had been roasting in coal dust over a portable fire; or baked sweet potatoes which we would eat skin and all; or my favorite, "ch-deu-wu-kehr", which were squares of soybean cake fried crisp on the outside but soft on the inside, three squares strung on a piece of straw with a blistering sauce dabbed over them, for two coppers. At that time we had metal coins in Shanghai, and three coppers were worth one penny, the rest of the exchange being on the decimal system. If there were school friends riding with us, they'd stop to watch in absolute horror while Annie and I enjoyed eating the "street-chow", saying that their parents would kill them if they were ever caught putting such filthy things in their mouths.

We were not excessively defensive about this criticism, but argued that the delectable goodies came either directly from a vat of boiling peanut oil or a bin of burning coals, and wouldn't all the germs have perished before we swallowed the forbidden treats? I rationalized their fears in terms of racial ignorance, deciding that the "foreigners" simply could not appreciate things that Annie and I, being Eurasian, were able to enjoy with impunity, coolly disregarding the possibility of contracting diphtheria, trench mouth or bubonic plague. Most of the children we knew at school were English, French, German, Russian and Dutch, a few Italians and Lebanese, many Portuguese and an occasional Estonian, all of whom lived in homes which served meals traditional to their mother countries and few of these culturally deprived youngsters were venturesome enough to keep up with The Four of Us.

Vincent was especially experimental and discovered a grimy shop which offered a plethora of "tucks." The word "tuck" is English slang which we used for preserved fruit, such as plums pickled in liquorice, salty olives hard and dry, or mango-bones marinated in a sticky red sweetness. My brother could keep a mango-bone in his mouth for a whole afternoon, and afterwards he would look as though he had been chewing betel nut, his teeth and gums a deep scarlet and his tongue fire engine red. There must have been a secret ingredient in these sweetmeats as one could easily become addicted to them and suffer terrible cravings which were only satisfied by more tucks. Even now, in the early autumn of our lives, we'd much prefer to have a box of tucks than a carload of candy.

The one Chinese girl I can remember who attended our school was a very pale, thin child with short cropped hair and a sorrowful face. She did not seek out anyone else in class except me, possibly because I could speak her dialect, and one day she shyly told me that she had saved a box of Moon Cakes for me and asked me to go home with her after school. Annie was not riding with me then and we bicycled to the girl's house, taking a circuitous route in the opposite direction of my apartment. We must have been almost eleven years old then, and I could never think of her name after she left the convent.

She and I, riding through the noisy crowded alleys, finally came to where she lived in the Chinese section of the city in a tenement-like complex. I had heard some gossip about my friend's background- that she made her home with her mother and was supported by her father who was very rich but unable to recognize them. It is possible that the girl's father was not Chinese, but she didn't look Eurasian and never admitted she was.

The halls of her building were heavy with the aromas of a hundred dinners cooking at once, not all of them pleasant. She led me to her door and I was impressed to see that she had a key of her own, a grown-up item which I never owned while living in the I.S.S. Building. The front room reeked of a sickly sweet smell and we passed through a curtain to see a woman lying on a bare mattress, the ticking torn and dirty, in a bed with a white enameled iron railing at the head and foot. A single light bulb hanging from an electric cord dangled over the bed. My friend looked at her mother sprawled on the blue striped ticking and said: "My mother is sleeping. She usually waits until I come home."

"Why does she wait?" I asked, trying to keep from retching. The noxious odor, the sight of the iron bed and that mattress, the light bulb swinging lazily in the fetid air, all but overcame me and I broke into a sweat as a wave of nausea swept over me. I could think of nothing else but to escape from that horrifying room. It all seemed so familiar and I felt as though I had been there before, but I knew I had not. I moved into the tiny kitchen to get away from the odious sight and smell and the girl came with me to put the Moon Cakes in a box which she tied with string so I could carry it home easily.

"What do you mean she didn't wait for you? I asked absently, not caring.

"Well, she waits until I get back from school and then she sleeps. She is afraid to be alone," the girl said simply. "Must be she couldn't wait for me today."

My friend smiled and handed me the box. I thanked her, smiling greenly, and said I would share her present with my brothers who loved Moon Cakes. We shook hands lightly and I stumbled past the prostrate woman, unconscious on that revolting pallet, and held my breath until I was once again outside in the open air. I rode away as fast as I could from that area, and as soon as I was well out of sight I slowed down in front of a group of beggar children and flung the box of festival cakes toward them. The ragged bunch swooped down on the box, tearing it open and rooting through the paper wrapping found the pastries and started squabbling over the booty.

Suddenly I began to cry and couldn't stop until I was in the elevator going up to our floor, when I felt safe again. I had seen worse things than that girl's mother on her dreadful bed, but the thought of it and remembering the light bulb swinging overhead made me violently ill and I ran into the apartment and heaved.

Soon after this incident, my Chinese friend came to school no more and we never heard of her again. I used to wonder what had happened to her but was afraid to stop at her house and ask. I never told anyone that I had been in such a hideous rom or that I had witnessed that abominable scene, and could not understand why I felt so much shame from having been there.

"Mary is very high strung," I heard my Auntie Ida say to Grandpa, and he murmured his assent.

The one activity which truly interested me was reading, and I read everything I could find. My Grandma insisted that I read the Lives of the Saints, a fat red book with pictures of Christians being subjected to imaginative tortures, (published, I am sure, by evil men catering to the prurient interests of sadists and masochists) which I thought fascinating and finished the entire volume in post haste. She had a copy of The Malleus Maleficarum (The Witch's Hammer) which was difficult to plod through, but Grandma explained it in great detail so that it became quite understandable. She was deeply interested in the occult, aside and apart from her own miraculous Catholic visions, and told me hundreds of stories of "happenings" with fortune tellers and seers. The one that has stayed with me was an account of a "true story" my Grandma herself experienced.

"It's this way," she'd say, and tell her story. One day, she discovered an expensive ring missing from her jewel case. She hunted high and low, and ordered the servants to turn the house upside down to find it. They searched for days without any luck, and finally the wash amah said that if my Grandmother would go to a certain man in the Chinese sector he might find the culprit if the ring had been stolen, or lead her to the spot where it might have been misplaced. The wash amah rode with Grandma in a taxicab, a most unusual circumstance, took her mistress to a door in a narrow alley and knocked loudly. An old man let them in and listened to my Grandmother's tale. He brought a pan of water and said to her, "Look into the water and you will see the face of the person who stole your ring."

Grandma would tell us in an alarmed voice, her hands held up in front of her, palms out in a show of great fright, "I looked in the water and there I saw the face of the Number Two Boy whom I had dismissed the week before! I was so angry that I raised my hand (like this) and slapped the water, PIACK! Like that." (We jumped.)

At this point, Grandma and the amah taxied to where the ex-servant lived, and pounded on his door. He came to see who was knocking so angrily and was startled to meet his former employer on the threshold who was even more shocked than he at the sight of her hand print across his face as though she had just slapped the thieving rascal. Naturally, the man confessed, returned the ring and presumably fled to Hong Kong, far removed from that insidious practitioner of hydromancy who had conjured up the culprit's face in his magic pan.

Buffeted by waves of cultural shock I pressed on "into the world of books, devouring the Anne of Green Gables collection and every segment of The Whiteoaks of Jalna; onward with Beowulf and Siegfried, those stolid epic heroes; held fast by Little Dorritt, Oliver Twist and Great Expectations. I read Gone with the Wind on the sly, stopping at a friend's house on the way home to read a chapter or so every day because I had heard my Grandma say what a "bad book" it was and that it should have been banned by the church.

I'd found an old copy of the writings of Ralph Waldo Emerson and dutifully read some of it because he was an American. I was pleased with the essay he'd done on the perfect gift being fruit or flowers and am still in agreement with those sentiments. I also read Big Little Books and comic books about the Submariner and The Human Torch which I found abysmally stupid but felt that I had to read them on pain of being considered un-American or unpatriotic as the only citizen of the United States among my peers.

Actually, I knew one other American girl who, like me, was a quarter Chinese and also being raised by her Eurasian Grandfather. Her name was Bunny Barnes and she is as lovely a grown woman as she was a child. I always thought her the prettiest of all my friends and wished that I could be more like Bunny, neat and well-behaved, an almost constant wearer of the Blue Ribbon. I envied her having such a fetching nick-name. I was simply "Mary" and it seemed so final and pedestrian to me. My Auntie Ida sometimes called me "Mariah Jane" but that would be because of my fussy ways and constant worrying, and she said it fondly as if to allay whatever fears I may be voicing. Grandma would say,

"Oh, you and your silly worries. There are four hundred million Chinese who don't care a fig about you, and who wouldn't be in the least bit interested in your fretting and stewing."

Nowadays, I worry considerably less since there are <u>six</u> hundred million Chinese who have never heard about me, and it does tend to bring one's worries into perspective to know this piece of information.

I didn't have any friends who were "real" Americans, born in the States, who spoke slang with a nasal twang, and I used to have twinges of jealousy for children who lived in the land of my birth having easy access to the secret decoders, Shirley Temple cups, Orphan Annie malted milk shakers with domed covers, signet rings and whoopee cushions (whatever they were) that were advertised on the back pages of the comic books. I must have known a good thing when I saw it because many of these items are now avidly sought by collectors of pre-war memorabilia.

The first Christmas that Annie attended school found us lined up in the chapel hallway holding potatoes in our hands. We were to file past the Crèche on our way to the Christmas service and were instructed to place the potatoes in a basket as an offering for the poor. I looked down the line to see Annie holding her potato at arm's length, wearing a disgusted expression on her round face. The little ones went first, and I watched Annie lob the offending spud into the basket, whisking her hands together as she left it behind. Later, riding home in the bitter cold, all muffled in scarves, I shouted against the howling wind,

"What was wrong with your potato?"

"Rotten!" my sister said. "Ugh!"

I laughed at her querulous reply, but felt sorry for the unknown child who would get only a rotten potato for Christmas. As I parked my bike in the lobby, Annie said,

"That was so DUMB," and I had to agree with her.

All in all, I loved school even though there were days when I was glad to be able to stay away, and I wrote denunciatory letters to Louise regarding the oppressive rule of the Convent. But I loved the beautiful grounds, the highly polished floors; I loved Mother Fitzgerald and Mother Lewis who introduced us to Caedmon and Bede, Cynewulf and Chaucer. In a report, I had written: "Cynewulf lived in the 8th century. He was a great writer, and wrote "Crist" "Elene" and "Fates of the Apostles" and "Judith." Nothing else is known of him. This pithy piece appeared in a folder I made, aptly titled "Lapses of Literature", which my Grandmother had kept these many years.

There were transoms above every door in the Convent of the Sacred Heart and I had a deep dislike of those windowed air vents, spending far too much time looking up at them, always expecting to see a face peering down at me when the doors were closed, and relieved when it never happened.

Because I was so involved in school, my Grandma liked to talk of the time when she was a girl and had gone to the Hanbury School in old Shanghai. She'd corner me and tell me long tales of her adventure, saying: "When I was a girl like you..."

I learned that my Grandmother had owned the first pair of roller skates in Shanghai, which was quite a distinction. (She also told us that our Grandpa Vincent had been the first man to own a horse and carriage in that city.) When she was sixteen years old, my Grandmother had been invited by the Princess Der Ling to spend some time at the Summer Palace in Peking at the court of the Empress Dowager. Grandma went, accompanied by her father, Frank Ferris, to teach English to a nephew of Empress Tzu His, and she told me that after the wealth and splendor of the Palace it had been difficult for her to return to her modest home on Bubbling Well Road. (There was a well on that road and it really bubbled, as I can remember it myself.)

When telling us stories of her past, Grandma seemed to have been fondest of the times she went to Coney Island and "looped-the-loop." The death-defying rides, especially the Barrel of Fun where everybody fell down and ended up in a tangle of arms and legs, had left an indelible mark on her memory, far greater than did the fabled Summer Palace and the tyrannical Empress Dowager in the legendary city of old Peking.

Grandma often remarked on the fact that swarms of the old Palace Eunuchs fled to Shanghai when the Empress Dowager left Peking when the new regime collapsed long ago. Grandma never missed a chance to denigrate those pitiful creatures when we saw them, and I would cringe at the sight of their fat, ponderous bodies, and especially at their huge but delicate seeming hands and fingers.

Chapter 10

We'd been living in the I.S.S. Building with our Grandparents and Auntie Ida for several months when Louise returned to Shanghai from Manila in 1939. At first, I thought she had come to take us so that we might make another home together, but I soon realized that it would be financially impossible. My mother worked for the Shanghai Evening Post and Mercury newspaper in the advertising department, and for a few weeks she stayed in the crowded apartment with us, using the little box-room for a place to sleep. One evening, I found her crying. She was sitting at a vanity table that Grandma put in the hallway for Louise to use, and she was brushing her beautiful brown hair in front of the mirror with the tears trickling down her cheeks. I was alarmed and asked what the matter was. My mother threw her arms around me and, burying her tear-streaked face on my shoulder, said,

"A friend of mine is in town but I can't see him now because he has his wife with him," sobbing.

Soon afterwards, Louise moved into an apartment of her own across the Garden Bridge, but we children remained with Grandpa. On weekends she would come to take one of us to spend the night with her there, which meant we each got a turn once a month. It was a luxury studio apartment with a lovely view of the Whangpoo River, and considered a very posh address. It seemed like forever until my turn came round again, and I looked forward to spending the night alone with my mother with such an intensity that at times I felt positively feverish when she'd come to get me. Louise had her own rickshaw and we'd ride to her place cuddled up in the tiny carriage. I loved being in her exciting presence; the smell of her hair intoxicated me; the warmth of her body close to mine was almost more than I could bear.

We spoke frequently of the day when we would all be together again and not have to live with Grandma, and my mother spun out my dream of that longed-for time in fine, sugary threads of promises, gathering them up in a shimmering ball of cotton candy on which I fed my hungry little soul, and waited.

It was my turn again and I fretted impatiently until Louise arrived. I couldn't wait to leave and paid no attention to my Grandmother's sneering looks which I put down as jealousy on her part since she invariably managed to say or do something sinister whenever one of us was waiting for Louise. I'd hover by the front door, dashing out in the corridor every minute or so to see if my mother was coming from the elevator, and Grandma would yell at me, saying,

"Keep that door shut. You're making me nervous."

I was fully aware that Grandma did not like any of us going to spend a night with Louise in her apartment. She had engaged my mother in a horrendous argument when Louise decided to move away from the I.S.S. Building, and it had seemed to be mainly over the expense of it; but a great deal more was said that had little to do with money. I knew what my Grandmother thought of Louise because whenever I did anything that displeased her, she would put on her most hateful expression, and using her iciest tone of voice would say, in deep disgust,

"You're just like your mother."

And I understood it to be the strongest insult she could deliver to me. I hardened my heart against Grandma when this happened and the opprobrium only strengthened my loyalties to Louise, giving rise to that deep reserve of protectiveness and partisanship I felt for her. It angered me to be forced to choose between these two women, both of whom I loved so vigorously, and sometimes I'd think fleetingly of how Smith must have felt, pinned as he had been between them. He had not fared any better than I in this regard, and now they had me to finish out the game.

Louise was late, but nothing mattered once she arrived. She kissed the boys and Annie as we said hurried goodbyes to Grandma, leaving before she could embroil us in another row. I chattered all the way and my mother listened absently. Sometimes Louise would ask me a question and look so interested and delighted, and as I answered I could see her drift off so that I might just as easily have spoken gibberish to her and she would have still looked at me with that veiled, somnolent expression and said, "How nice,"

as though I'd told her I had received a perfect report card at school. It dismayed me, but I knew she had a lot on her mind and was certain that all she ever thought about was how she could make a home for us and have us together again.

We came into her well-appointed little flat and before I could catch my breath my eyes fell on the coffee table where I saw a man's pipe in the ashtray. I was stricken; but the molten metals of my interior hissed into the frigid waters of suspicion, hardening into sheets of armor plate. I said nothing. I ate little, smiled not at all, and can't remember how the rest of the time was spent there with her. No one else came to the apartment. No one called her on the telephone. Louise maundered gaily, peering at me every so often with a quizzical and amused look in her large brown eyes.

The next morning, as I readied to go back to the I.S.S., my mood had not changed with sleep and I was angry that the pipe had spoiled my long-awaited visit with Louise. I must have looked at the hated briar dozens of times, but I had not gone near it or touched it, nor had I asked any questions about it. As I stood at the door waiting for my mother to get her things, she walked over to the low table and picked up the ashtray. She held the pipe in her hand and I saw immediately that it and the ashtray were all of a piece, the pipe being only an ornamental one made from the same ceramic as the ashtray. It was just a decoration! I had agonized over nothing and wasted my precious time with her all because of a cleverly wrought bit of clay and glaze, and she had let me suffer over it, finding my jealousy flattering and funny. My mother said,

"You thought this was a real pipe didn't you? You thought there'd been a man here, didn't you?" she laughed harder than I had ever remembered her laughing, shaking all over and screwing up her face the way Grandma did when she was overcome with amusement. Louise sat on the couch and laughed uncontrollably, and I, standing at the door, consumed with rage and bitterness, feeling utterly helpless and foolish, loved her still. But I had been warned by that experience and it lodged in my mind to serve as a reminder that treachery lay in the least expected places, that cruelty wore a loved one's face, and that the hand striking a death blow might well be the hand of someone trusted and cherished.

Forewarned is forearmed, it is said, but to sally forth each day of one's life armed to the teeth, in full battle array, with flags flying and sword glistening, visor clamped tightly over the face, is totally immobilizing and a most exhausting way to live; too much energy is expended in guarding against the moment when one might be attacked or ambushed, which leaves little time for getting on with the job of living. I learned that to be sane is to live as though things were going to be all right, even if they didn't make sense, and that if they were not all right, then to do whatever I could to make some sense out of it and get on with my life. It is a bit easier to do that now, but at the time of the pipe-in-the-ashtray, when I was nine years old, I had not perfected the system.

Louise had smote me.

The wound was mortal, and there was no balm in Gilead.

Vincent and I used to stand on either side of Grandma's double bed and toss Annie back and forth across it, much to her delight, but to the horror of the amahs who thought we'd surely kill the child. Whenever we played hide-and-seek we'd crawl under the beds, and I can still hear Grandma droning her exasperated admonition,

"You kids will BREAK YOUR BACKS coming out from under the bed!"

Whenever she had to discipline us orally, (she never excused herself when she was throwing books at us or hitting us with her slipper or a coat hanger), she would tell us the story of the man whose mother had never said one word when he was a child about his lying, cheating, and stealing. When he grew up he became a thief and a murderer and was caught and put in prison under sentence of death. As he went to the gallows to be hanged, the prison authorities allowed his mother to visit him for the last time, and the old lady tottered up the steps to give her criminal son a last kiss for goodbye. She came to him and as she put her arms around him, he bit off her ear, saying, "If you had only been strict with me, I would not be dying here today."

"So, you see," our Grandma would tell us, "I have to be strict with you children so that doesn't happen to us."

The story made a vivid impression upon The Four of Us and we have been careful not to engage too heavily in the arts of lying, cheating, stealing and killing to this day.

Louise would come by our apartment for dinner, in between our turns, and sometimes we would reminisce about our days in other places. She reminded us of the time I had saved twenty-five centavos and wanted to buy something very special with the coins. I'd gone to a drug-store in Manila, where we lived then, and of all the things in the shop decided upon a blue Tek toothbrush. But once I'd gotten it home and unwrapped it I'd dropped it on the floor and was heart-broken that the prized purchase was no longer "germ-free." Tearfully, I'd sobbed out my pitiful story to my mother and she'd advised me to dip the thing in boiling water and have it in pristine condition once more. Reasoning that if a "dip" would do it good, a "boil" would do better, I'd dropped the toothbrush into a pan of boiling water and let it cook for several minutes. The resulting twisted, misshapen piece of plastic was such a horrible surprise to me, and such a grotesquely funny thing to my mother, that she laughed again to think of my shocked face as I came to show her what had happened to my beloved treasure, and my brothers and Annie chortled in glee at the vision of Big Sister having to endure that humbling experience.

Another adventure which took the wind out of my sails occurred at this time. The paper for which Louise worked started a contest and the person who sold the most subscriptions to the Shanghai Evening Post and Mercury would win a bicycle. With high hopes, I made the rounds of every apartment in our building and did not sell one subscription. Days went by and my depression mounted as my failure became absolute. Again, in tears, the next time Louise showed up I rushed at her wailing my disappointment and she promised me that she'd get the prize in my name. And she did! I don't know whether she sold the most subscriptions, but she brought me a gorgeous red English bike which opened up a whole new world for me, and which I loved more than anything else I had ever owned.

I had not had my tenth birthday when Louise left us again and returned to Manila, and I did not know at the time that when I was to see her next, it would be as an almost grown woman of fifteen with a war behind me and a mind of my own. My mother used a special whistle whenever she wanted to call us together and it was the sound of that whistle that I missed with a sharp ache. Annie and my brothers and I would then whistle for one another, using the same notes Louise had, and we call each other that way yet when we visit, whistling as we come up the walk to one another's houses and time stands still for us for a moment at the sound of that short trill.

My mother kept all the letters I'd written to her during these next five years and I found them in my sister's collection of family memorabilia. Reading them over, thirty-six years later, brought back so many memories and things I'd long forgotten flooded back in high tide. This far removed from the child who'd penned those grubby pages, I could see that they were close to being "fan letters" and must have afforded their recipient a great boost to her ego; but they were also outpourings of emotion, filled with flowery declarations of love, stereotyped dreams of white cottages and climbing roses, descriptions of the bright future when we would live happily as a family, obsequious apologies for being impatient and lacking faith in the realization of our dreams. They were passionate letters for a child to have written and the expectations they revealed were so utterly unrealistic that the devastating disappointments which ultimately followed were guaranteed to be of a critical nature. My mother's letters to me, left behind when we kids went to camp were lost, I can remember as being full of hope and rosy descriptions of what it would be like when we finally came together, and they fed my fantasies which in turn sustained me through the next five years of my life.

Soon after I reached my tenth birthday, we got word that Louise had married in Manila. She sent us a full length picture of herself in a formal gown, standing alone in a spotlight, with her hair tightly curled and a posed smile on her lips. The only picture we ever saw of the man Louise had married was a tiny snap shot which showed a group of people around an airplane, with her husband in the center, short, fat, bald and heavy-lidded, pointing to a piece of paper in his hand. He wrote not one line to us, but Louise never failed to say that he sent us all his love and longed for the day when he could see us. I snarled, reading that.

I think that as far as she was able, my mother sent money to Grandpa for our maintenance, but I doubt that it was regular in coming, and the war, later on, made it quite impossible to send drafts to Shanghai from Canada and the United States where Louise and this man eventually settled.

In my mother's absence, I turned needfully toward my Auntie Ida who had developed a very real concern about me and my siblings. Ida filled a void in my existence and it was she who made sense out of the chaos. She had not married then, although she was a quietly beautiful woman, and made her home with her parents until she married Arne Helleryd, a Swedish diplomat in Shanghai.

Ida could empathize with a little girl whose mother had gone off and left her behind. She had been such a child as I was, and she had not forgotten what it had been like for herself. My aunt had every reason to be resentful of our boisterous presence in the crowded apartment, but she always treated us fairly and with much kindness, although I know that our noisy ways and unmannerly behavior grated on her nerves and at times drove her to distraction. She scolded us frequently, but her posture was firm and reasonable, and she did not resort to the dramatic bleatings of her mother and sister in airing her grievances. Ida was more like her father, Vincent, than anyone else, and she held a responsible position in an office downtown, working hard and contributing to the household expenses, and many times seeing to it that we children had what we needed by paying for it herself. She was, understandably, bitter toward our father, Smith, who had created such havoc in her family's life, but she bore his children no grudge and, indeed, loved us in her own way, enhancing the quality of our lives as best she could under the circumstances.

My Grandfather had suffered financial reverses caused by the war in 1937, and Louise did not seem able to send enough for our many needs; but we managed to have serviceable clothes and shoes, and never went hungry while we lived at the I.S.S., all of which can partly be laid to the good offices of our Auntie Ida. She used to have new clothes made especially for us once a year, and brought Annie and me wide, satin ribbons for our long hair. Then she'd take us to the photographer to have our portraits made so that Louise could see how we were growing up and that we looked well and happy. There was always a great fuss made about the picture-taking sessions and we considered the sittings to be the one important event of the year. We knew why it was being done and all cooperated as best we could. Grandma would say petulantly,

"Fat lot that one will care about having pictures of her kids."

But I knew Louise cared and would be proud to see how much we'd grown and how nice we looked, the boys in their neat suits and ties and Annie and me in our tucked-bodice blue dresses with our hair brushed and be-ribboned.

Ida was the antithesis of her sister. I recognized that there were differences between the two but was unwilling to admit that it felt safer to be in the care of one who was sensible, reliable, tidy and cautious. Ida might not have been as romantic a figure as Louise, nor did she possess her flair and flamboyance, but a little of that goes a long way when one is trying to grow up, even though "colorful people" are more fun, and as I did with Grandpa so did I appreciate in my Aunt the considerate, honest, conservative nature which she evidenced. There were times when I secretly wished she had been my mother instead of Louise and I sought to emulate her, knowing that she was the best example I would ever have upon whom to model my own demeanor. I felt that Ida loved and liked me very much and I was comfortable in her crisp company, knowing exactly where I stood with her. She made everything very plain and took the guesswork out of my relationship with her. She said what was on her mind and stated it clearly, without one devious syllable.

Whenever she'd see that I had grown out of my school clothes and took me to get replacements for my uniforms, Ida would stand aside and look at her "finished product" and say with a proud smile, patting my back,

"My, how sweet you look," and put her finger up to her lips, musingly, cocking her head and appearing so pleased with me. I'd swell with self-importance and a sense of wellbeing, and these trips to the shops made me feel that I was cared for by a woman with a fine eye and a steady hand, and it did a great deal for my self-image.

Ida was unfailingly well-groomed, wearing clothes which suited her admirably. Her hair, always clean, shining and glossy, looked so attractive to me, and her taste in all things was impeccable. She knew what was good and she never lied to me or let me down and best of all, my Aunt did not promise me anything that she knew she could not deliver. In many ways, she took my mother's place, doing all the motherly things we needed, but she made no attempt to usurp Louise's place in the hearts of her children as Grandma did often enough, without success. In all truthfulness, I think Ida felt differently towards me than she did the others. She ministered to the boys and Annie, but I used to feel that she truly loved me and shared more of herself with me. Ida was never unkind or cruel to the boys, but she did not have much time for them and they were extremely annoying, as small boys often are, and not as lovable as Annie, who was everyone's pet and darling.

My Auntie Ida played a smashing game of tennis and she would sometimes take me to the French Club where I'd watch her play, so proud of her slim, athletic figure on the courts, so pleased with her when she'd win the match. The women in my family were small and well-formed and I dearly hoped that I would grow up to look the way Auntie Ida did in her white tennis dress. In the company of others, she treated me in a manner which made me feel as though I were a special person, never ordering me around or causing me to feel small and insignificant. She gave me confidence and I basked in her approving glances, so pleased to be seen in her company. I liked the sense of belonging to her and trusted her implicitly in every way, not only in the sense that she would be honest with me, but also that I could depend upon her, and in all of my life, Ida has never let me down.

When I came to realize the influence Ida had had on me as I grew to young womanhood, it has since crossed my mind more than once that the fact my father died and our mother left us as she did was not the terrible misfortune I had originally thought it to be. How much better for us all to have remained in one place, under my Grandfather's aegis, and to flourish in so steadying an atmosphere as provided by our Aunt.

Grandpa was the Roast Beef, Ida was the Yorkshire pudding and Buttered Vegetables, and Grandma was the English Trifle of my life in those days. How lucky we were to have had it all; but I did not think of it in these terms while I was growing up in the apartment, and spent my time mooning over my absent mother whom I missed so painfully, idolizing her beyond all reason, and counting the days when we would be reunited once again.

CONSULADO GENERAL DE ESPAÑA EN SHANGHAI

Certificado de Nacionalidad n.º ....

Left: Louise's 1939 Spanish passport when she left for Manila and we did not meet again until December 1943 in California.

EL CONSUL GENERAL DE ESPAÑA

CERTIFICO: Que en el Registro de matrícula de españoles que existen en este Consulado hay una partida señalada con el número .... que dice:

Don ....

nacido en .... *provincia de* ....

el ...... *de* .... *de 19* ...... *profesión* ....

estado .... *residente en* ....

Y a fin de que el interesado pueda acreditar su nacionalidad expido el presente a ...... *de* ....

de ....

El Cónsul General de España,

Clase
GRATIS
Art.........del Arancel
Disposicion 5ª del Arancel.
Derechos..............

....
Firma del interesado,

Above: Anne and Mary, Shanghai, 1940.

Vincent Vizenzinovich
1940

Spanish Consulate document for Grandpa Vincent 1940

CONSULADO GENERAL DE ESPAÑA EN SHANGHAI

Certificadó de Nacionalidad n.° ..[illegible]..........

EL CONSUL GENERAL DE ESPAÑA

CERTIFICO: Que en el Registro de matrícula de españoles que existen en este Consulado hay una partida señalada con el número.795..que dice:

Don..Vicente [illegible] Zen.......

nacido en..[illegible]........ *provincia de*.[illegible]

el.10.*de*..Septiembre *de* 1866...*professión*.[illegible]

estado..casado. *res dente en*......Shanghai.......

Y a fin de que el interesado pueda acreditar su nacional dad expido el presente a..12.*de*..Enero.......

de..1940...........

El Consul General de España,

Sello

Clase...............

Art. GRATIS del Arancel

Derechos. Disposición 5ª del Arancel

....

Firma del interesado,

Anne's First Holy Communion 1941.

Chapter 11

Vincent had discovered a Chinese nonsense song which he would sing all day long until we begged for mercy or threatened to have him disemboweled in the front lobby in the presence of his enemies.

"Ja-li-ma-li
Toong-toong piang
Ja-li-ma-li
Toong-toong piang"

He'd sing, disregarding the threats and entreaties alike.

"Ja-li-ma-li" was a Shanghai dialect slang word for the Indian Sikhs who served as police in the British Settlement, and the servants told us that it was the way their language sounded to the Chinese ears. It was probably a racist song and not meant to be complimentary, I'm afraid, and I never knew exactly what the words meant.

As much as we hated his singing it, discovering that Vincent's incessant song irked our Grandmother far more severely than it annoyed us, we'd egg him on, and then the two younger kids would join in a chorus while I went into paroxysms of laughter to see Grandma's face draw into a tight grimace. It was a harmless amusement for us but Vincent's song grew into a vexation of major proportions for Grandma.

It was a hot, muggy night, the windows were open, and my brother was singing his simple-minded lyric while he and the two younger ones jumped rhythmically on the beds in our room. The song lent a proper cadence to their jumping, the creaking bed springs making just the right accompaniment for his song. Grandma, who had been sitting in the outer room, transfixed against her will by Vinnie's hypnotic ditty, suddenly erupted in a volcanic fury and burst into the bedroom where my brothers and Annie were mindlessly bouncing themselves to sleep as I read quietly to myself.

Grandma charged in, armed with a bamboo fly swatter, and flailed vigorously at the three unsuspecting brats who had all but sung and bounced themselves into a stupor. They fell in a heap on the bed, cowering together, trying to ward off the swift and terrible punishment meted out by that Oriental pest controlling device which bit into their legs and stung painfully. Grandma, whacking them indiscriminately, shrieked at the top of her lungs,

"STOP THAT SINGING! There is NO SUCH A SONG! Stop it RIGHT NOW YOU STUPID BOY! There is NO SUCH A SONG AS THAT SUPID SONG! Do you HEAR me? NO SUCH SONG!"

Her eyes watering in rage, Grandma stopped for a moment to catch her breath and as she inhaled to allow for further venting of her spleen, there came the unmistakable strains of

"Ja-li-ma-li
Toong-toong piang"

wafting from the street below. We were thunderstruck but pricked up our ears. Grandma, fly swatter poised for a renewed onslaught, heard The Song being sung by an unknown strolling Chinese passing beneath our very windows and she rushed towards them to hurl a few choice epithets in the songbird's direction. We also looked out across the street to see who had unwittingly saved the day for us, and saw a young peasant fellow under the street lamp carrying a basket. He looked up shading his eyes to see who it was heaping abuse on his head, and when he spied our furious grandmother shaking her fly swatter at him, he responded with a rude finger-sign which I have discovered to be a universal salute whose obscene definition does not vary from country to country, and whose meaning, which neither the passage of time nor the usage of language has impaired, remains intact.

No one dared look triumphantly at Angry Lady with Bamboo Fly Swatter. We muttered our good-nights and crept into bed quietly as Grandma swept out, her face flushed, banging the door as she left. We quaked in our stifled laughter, choking on the delicious waves of hysteria as they rose uncontrollably in our chests, our faces contorted and buried in our pillows and our stomachs aching with the spasms of convulsive silent cackling.

The Song was sung again many times after that hot summer night, but never within our Grandmother's earshot.

She, on the other hand, did not have the self-same consideration for us because one day she came home from S. Moutrie and Company on Nanking Road, where she liked to browse and buy sheet music, and had been introduced to a song called "Nola" with which she had immediately fallen madly in love. Grandma played "Nola" for days. We'd stand around the piano singing snatches of songs that had no relation to "Nola"

"...of gladness
Fall on the ea-ear.
Voices long hushed
Now their full notes prolo-ong
Echoing far and near."

Hoping to throw her off, but she played on, and she played "N O L A". Have you any idea how difficult it is to sing any other song to the tune of "Nola"? We tried them all, all that is except Vincent's famous ditty. We were none of us that inspired. Clustered about our Grandma as she sat rooted to her piano stool we would sing as loudly as we could and as much in harmony as was humanly possible:

"There's a Long Long Trail A-Winding"

And

"It's a Long Way to Tipperary"

which she had taught us, and in a speeded-up tempo we'd rattled off that lullaby

"Just a song at twilight
When the lights are low
And the flickering shadows
Softly come and go.
Whipporwills are singing
Robin's in his nest.
Just a song at twilight
Lulls me to rest.
Lulls mee-e-e to sweet rest."

giving a maniacal rendition of that faintly saccharine composition, complete with foot-stampings and a lot of very ugly faces which we were expert in making. Annie was especially adept at facial expressions which called for the tongue to be sticking out in a variety of positions. Of course, much of this behavior was executed facing the piano, and Grandma, intent on her keyboard, missed seeing some of the nastier grimaces we offered.

Our singing other songs and her playing that one maddening piece, "Nola", became a duel in cacophony, and it was the best fun I can remember us having in the world of music, with one exception.

I can't recall whose original idea it was, but quite often when it rained and we couldn't go out to play on the roof-garden of the apartment building, Grandma would get out sheaves of Grand March Music and while she played "The Double Eagle" (our favorite) and other martial airs, we would scurry into the kitchen and fit our heads with whatever pots or pans the cook was not using at the moment, and with the lids for cymbals, we'd parade around the rooms, circling through the hallway, the bathroom, the bedroom, the living and dining room, and back into the hall once more. We marched like determined soldiers and clanged our cymbals to our own private rhythms, stamping our feet down hard on the floor. This was all very well during the daytime when the people who lived in the apartment below were out to work, but there were a few occasions when it wasn't even raining that I remember us marching and clanging about at night. I don't know whether it was because Grandma felt like playing that particular kind of music or whether we could not control our urge to march, but we did give a few performances during the nighttime hours. It was one of those things that one is never sure of explaining how it got started, but once begun it was hard to stop.

My Grandfather always looked very surprised when we appeared with the pots on our heads and in deference to him we eschewed the lid-banging when he was at home, waving at him as we marched by each time while the poor old gentleman sat in his chair trying to read his evening paper. I doubt that the day's events included such bizarre accounts as the report of marches held in the city which equaled ours.

Once, my Grandpa said, "I think that's enough now." and Grandma said pettishly, "Oh, leave them alone. It keeps them quiet and happy!" and launched into another stirring Sousa arrangement. He had learned, long ago, not to expect rational answers from an occasionally irrational piano artist, and went back to reading his paper amidst the din.

Grandma did not teach me a great deal about music, but I learned something about tolerance from my Grandpa, and could recognize the difference between sullen resignation and willing acceptance, which knowledge was his greatest gift to me.

The last favorite song my Grandmother had was "Raindrops Keep Falling on My Head." I got her the recording of the sound track from the movie about the two desperadoes who died in a blaze of gunfire, and she had shaken her head and said,

"What lovely music for such a horrible story." After her death I found that she had made a note to herself on her check register which read: "Raindrops Keep Falling'-must get sheet music for piano." It was the last item on the list of things-to-do that she made in her life, and in many ways that was truly "her song."

Chapter 12

Grandma played the stock market the same way she played the piano. She had made and lost small fortunes through the years and considered herself an astute businesswoman, but Hetty Green she never was. Every other month or so she would announce to me that I was not to attend school that day but to wear my usual uniform, nonetheless, and when I was ready she'd have me lift my skirt and petticoat, pull down my black bloomers, and between my singlet and red hug-me-tight she would strap on a canvas money belt into which she'd zipper thousands of dollars in Chinese paper money. The reason for this, she said,
"...is because no one will suspect a little girl like you to have all this 'dung-dee' around her belly."

She and I then took the tram downtown to a brokerage firm called Swan Culbertson & Fritz where I'd spend the day sitting around the smoke-filled, noisy counting house until Grandma decided she wanted to buy something like Anaconda Copper or rubber shares, or whatever. At that point, she would signal excitedly to me and I'd trot out to the ladies' room where she'd lock us into one of the cubicles and proceed to dig furiously into my clothing, flinging up my skirts for me to hold in front of my face while she rooted in the money belt, getting what she needed for the transaction she was about to make. Any perceptive brigand could easily have figured out what we were up to, and I used to feel uneasy when anyone looked at me, not considering that the presence of a small foreign girl in a convent uniform was an unusual sight in that frenetic setting. (In my Shanghai days there were only two categories of people – Chinese and Foreigners.) It occurred to me that some nefarious type might take it in mind to kidnap me while my Grandmother was turned the other way, but she had taken precautions against that contingency by pinning medals of St. Jude, St. Christopher and the Blessed Virgin to the outside of the bulky money belt I wore, so really, I was quite safe from all harm in that respect.

She kept me busy popping up and down for hours, and sometimes she even stuffed more money into the belt instead of removing it. During these forays, Grandma would completely forget that I was flesh and blood and regarded me as nothing more than a walking depository with a handy zipper. It was hot and uncomfortable in that busy place and the chairs were so hard that I would be quite stiff at the end of the day, hungry, restive, bored and truculent. To make up to me for all my inconvenience, Grandma would promise a treat at Bianchi's or the Chocolate Shop when the market closed, and she was as good as her word.

Bianchi's was a luscious confectionary shop, a paradise of cream cakes and éclairs, Napoleons and glazed fruit tarts. She'd buy me a box of "marrons glaces" or a fistful of barley sugar sticks to take home after I'd stuffed myself on pastries and hot chocolate with whipped cream. The "babas au rhum" were delectable and my mouth waters even now to think of Bianchi's meringues and cream horns, the like of which I've not found since.

The Chocolate Shop was more of an ice cream parlor, and I was mad for their banana splits and sundaes. Sometimes Grandma would take me to the Palace Hotel on the Bund and we'd sit by the enormous windows looking out on the street. A small ensemble would play "refined" music as a foreign waitress in a French maid's costume served a staggering variety of pastries in fluted paper cups from a silver tea-cart. Everything was so elegant and tasteful and I loved every minute of it except the moment before we began to eat when Grandma, making the sign of the cross in great sweeping gestures, would say loudly for everyone to hear, "In the name of the Father…" and proceed to say grace. I would be mortified and bury my eyes in my fists, hoping no one noticed this bizarre ceremony in public. I thought it almost as bad as when my father had come into the lobby of the Palace and done his Tarzan of the Apes act on their chandelier, and I prayed that no one would know of my connection with him, especially now that I was back with yet another person who was given to strange behavior.

On our visits to downtown Shanghai, we had to pass an American bar or two on the way, and the dank, moldering smell of stale liquor and cigarette smoke emanating from these dens of iniquity triggered a small memory which I refused to acknowledge but which made me more than slightly queasy. Once, as we passed by, I looked inside and saw the bar stools lined up against the long counter in a saloon that had dusty Polynesian décor; the sight sickened me, and I turned away quickly.

Swarms of beggars thronged the crowded streets and my Grandmother clutched her bag tightly since there were so many incidents of purse-snatchings in those days. She would take me to the Hong Kong-Shanghai Bank, a hallowed building with marble pillars and floors, and high Carrera tables at which one stood to write important things in little black books. Sometimes Grandma took all of us downtown on an errand, and at the bank, while she conducted her business, we'd play underneath the tables and slide on the glassy floor, twirling around the pillars and making a general nuisance of ourselves. She was extremely permissive about this behavior of ours, and I don't remember her ever telling us to stop in spite of all the disapproving looks we got from the staid customers and clerks.

The bank had large, deep windows with iron grillwork in front of the massive panes and the outside sills were big enough for several people to sit in. Some beggar families took up their abode in these windows and lived out their lives in them, their abject poverty and misery on display for the world to see and pity with a coin or two thrown their way. Many of them were what my Grandma called "professional beggars" and they had regular stations so that one got to know them fairly well. Whole families of maimed children, some without legs and arms, some with running sores covered with flies, all incredibly ragged and filthy, had a sort of squatters' rights to the bank's outside window sills, and we, inside the building, could stand right by the glass and watch them without being seen. One group had a father who kept the stump of his severed knee on view for the passersby and the wound had never seemed to heal as I saw it from time to time in a state of constant fester. The mother sat cross-legged on the ledge and emitted a screeching yowl in which she described their plight, and at regular intervals she'd bang her forehead on the stone sill beneath her knees. This poor woman had a permanent lump where her head met the cold hardness each time. They had five children afflicted with various stages of skin eruptions, each with a runny nose and inflamed eyes, hair growing in tufts from their heads and all in a general ghastly condition.

My brother Vincent and I, safe on the inside behind the grille, would peer at them through the glass, and watch these wretched children playing behind their parents' backs, doing the mysterious finger games that Chinese youngsters perform so deftly, laughing together, nudging one another, seemingly oblivious to their unbelievable state. Then, the father would notice a well-dressed and probably rich man approaching and he would turn around and hit the children behind him, and they immediately took up a supplicant attitude, stretching out their hands and braying pitifully for the wealthy man passing their stall to toss them a few coppers. As soon as he had gone on his way, the beggar children would resume their cunning quiet games and be giggling and smiling once more, only to start the performance again when punched into action by their parents. Children will play anywhere, in the most appalling situations, finding a bit of "joie" in any one of a thousand hellish days.

We never thought this heartbreaking scene to be funny and I grieved for those poor little lost souls who had nothing to look forward to in their lives. The amahs used to tell me that many professional beggars bought children from the country and trained them to be useful in that business, breaking their legs and arms, or disfiguring them in obscene ways so as to incite pity in those who gazed upon them, and the more fearsome their appearance the more valuable they were to their owners.

When the Chinese Communists took over the government I heard that one of the first things on their agenda was to clear the streets of the beggar population, and overnight these unfortunate beings disappeared. I trust and pray that they were rehabilitated and that work was found for them, and that the pile of human refuse was salvaged and given some hope for a decent life in the New China, no more to debase themselves or corrupt and destroy their children for the sake of a mouthful of swill. There must be people now alive in Shanghai who are my age who lived in the deep windows of the Hong Kong-Shanghai Bank, and I hope that they have fared well and are still alive to the glory of their nation.

As much as I deplore the offensive term "coolie", that is what laborers were called in those days, and the rickshaw coolies were a special breed. We often rode in these hand-pulled carts and I looked closely at their bulging legs, thick with darkly broken veins and ropey muscles, as they ran ahead of us. They wore woven straw sandals which lasted not longer than a day, and in the rain they used straw hats and coats which gave them the appearance of thatched huts jogging through the Shanghai traffic. Some of them were too poor to afford the straw sandals and wrapped their feet in newspapers in a most ingenious way. The amahs said these rickshaw men rarely lived beyond the age of thirty and it was easy to believe that information. In the summer, many of them dropped in the streets in exhaustion, dying from heart seizures in the muggy heat, and from malnutrition, one can be sure.

I remember blistering summer afternoons watching the sweat pouring down their naked backs in streams as they puffed along, dodging one another and cursing anyone who got in their way. Our Grandparents took us with them in rickshaws whenever we had to go somewhere where there was no tram line, and, although they sometimes remarked on the plight of these coolies, it didn't stop them from using their services. During the cold weather we'd see knots of them huddled around a fire someone had built in an old kerosene drum, and the men would try to warm their gnarled and calloused hands in front of the blaze before some new customer called out.

There were stories about the cruelties the rickshaw men were subject to, such as one person who laughingly told of how he had run coolie all over town, and then had left a five-cent piece on the seat and dashed into a building, cheating the man out of his rightful fare. Once, we heard that some drunken sailors had set their rickshaw coolie on fire as he pulled them through the alleys, and I had not wanted to believe that these had been men belonging to the U.S. Navy amusing themselves in this fashion. In passing, I must note that when Shanghailanders got the word that the Fleet was in, the news struck terror in some hearts and many of us went warily and cautiously through the streets. Others, with commodities to sell to sailors on leave, rubbed their hands and set out their wares, and in Shanghai there was nothing that money could not buy.

My brother Jordie insisted that he be allowed to pull the cart after a short trip we'd made with Grandpa, and the rickshaw man was good enough to let the little fellow have a go at it. He got between the long shafts and as soon as he had raised them off the ground he found himself dangling high in the air as the cart tipped over backwards, and we laughed to see that his small body did not have the necessary weight to keep the rickshaw at the proper angle for pulling and riding.

Another time, Annie and I were standing on a corner waiting for the tram, and in the window under which we stood was a large, multi-colored parrot in a cage. It had been taught to say, "Wom-pah-tsoh" which means "Rickshaw" in our dialect, and it called out loudly several times. At this signal, a dozen rickshaw men raced up to us, (they were highly competitive and aggressive), and we had an embarrassing time of it explaining to them that it was not us who had called but that bird in the window. Of course, the miscreant fowl never said another word, and Annie and I were roundly sworn at and cursed in the sulphurous epithets of Shanghai gutter language.

The pulling of human beings in rickshaws by other human beings has been outlawed in China. I applaud that action. Rickshaws may have seemed romantic to the tourists, to readers of the National Geographic, and perhaps to travelogue aficionados, but they were never picturesque or quaint in my opinion, and I am relieved to know that the brutal custom has been abolished.

That profession, which was a notch lower on the social scale to the one I have just described, was the business of what my Grandma referred to as the "Honey Cart" gatherers. In the early mornings one could see columns of Chinese, women and children among them, pulling rough wooden carts through the roads. Their employment was to go from house to house where there were no flush toilets and collect the contents of the commodes, which would then be poured into the rumbling "Maw-doong" carts, as they were called. When filled, the people took their loads to the countryside whether farmers bought the "night soil" to use as fertilizer. The smell was indescribable and unforgettable, and if travellers went to the Orient and did not encounter this overpowering odor they could not truly say that they had been to China. Perhaps there is a better quality of indoor plumbing in that country today, and perhaps the Chinese have devised a less unpleasant way to deal with their waste. Knowing whence our fresh vegetables came, our Grandparents insisted that the cook wash every leaf in permanganate, and I don't recall one instance of our being indisposed because of that ancient style of the fertilization of crops.

On the way home from the Palace Hotel on one of my "counting house days", the tramcar was crowded and I stood against the glass panel which divided the first class from the second class section as Grandma took a seat. I looked down and saw a person through the divider window, sitting with pudgy hands folded on a protruding stomach. It was hard to tell whether the person was a man or a woman since most Chinese dressed alike, regardless of sex, and I couldn't see what it was by the gown it wore. A beardless, puffed face stuck out from a billiard-ball head which sat directly on a pair of rounded shoulders, the neck having disappeared, and the body, which looked doughy and soft, pushed out against the frayed silk tunic. The person wore an impassive expression, staring straight ahead, looking at nothing, and our eyes never met. Its fingernails were long and curved over, and there were rings on each of the fingers of its milky hands. It sighed from time to time as I could see from the slight heaving of that prominent flabby breast, but otherwise was totally apathetic. I stared, fascinated, transfixed, a mongoose confronting a cobra, and I would have run, screaming, but for the crush of passengers and my Grandmother sitting on the tram. I edged away from the glass panel, pushing my way to the other end of the car so as to be as far from that creature as I possibly could that moment. My heart thudded in my throat and tiny sparks of light burst behind my eyes. I watched each stop and finally saw the person get off the tram and waddle away into the dusk, and I knew him even though I had never seen him before in my life.

Later, my Grandmother said,

"Did you see that strange looking man get off the tramcar? That was a eunuch. They all look alike. There are still a few of them around from the old days of the court. Pitiful things."

Whispering in my ear, Grandma would say,

"Let's Grandma and Mary get up early in the morning tomorrow and go to the Zikawei Cathedral for Mass and Holy Communion. It's the First Friday of the month, you know."

I'd say, "Okay, but why are we whispering?" and she would answer,

"So the Devil can't hear us and try to prevent us from going."

It never failed to raise the hair on the back of my neck when she spoke of Beelzebub as though he were present, lurking at our elbows, trying to hear what we might be saying. The Devil was very real to Grandma and she spent more time engaging him in mortal combat than she did in giving praise and hosannas to the Almighty. Satan kept Lady Georgina very busy and proved to be a worthy opponent to her life's work.

Zikawei Cathedral was built on the banks of the Soochow Creek, an ooze of green slime jammed with sampans, and the Boat People who lived on them rarely, if ever, set foot on dry land in their lifetimes. It was not unusual to see a man urinating into the water while an old crone threw a bucket of stinking garbage overboard at one end of the boat, and to watch another woman washing rice in a basket in the same creek on the other side of the sampan. It is a marvel to me that these Boat People contrived to live at all, much less to notice that many of them had reached a ripe old age, and sat contentedly sunning themselves on the narrow decks, smoking their pipes and playing mah-johng.

The Cathedral, built by Catholic missionaries, sat imposingly in a flagstone square and was part of a complex of buildings which housed a school and an orphanage. The girls in the school did fine, intricate, eye-blinding embroidery and needlework, and we would visit their cold work-rooms to watch them painstakingly create pieces of delicate art in silken thread. They wore woolen gloves with the tops of all the fingers cut off at the first joint, so that most of their hands stayed warm. After Mass, we'd visit the dozens of babies who were kept in a huge hall, and the row upon row of iron cribs containing these wistful, benumbed little people, who never smiled or cooed as babies are supposed to do, made my sister Annie and me want to take them in our arms and bring them home for proper care. Their listless faces and thin, limp bodies were pitiful, and we thought they needed hugging desperately, but all we could ever do would be to look into their beds and make clucking noises because our Grandma didn't want us to touch them for fear that we would "catch something." Most of these babies had been thrown away at birth, and the orphanage did the best it could, I suppose, but it is always difficult to give so many children the affection we need to develop properly when the numbers are so great and the help so minimal.

Zikawei Cathedral did not have too many foreign worshippers and when we would attend Mass there we were invariably stared at as though we had just landed on earth from another planet, and I would hear the Chinese discussing our light colored hair and skin, remarking on the green of my eyes. They would say, thinking we did not understand the dialect, "Foreigners smell like mutton!" and screw their noses in disgust. Once, I could not restrain myself and retorted, "And Chinese people smell like bean cake and peanut oil!" and everyone laughed in surprise to hear me speak in Chinese, clapping their hands as we entered the church.

The women and men sat on opposite sides of the aisle, and we did likewise when we were among them. One hot day I'd gone to the Cathedral with Grandma, and I wore a short-sleeved summer dress. When it was time for Communion, I approached the rail and knelt down, only to be passed by when the priest distributed the hosts. My Grandmother kept pointing to me, hoping to remind the priest that he had forgotten me, but he looked at me with a frown and shook his head. I thought he knew some dark secret I had, or something frightful I had done, and I racked my brain to think of what it was. At the end of the service, he called us into the sacristy and said in his French-accented English that he had purposely refused me the Eucharist because I had come to the altar with bared arms, and since he would not honor a Chinese woman in such a flagrant departure from decorum, so was he constrained to reject me with my naked extremities on display in such vulgar fashion. I was furious, but Grandma said she understood his position and went on to say,

"Please forgive us as it will never happen again."

I told her she might have stood up for me, but she insisted that the good Father was correct in his thinking and that she should have known better than to have allowed me to go to Mass "looking like that." I said that this priest ought to meet the nun in Manila who'd made me wear a Mother Hubbard into the bathtub, and Grandma laughed all the way home in the rickshaw.

We had an amah who was Nee-Doo's daughter and when she was to be; married Grandma insisted that she take her vows at the Cathedral even though neither she nor her husband-to-be was Catholic. I think Seh-mee, for that was her name, was patronizing my Grandmother, her employer, when she agreed to it, but it was arranged, and after the traditional Chinese wedding at the joss house the party came to the Zikawei Cathedral to be married again in front of the priest.

It was the only wedding I can remember attending in my childhood, all others paling in comparison, even now. Seh-mee, resplendent in a red silk gown, wearing an ornate headpiece that looked like a tasseled lantern, was borne to the church in a sedan chair and stepped forth from the curtains, proud but shy. She was followed by a group of musicians playing flutes and drums, with cymbals clanging to ward off evil spirits and bad omens. Banners on long bamboo poles fluttered in the breeze as the bride's family brought up the rear. Annie and I, on either side of Grandma, walked behind the wedding group as clutches of curious children, their thick pantaloons slit conveniently from buttocks to crotch, pointed at us in our foreign clothes. We'd look back at them with wide, staring eyes in mock threatening expressions and they would laugh shrilly, hiding their faces in their parents' floppy trousers, and squeal in that universal delight children find in one another.

Afterwards, there was a feast at someone's house and the table groaned under the spread of cakes and sweetmeats, steamed dumplings and glutinous rice wrapped in palm leaves, as the guests paid homage to the "sing-yang-tz" (new bride) and her bashful groom. Nee-Doo made sure that we were given a large box of goodies to take home because she knew that the "Tung-kah", her Master, was very fond of Chinese wedding confections and did not wish him to miss enjoying them, even though Grandpa had not been able to come in person to her daughter's wedding.

My Grandpa said, regarding servants: "You can always tell the 'nouveaux riches' by the rude way they treat their amahs and boys. A real lady is just as courteous to her servants as she is to her family and friends."

However, Grandma paid no heed to this maxim when she was hell-bent on doing us bodily harm with a fly swatter on those occasions when we behaved like monkeys' but it must not have applied if she saw any danger of us being on our way to the hangman's noose, fearing for her ears.

Not a day went by that I did not think of Louise, and not a moment passed that I did not miss her. Once, when she had stayed for a short time in the apartment with us, she'd opened a can of peaches to find that there were only four pieces of fruit in it. She said: "Here's a peach for each of you children to eat, and I will go without."

Louise mentioned that incident many times, and she reminded us of it again when we were reunited some years later.

Chapter 13

There are times when children become restive and quarrelsome, and we four were no exception. My Grandmother never failed to take this as a sure sign that we were in dire need of a dose of "opening medicine" and would tell us to get dressed for a trip to MacTavish and Twigg's, a reputable and formal pharmaceutical shop in downtown Shanghai.

The first time I remember making this journey we'd looked forward to it as a mysterious treat, because that is the way it was presented to us, and we bustled happily off with Grandma on the tram thinking we would meet with high adventure; but it turned out to be a very low trick.

Upon arriving at Twigg's (the shop was also famous for a toffee we had enjoyed many times), my Grandma made a sign to the druggist, and he ushered us into a back room where we were asked to be seated on ornamental metal chairs. While waiting for the man to serve us a special delight, deceptively called by Grandma a "Castor Oil Cocktail", she announced that she had a riddle with an answer for each of us. The question was,

"Who were the four most constipated men in the Bible?" and, squealing delightedly at each of the responses, she delivered herself of these next lines, counting them on her fingers;

"There was Cain who wasn't Abel."

"There was Balaam whose ass wouldn't work."

"There was Solomon who sat on the throne for forty years."

"And there was Moses who took two tablets and fled screaming into the hills."

Of course, the answers had to be explained in detail to us, our knowledge of Biblical stories sorely wanting, and while we were trying to puzzle out this portentous parable, the old druggist appeared bearing four dainty crystal vials filled with what I would now recognize as a *pousse café*. For the uninitiated, a *pousse café* is an after dinner concoction of several liqueurs of different specific gravities poured so as to remain in separate layers, the castor oil floating innocently somewhere between the grenadine and the *crème de menthe*.

"Down the hatch!" she shouted as we gulped the colorful libation in one quick swallow, licking the sticky sweetness around our mouths and looking sheepishly at one another. Grandma was then in a great rush to get us out of the shop, the druggist anxiously helping to herd us to the sidewalk where she would hail a taxi-cab with an energetic flapping of her arms and much ado.

"Why don't we take the tram home?" I asked.

"We have to get back as soon as we can," she replied, looking frantically about and not trying very hard to suppress a particular giggling chuckle she had when she was especially amused.

The taxi ride back to the I.S.S. Building was uneventful and anti-climactic, except for the very interested looks Grandma would shoot at us from time to time.

"Aren't you kids feeling anything?" she asked.

"What are we supposed to feel? Sad? Surprised?" I asked in return, suspicion rising in me as if it had a life of its own. She laughed out loud then and, taking a handkerchief, dabbed at her streaming eyes.

"Are we supposed to be DRUNK or something?" I yelled. "What is this all about?"

The apartment had one bathroom and when the full force of the "opening medicine" struck our unsuspecting innards with its stunning impact, we forgot that thin veneer of civilized behavior with which we had been so haphazardly daubed, and the air was rent with frenzied bleatings as we did the short jerky steps of the MacTavish Twiggs Tango and danced around each other waiting to take our urgent turn on Solomon's seat.

My sister, Annie who was first introduced to these horrors when she was only four, exhibited an extraordinary talent for problem solving, and instead of getting caught in the rush in the over-crowded bathroom had cunningly availed herself of a waste-paper basket she found. Afterwards, she carefully hid the evidence of her impatience behind the sofa, and for many days the household was plagued by an indescribable but very recognizable aroma which made life in such close quarters difficult to endure.

Grandma would wait for a long time before staging that hilarious episode again, hoping that we'd have forgotten about it. The next time we were taken downtown to the druggist's it was on the pretext of having us wormed with pink lozenges shaped like candy kisses. But, once there, she ordered the Castor Oil Cocktails again which I adamantly refused to accept and, pitting my will against hers, budged not an inch.

"Once bitten twice shy, eh?" she taunted me, and just to make amends I agreed to taking the worm medicine whose ultimate action convinced me that the efficacy of the arts of pharmacology as practiced by the Messrs. MacTavish and Twigg far exceeded their advertised promises; and when in control of my own destiny, long after my feet had touched the tram-car floor, I avoided the dependence on so much as an aspirin and prefer to do imitations of the Little Spartan Boy than admit to a ruptured appendix.

Grandma did not believe in taking us to a doctor for any reason whatever except the Pasteur treatment, and when we came down with any of the childhood diseases she tended to us herself, with considerable help from the amahs and the Chinese herbalist. She would force us to drink bitter and nauseating teas as a first line of defense. Each spring she would buy a bag of yellow sulphur powder from Twiggs and set me to work mixing it carefully with a large tin of Lyle's Golden Syrup which came from England. I used to study the tin container with interest, finding the picture on the label so very intriguing. It showed a dead lion with a swarm of bees hovering over it, and the caption read,

"Out of the strong came forth sweetness."

Grandma explained that the bees were making honey in the dead lion's carcass, and I could never understand how the firm of Abram Lyle and Sons, by Appointment to His Majesty the King, Sugar Refiners, ever fixed upon such a macabre image with which to advertise their wares; but the Messrs. Tate and Lyle must have known something about merchandising that escaped me. I would mix the yellow powder with the treacle with great care and when it was stirred in so that the sulphur was well trapped in the sticky stuff, she would call the other three children in and have us take a large spoonful of it, saying that a spring tonic is just what growing children needed when the winter was over and their blood had turned thin and become diluted in the cold weather. We never questioned her medical expertise.

Oftentimes she would resort to ancient Chinese methods of welting and cupping, and if any of us caught a cold we had to plan on being kept out of school for many days until the large red welts on our throats had faded. That particular treatment was called "qua-soh" and it was administered by one of the amahs who would bring a bowl of peanut oil and a large copper coin to the bedroom. The patient would endure the discomfort of having the amah dip the coin into the oil and raise welts on the neck, back and chest with a series of quick rubbings, back and forth, of the oiled coin. It didn't really hurt but was most unpleasant, the worst of it being the ugly red marks the coin left on the tender skin. Sometimes I would have to attend school with a long scarf wrapped around my throat, pretending to be hoarse, so that no one would see the evidence of the primitive medical attention to which I had subjected myself, and as I got older I put up a mighty resistance to this treatment, allowing them only to do things that didn't leave marks which were difficult to explain to friends whose mothers always took them to a "proper" doctor whenever they chanced to fall ill.

Cupping called for outside help in the person of a Chinese herbalist who made house visits, and he would come to relieve my Grandfather of his high blood pressure. It should come as no surprise to anyone to know that this good gentleman suffered from that condition, things being what they were in our house. The man would bring a suitcase fitted out with bell-shaped glass cups which he held over a spirit lamp, and when they had been thoroughly heated, he would slap them onto my Grandpa's chest and I could watch the skin rising up in little mounds inside the glass. It was a more sophisticated form of "qua-soh" and far more efficacious, my Grandpa becoming immediately better and the pressure of his blood reduced before the practitioner left. The man would pull the cups off the patient's chest or back with some force, causing the cups to make a sucking noise as they were lifted away. Once, the man brought a jar of loathsome looking creatures that seemed to be snails without their shells, and he distributed them evenly over my Grandfather's chest. They swelled up and turned a dark color and then seemed to fall off, and my Grandmother said,

"I think the next time you should do the cupping again and not bother with those leeches."

Acupuncture was a method employed in barbershops and we knew about it but never saw it practiced in our home. I would hear the servants discussing the treatment and believed that it had much to recommend it, but I had no firsthand knowledge of the needle therapy in my childhood. As an adult, however, I have found acupuncture to be of great help when afflicted with bursitis as I was some years ago. The Chinese doctor in San Francisco said that in all the centuries it has been practiced no one yet knows how acupuncture works; it just does.

Grandma was ever on the lookout for any of us to have the slightest thing go wrong because the moment she'd discover that there was anything amiss, her eyes would light up in a Hippocratic fervor and she would set about to cure whatever it was that ailed us. If the boys sprained an ankle she made a poultice of what I am certain was fermenting chicken manure and straw, plastering the nasty stuff around the sprain and wrapping the lot in a red flannel rag. The red rag was an integral part of this method for dealing with sprains, and somehow in a day or two, or as long as any of us could stand the dreadful stench given off by this poultice, it would be removed and there would be no sign of discoloration of the skin or any after-effects of a sprain. Either it was a genuine miracle drug or there never had been a bad sprain in the first place, my brothers being infamous malingerers, always vying for our Grandmother's attention.

During the years I lived in the I.S.S. Building with my grandparents it happened that I often had a bad cough and would wheeze at night frequently. At first I was doctored with generous applications of Elliman's Embrocaton, an icy cold, white, creamy substance which Grandma spread on a large piece of cotton wool and would then place it on my chest, covering me from the top of my neck to my waist. The shock of the initial frigid contact with my skin was enough to stop me not only from coughing or wheezing, but from ever breathing again, and presently the whole thing would begin to heat up and burn my chest relentlessly, giving off fumes that seared my nostrils and caused my eyes to water.

"Take this thing off me!" I'd wail.

"Just a little longer, darling. It's only begun to do its work," Grandma would say, and watch the clock until the prescribed time had passed. Then she'd peel away the fire-and-ice plaster and say,

"What a brave girl you are. Now you will be well."

But I wasn't well, and I wheezed on, coughing and hacking into the night. We never heard the word "asthma" so I didn't learn that asthma attacks were often triggered by emotional stress and anxiety until I was a grown woman.

My Grandmother, seeing that I was getting no better, decided that I had The Dread Disease, and she came to me a bit tearfully one afternoon after the Elliman's had not relieved my breathing and said,

"Don't be afraid, but you might well have what is called 'Galloping Consumption.' You see, the reason you are wheezing is that there is a small hole in your lung and the air going in and out of it makes that noise. It's like a toy whistle, don't you know."

I was afraid and didn't want to die from a terminal case of whistles; but my Grandmother devised a solution. She said, "What we have to do now is plug up that hole in your lung."

And I wondered what with, hoping that she had something more substantial in mind than chewing gum. For many days she saw to it that I had a pot of the heaviest whipping cream with sugar stirred into it three times a day, and that, she said, would stop up the hole in my lung. It must have worked because I did not die from Galloping Consumption, but almost expired from a surfeit of heavy cream and sugar thrice a day. Before the cream had any effect on that hole in my lung I was still wheezing badly. I'd taken a long look at myself in the mirror. My face was ashen, dark circles had formed under my eyes, my hair was dank and lifeless and I could think of nothing but that Louise had married again in Manila. I crept back into bed, hurting in every fiber and sick at heart, when Grandma came into the room with a worried look on her face. She gazed at me lying there with my chest heaving up and down and that dreadful noise whistling through my lungs, when she suddenly knelt down beside my bed and clasped her hands as if in prayer, saying,

"If you should die from this, will you promise to be my own special little saint in Heaven, and I shall pray to you and you can intercede for me with God?" and she burst into tears.

I thought about that for a long time, and as soon as I was able to get up I wrote my last will and testament, the first of many I wrote during my childhood, leaving my pitiful belongings to my brothers and sister, and enjoying every minute of my anticipated demise. I suppose I must have thought that Louise would be sorry when she heard that Mary had died and gone to Heaven, but I was only eleven then and did not realize that everyone is expendable.

All during the time I lived in the I.S.S. Building I wheezed off and on, but stopped abruptly when we left that place to enter a Japanese prison camp during World War II, leaving our Grandparents behind since they held papers of a neutral country and were not considered enemy nationals by the Japanese authorities in Shanghai.

Grandma's bureau was filled with a variety of distinctive odors, the main ones being Elizabeth Arden's Orange Skin Food and Tiger Balm, the latter being a Chinese panacea for any external symptoms. She was fond of tincture of benzoin too and also bought cases of carbolic soap which burned our eyes, and Life Buoy soap for relief. We were taught to brush our teeth, which surprises me since I never paid a visit to a dentist until I was eighteen years old and on my own in America after the war. My Grandmother insisted on a brand of toothpaste known as Kolynos, which I hated, but it must have done us a lot of good because that first visit to an American dentist turned out to be a red letter day. I'd been hearing the propaganda phrase "See your dentist twice a year" and since I had not seen one in my life, I went for an examination. The dentist looked into my mouth and saw what he appeared to think a most remarkable sight – a set of virgin teeth without a filling in the batch- and he called in his nurse and three patients who were waiting to see him, and they peered into my open mouth, clucking and remarking as to the wonderment of my hitherto unattended choppers. There was another preparation we used for brushing our teeth called "Little Flower Tooth Powder", but that was more of an entertainment than a dental nostrum, although it was that too.

Whiteaway Laidlaw's advertised something called an Iodine Locket and the ad claimed that if "you wear a Simpson Iodine Locket near your skin you can laugh at flu colds and rheumatism." Grandma glued a small tin medal of the Immaculate Heart of Mary to the Iodine Locket and made me wear it with the collection of other holy medals I wore on a chain around my neck.

We didn't take any chances.

In the event that we were just feeling seedy and out of sorts, Grandma would give us teaspoonful of Benedictine, a liqueur purchased at Caldbeck MacGregor's on Foochow Road, which she knew to be perfectly safe because there was a drawing of a monk on the label, and she'd heard that real Benedictine monks actually brewed the medicinal tasting liquid, which made it all the safer.

We never knew whether friends of ours were ever wormed, but we certainly were once a year. The worm medicine tasted like candy and came shaped in little pink cones. I never wanted to know whether it had an effect on me, but one season my brother Vincent produced a "parasite" as Grandma called it, which he fished out and kept alive in a glass bowl. I am appalled, at this stage of my life, that such a horrid thing was allowed, but at the time it seemed perfectly ordinary, my Grandma being extremely permissive at times, and we would watch the ghastly thing slither around in the bowl, Vincent quite proud of having "borned" it. One day, he had an angry fight with Jordie, and because Vincent was bigger and stronger he won the tussle handily. In revenge, Jordie cut Vincent's worm in several pieces with a pair of scissors, (a marvelously symbolic act and worthy of Jordie's imagination); no pet was ever mourned so elaborately to this day. Vincent has turned his present attention to the canine species since it appears to be more acceptable in polite society to keep a dog around the house, and he does not receive strange looks on account of his Labrador retriever.

There were a multitude of quick cures Grandma had for any number of ailments:

For depression: a new hat from Lane Crawford's.

For headache: a slice of fresh ginger rubbed on the temples and forehead.

For wrinkles: a pound of butter("real butter" not margarine) to be eaten in one week. "Butter on the inside is better than Elizabeth Arden's on the outside," she'd say.

For a sore throat: an iodine swab followed by a spoonful of honey.

For flatulence: her advice that there was "more room out than in."

For pimples: a dab on each one with tincture of benzoin.

It was the benzoin which I hated the most. Every so often I would be beset by an outbreak of tiny red spots on my face and she would follow me around the apartment with a small bottle of that sticky, brown, evil smelling stuff saying, "Just one dab, come on." But I would avoid her angrily and insist on being left alone, and after an hour she would seem to give up and put the medicine away. I'd go to bed thinking I had won the day only to wake up the next morning and find my face covered with small brown splotches which would not wash away. She had painted my face while I slept unsuspecting so that I looked as though I were in the initial stages of the pox. I'd be furious and she would just laugh and say, "Well, I had to get at you some way."

The one thing over which Grandma had no control, and for which she could find no cure was the time my brother Vincent developed a tic. I think he just did it to get attention, and he was rewarded for his trouble if that had been his intent. He started, all of a sudden, to twitch his head upwards to the right and roll his eyes in the same direction simultaneously. It had a decided effect on our Grandmother who over-reacted to everything, and to this tic of Vinnie's she threw in all her disapproving energy.

"STOP DOING THAT!" she'd shout at him, and he would roll his eyes and jerk his head upwards saying,

"Stop doing what, Grandma?" doing it regularly every two and a half seconds, driving her crazy. (He only seemed to be thus afflicted when school was over for the day.) She'd shake him violently as his eyes lolled in his head. She took to popping paper bags filled with air in his face. She painted him around the eyebrows with mercurochrome. She made a kind of Plaster of Paris mixture out of flour and water and caked his face with it. She made him drink salt and barley water. She wrapped him in cold wet sheets. She syringed his ears with baking soda and mineral water. She forced him to gargle with Burdock root tea. She stuck triangular wrinkle plasters all over his face and made him go to sleep wearing them.

My Grandmother did everything to stop Vincent from exercising his tic, but nothing worked. Nothing. She even rigged up a harness which she had him wear after school and the tic-ing boy would have to walk around the house all trussed up about the head and shoulders like a Christmas goose. He was also given several soapy enemas.

One day he simply stopped doing it and never did it again in his life.

Chapter 14

My two brothers were the Katzenjammer Kids. The older one was accident prone, and no one thought he would live long enough to grow to manhood. One night, when the hot bath water had steamed the windows in our bedroom, he stood on his head and put his foot up to the misted glass to make a footprint there; we watched in helpless horror as Vinnie's foot crashed through the pane tearing a huge hunk of flesh from the back of his ankle as he stood, poised on one leg, blood streaming from the gaping wound. It caused quite a sensation in our household and Grandma and the amahs ran around in hysterics while Vinnie, holding out his foot, bled all over the room. Luckily, Ida was at home and she had the good sense to wrap the injured foot and take the boy to a doctor who stitched it closed. He still has the scar, but it did not injure him permanently.

Coming up in the elevator one afternoon, Vincent had been bouncing a tennis ball. He missed a stroke and the ball rolled toward the metal action-gate of the lift, and he dived at it, grasping it just as it rolled down the shaft between the floors, saving the ball but mangling his hand rather badly, and he bears the scar of that accident as well.

There was a tough kid in the apartment building whose name was Miguel Campos, a handsome boy whom everyone feared. At school he and Vinnie had been matched in a boxing competition and my brother had won; but later, Miguel's brother Mario, got hold of Vincent and said,

"Let's see how tough you really are." An informal match between the two boys was set, and the entire population of kids in the I.S.S. turning out to see the fight. Miguel delivered a vicious beating to Vinnie, blacking both his eyes, giving him a bloody mouth and thrashing him soundly. It made for a bitter feud between the supporters of both parties and that war did not see an armistice. Miguel Campos died of meningitis when he was seventeen years old, and when I heard this news from a cousin after we had come to America I was sorry that a boy of such promise had not reached maturity, and doubly glad that Vince had survived.

A few times I would have been pleased to have killed Vincent myself, and indeed, probably tried to accomplish that feat on several occasions. He knew just what to do to instantly turn me into a raving harpy, and I rose to the bait every time. His favorite, sure-fire method was to ring my bicycle bell while I was taking a bath, unable to come immediately to prevent him from touching my precious possession. He'd stand in the hallway where it was parked and ring that bell incessantly until he heard me crashing around in my haste to get at him, and then he'd run out of the apartment, knowing I couldn't chase him with only a towel around me. We had many fights over this, and it was not too long before I realized that he was a good bit stronger than I.

Vincent found a picture of the Gerber baby in a magazine and colored it with crayons, writing the name "Root Smit" under the sweet angelic face. He stuck it on a wall and seemed to be terribly fond of that nonexistent infant. I taunted him about the misspelling of the name when he said he'd called the baby Ruth Smith, and he was so enraged at my teasing about his error that he locked me in a desperate struggle, after which, the fight ending in a draw, he tore the picture in shreds and threw the pieces in my face as I laughed in derision at his anger.

He got back at me royally, however, and sometime later I noticed that he was snickering at me and casting surreptitious looks my way. I thought I heard him muttering some words I couldn't make out, and finally he said, out loud in a mocking sing-song voice, the most devastating words I had ever heard:

Dick and Mary went to the dairy.
Dick took out his big canary.
Oh, said Mary, wot a whoppa,
Let's lie down and do it proppa.

He delivered this recitation from across the table and I, upon hearing the ghastly rhyme, flung myself toward him, sliding over the smooth surface of the tabletop and catching him by surprise by the hair. We toppled to the floor in a great tangle of fists and elbows, and I gave him the beating of his life. Vincent, helpless with laughter because he had pierced my armor in a most vulnerable spot, enjoyed that fight enormously, and although he cried loudly he also found it to be the most amusing thing that had happened to him in a long while. From then on, all he would have to say to me was, "Dick and…" and I'd erupt in a rage and chase him about the flat screaming at the top of my lungs.

The amahs were mystified, not understanding English, and thought we were deranged, which I certainly was when my brother repeated that horrid jingle to me; but there were times when Vincent and I collaborated in mischief. The amahs, innocent beings that they were, would ask us to teach them English, and, if they were new to the household, we'd have them on and instruct them in a few nice phrases such as, "Dinner is served," or "Someone to see you," and "The mail has come," which they would go in and say to our Grandma, receiving an approving look from her at these announcements. Then, when the amah had come to trust us, we would have her say other lines and hide behind the door to watch Grandma's reaction to the little country girl smilingly invite her to "Please go to hell." Grandma rarely failed us and overreacted splendidly with loud shrieks of "Where are those ruffians!" and we were punished for our trouble with a few hard whacks of the fly swatter, or a clout on the head with the 'phone book while the puzzled amah looked on in dismay, wondering what it was she had said to her mistress to cause such a scene.

Jordie and I were not given to being locked in mortal combat as children, although he and Vincent cuffed and tormented one another at every opportunity, the older of the two generally emerging the victor. Jordie had been blessed with the most innocent face on earth, and looking into those wide guileless eyes no one could believe that he was the perpetrator of high crimes or low deeds as well he might have been. I am certain that long before Vincent discovered tobacco, Jordie had smoked cigarettes in the basement garage with the gang in the I.S.S. Building, starting at the age of six or seven. What other initiation rites performed in those dark and cavernous stalls have never been revealed to me, and my brothers will have to write of those things themselves.

Before Jordie was fully accepted in the world of boys, and before he'd had his mass of curly hair cut away for good, he and I played a game we called "Peggy and Alice." He'd be Peggy and he would call me "Alith" because Jordie had a pronounced lisp which has not entirely left him. He was the most affectionate little chap and had such winning ways, and we played the game for weeks, bringing it into our "real lives" and mixing our fantasy with the reality of our days. Jordie would allow me to deck him out in scarves and ribbons, and wear odd little hats I'd make for him. We'd stage tea parties with my dolls and he played so earnestly, offering our mute companions another cupful and "...do you want milk and thugar in it?"

Grandma had allowed me to take the box-room for my very own, and I'd arranged the trunks in such a way so that there was ample room for us to play quite comfortably in that tiny space. It had its own door and a window which looked out onto the roof-garden built over the garage. Jordie and I would shout insults to the kids playing down there if we saw a group we did not like, and we even threw old lemons and bits of soap at them, hoping we wouldn't get caught.

One day Jordie came home from school with red eyes and Grandma said: "What's the matter with your eyes? Have you been peeking through keyholes again? That's how people get red eyes, you know."

And we believed that for years. Grandma also told us that bathing was of extreme importance, and she'd point at the beggar children on the streets as we passed by, telling us that the reason they picked through each other's hair and rages for vermin was because lice sprang from filth, and it was not until I had grown up that I realized the theory of spontaneous generation was not universally accepted as valid.

Whenever Jordie did any of his mysterious tricks or was caught in a lie, or if his behavior was in the smallest way considered peculiar by Grandma, she would have him stand between her knees and study his eyes with a delving expression, searching his face, shaking her head slowly, pursing her lips and frowning;' and she'd say with great solemnity and dramatic concern, jabbing her finger in his chest,

"I can see it in his eyes. There's consanguinity in the family. Smith's mother and father were first cousins and I think it is 'coming out' in this one."

He would widen his eyes, poor doomed, misbegotten little imp, and look sorrowfully about at us. I think my younger brother was convinced at an early age that he was capable of truly inspired evil-doing which, coupled with his ingenuous face,, allowed for a life of colorful adventure pursued with impunity, and I know that, far more than Vincent ever did, Jordie grew up with the notion that he was unredeemable and behaved accordingly, with great style and abundant charm.

Vincent secretly called Grandma "Madame Fatima". She punished him once for some misdeed by making him wash the woodwork in the hallway. She stood over the unwilling boy shouting instructions and brandishing a wooden spoon; he forgot himself and said, "All right, Madame Fatima."

Grandma sucked in her breath in shock and gave him a knot on his head with the heavy spoon.

Out in the fields, with our friends Enrico and Nina Pagani, we played on the burial mounds, leaping from grave to grave, whooping and hollering. The amahs said it would bring us much bad fortune to defile the places of the dead, but it did not worry us during the daylight hours, our fear coming alive only in the dark and gloom of night. Annie was shot in the leg with a bee-bee gun by a nameless sniper during one of these "field trips" and we stayed away for a week or two. She found a dead baby in the bushes one afternoon and we inspected it thoroughly before we told the servants of our discovery. It was not an uncommon event, in those days of famine and poverty for the Chinese peasantry, to find such a pitiful bundle. We used to hear that people smuggling arms through the lines guarded by Japanese soldiers sometimes gutted dead babies and filled their bodies with bullets, then carrying them across the barricades without fear of being searched in such an unlikely place.

It rarely snowed in Shanghai, but it did one year when we were children, and we had the chance of making our one and only snowman.

My brothers became adept at certain Chinese games. There was one which used a large spool that was kept balanced on a string attached to two sticks, and, holding a stick in each had, the player kept the spool spinning in the air. The boys learned to juggle with three bamboo sticks, again one in each hand, and the third kept in the air, making sounds of pok-pok-pok as the bamboo clicked against itself, hitting accurately dozens of times. We played hop-scotch too, and other English games like "Wind and Flowers" and "Bobbies and Thieves" (our version of "Cops and Robbers") with the other kids in the building, and we spent many exciting evenings fraught with intrigue hiding from one another in that rambling structure of corridors, stairwells and cubby-holes.

We loved the movies, but our Grandmother said that most of them were sinful, so we sneaked out to see Jeanette McDonald and Nelson Eddy in their lyrical romances, coming home with our heads filled with love songs and visions of stout-hearted men on horseback riding to the rescue. I often went to the show with some of our cousins, the children of Grandma's sisters, of which there was a multitude, and I think I saw every Shirley Temple movie ever made, and can still remember the words to "You Gotta Eat Your Spinach, Baby" and "Goodnight, My Love." Grandma didn't mind Shirley too much, and would grudgingly allow us to see her films, even though she said they were asinine and caused men to have evil thoughts. I didn't care what she said, and I loved every second of "Baby Take a Bow", "Stowaway", "Poor Little Rich Girl" and "Stand Up and Cheer." She meant a great deal to me, little Shirley Temple did, and I am pleased that she grew up to be a rather good sort.

The movie, "The Sign of the Cross", was one that my Grandma actually took us to see, although she disapproved highly of Claudette Colbert showing so much of herself and taking a bath in asses' milk. We thought that was marvelous, and would play Crucifixion for a long time afterwards, stripped to the waist on imaginary crosses, my brothers as the good and bad thieves on either side of me as Jesus of Nazareth dying on Golgotha. (A scant year later I'd not be caught dead half naked.) Sometimes, carried away with religious fervor, we'd play at having a Mass and the two boys would act as acolytes to my priest. Annie was the army of faithful who came to the rail for Holy Communion which I dispensed, using flattened puffed rice or rounds of ironed bread as hosts. We set the piano as an altar, lit candles and votive lights, and our Grandmother doted on this game, looking for things we could use as platens and chalices, finding a bell for Vince to ring as altar boy, digging through her trunks in search of stuff we could turn into a surplice or a chasuble. She even let us use mosquito repellant punk sticks to burn as incense, and would order the cook to hold off dinner so as not to interfere with our sacred masquerade. The amahs would think us quite mad, watching us ironing the bits of bread to be given out at our "gray Masses," and I'd hear them telling one another about the strange practices of "Tung-kah's" grandchildren.

Because there was an allusion to Our Lord in the title of a movie called "One Million B.C." my Grandma, knowing what B.C. meant, recommended this film as one we ought not to miss. We saw it several times, and when we had it down pat, we went home and played our Caveman Game draped in Grandma's old furs, brandishing bones we'd salvaged from dinner roasts, and growling at one another in feral snarls, baring our teeth and crouching around the house, dragging Annie by her hair across the floor, leaping at each other from atop the back of the sofa and crawling through the "underbrush" of drapery and tablecloths. I think Grandma kept looking for some religious symbolism in all of these performances and remained quite baffled since she did not see the movie herself; but no one ever stopped us from doing these absurd charades and we enjoyed acting out whatever we saw on the screen. We were a participating audience, and did not consider the movies solely as a spectator sport.

We were allowed to see Spencer Tracy in a film called "Boys Town" and we loved Mickey Rooney in it. Vincent would carry Jr. around on his shoulders, staggering, and say,

"He ain't heavy, Father. He's my brudder."

We used to laugh at them doing this routine, but little did we know that when we were finally to come to the United States, both of my brothers would spend several years at Father Flanagan's refuge for homeless boys where they finished high school as stars on the football field and in the Boys' Town Choir. Their memories of those days were not happy ones.

Annie was a small girl who knew a lot of big words. Grandma was delighted one day when she asked Annie why she was crying and received the following answer: "I am crying because Jordie has been all day antagonizing me."

A legion of forces combined to make my brothers and Annie and I what we are today, and so many impressions, mistaken and otherwise, formed to mold our personalities and set us in our ways. In our young days, space travel was unheard of and I still marvel at the thought that my brother Vincent, that dreadful boy, helped to design the hydraulic valves in the rocket which carried Neil Armstrong to the moon in the Apollo program.

Chapter 15

Jordie turned seven, and a birthday party was arranged for him. We invited a group of his friends, and Auntie Ida brought him a cake with candles and a bag of favors, toy whistles and paper hats. He got so excited when the guests arrived that he climbed onto the table and made a leap to catch a curtain rod above one of the doors, missed the rod and crashed to the floor, knocking himself out. He suffered a slight concussion for showing off, and remained unconscious the whole time we celebrated his birthday, eating his cake and opening the presents and playing Pin-the-Tail-on-the-Donkey for prizes, yelping loudly. After everyone had left, Jordie came around and looked at the shambles we'd made of the sitting room and asked,

"Where's the party?"

We attended other children's affairs but I would feel self-conscious and uncomfortable playing silly games and wearing ridiculous gold and silver foil hats. There is a picture of us at such a gathering, and the look on my face suggests that I was on my way to the abattoir wearing a lace dress and black patent leather shoes, although the other three seemed to be having a good time. Whenever Charlie Chaplin movies were shown at someone's birthday I did not consider the event a total loss, and was even more pleased when the films were of Laurel and Hardy.

Annie was invited to the home of a wealthy South American family for a kiddie party and there is a photo of her wearing a hideous dress in a garish pattern. I remember the dress coming well below her chubby knees and thought the color-maroon and lime green- a ghastly combination for a small girl; but it had been Grandma's choice for my poor sister, and the snapshot we have of that celebration shows Annie standing out like a sore thumb in the front row of a group of other little girls who are decked out in short, frilly white frocks with big bows in their hair. This was the birthday of Carmen Prieto, whose older sisters, Margarita, Maria and Graciela, attended the convent with us. Maragarita Prieto was an elfin child, religious to an extreme, whose family believed that she saw visions. She died unexpectedly at the age of twelve, leaving her mother and sisters distraught, and me wondering if she would be canonized.

Grandpa loved snails and he'd have the cook boil a bucketful for him whenever there was a good crop of them available at the market. Grandpa would sit at the table with a large basin of steaming mollusks in front of him and suck them noisily out of their shells with great relish. We eschewed joining him to share this feast and regarded his taste for them as quite disgusting, it being on a par with Grandpa's fondness for the eyes of steamed fish which the cook often served. One day, as we watched him enjoying a particularly succulent batch, we asked him how he could bear to eat snails, and he said, "If you think eating these slimy things is peculiar, let me tell you about a really unusual dish I once had."

In 1915 President Yuan Shih-kai had conferred upon our Grandfather the Fifth Class of the Chia-ho Order in recognition for valuable services he had rendered the Chinese government. There was an article Grandma had saved from the Shanghai Mercury newspaper, dated October 10, 1915, which gave the details of this presentation. In his honor, the officials had given a feast, at which dignitaries of the day were assembled, and an elaborate dinner with dozens of courses was held over a period of many hours. Grandpa told us that in the center of the main round table where he was seated there was a brass domed cover which was not touched during the festivities until the high point of the evening arrived when, after many toasts, the cover was lifted off ceremoniously to reveal the "piece de resistance."

"You must remember," he told us, "that I had been brought up in the Chinese section of this City by my Chinese mother, and I thought that I had heard of everything there was to know about my people. But I was not prepared for the great delicacy before me, of which I, as the guest of honor, had to take the first helping."

Sitting beneath the table under the metal cover was a live monkey in a cage with the top of its skull carefully sawed away. The moment a pair of chopsticks was put to its brain it died, and it was our Grandpa's place to deliver the *"coup de grace"* in taking the first morsel. Grandpa said: "And even I, no stranger to things Chinese, was hard pressed to do this. I did as I was expected to, but I confess that it made me quite ill and I had to put on a good show for my hosts at the banquet in my honor."

The supreme delicacy was in having the animal's blood still coursing through its veins as the brain was picked over, and my Grandfather told us that ever after that experience there was no food in the world he considered of a less savory nature. I have not heard of this practice in any other quarter, and I wonder if Grandpa didn't invent the story of that toothsome final course for us to justify his bucketful of snails. The validity of his having received the Chia-ho Order, however, is beyond dispute.

At my Grandfather's table each place was set with the plates, knives, forks and spoons one might expect, but on the upper left hand side we also were provided with a bowl and a pair of chopsticks resting on the rim. We would have a leg of lamb and mint jelly with roast potatoes in the company of a dish of Shan-tung cabbage or long Chinese beans and a tureen of steaming rice; and we ate the first part of the dinner in Western style, finishing up with a rice bowl in the left hand and a pair of chopsticks in the right, shoveling white rice and vegetables into our mouths very neatly, without dropping a grain. Grandpa said that we were never to waste food, and told us that for every grain of rice left in our bowls there would be a pock mark on the face of whomever we might marry when we grew up, and so successful were we in cleaning our bowls that not one of us married a person with a blemished face.

Grandma developed a bad habit of chewing the taste and texture out of her food, and then removing the bits from her mouth would make little mounds of chewed meat and other things all around her plate. It turned my stomach to see her doing this, and I contrived to sit as far away from her as I could during meals, and did not look at her while she ate. Grandpa's manners were faultless and if we learned any of the social amenities it was surely from that good man who sheltered us in our childhood.

Mrs. Vincent (as Grandma was often called), was a difficult person for whom to find an appropriate gift. Louise told me that when she and Ida had been children they'd saved their money to surprise their mother on her birthday, and had bought an armful of long-stemmed yellow roses which they proudly presented to her as she lay in bed that morning. From what Louise said, Georgina turned around to look dolefully at the beautiful flowers and said,

"You know how I hate yellow" and sent them away in tears. Louise had many strange memories and I wonder how much of what she remembered actually took place; but her story stuck in my mind and I felt it was safer to present my Grandma such gifts as a pretty card stating that I had made a special novena for her, or that I promised a set number of rosaries to be said in her name. She was pleased with such presents, and they cost me nothing except time, of which I had a more than goodly amount.

An ugly friend of Grandpa's came to dinner one night. The unfortunate man had a red, bulbous nose and bloodshot eyes which stared out from a craggy, rutted face. His skin looked raw and cracked, his thick lips were chapped and broken, and he had deep furrows on his brow. Wisps of copper colored hair grew in tendrils from his huge misshapen ears, and when he smiled, which he did often, he exposed a mouthful of chipped, uneven teeth, no two of which seemed to be the same color. There was a large wart on one of his cheeks, but for all his fearsome appearance he had a pleasant voice, deep and manly, and most courtly in manner.

Jordie stood with his chin resting on the table, his eyes fixed upon our spectacular guest as the rest of us tried to finish our dinner without looking too closely at the unusual man sharing our meal. Jordie listened to the conversation, never once taking his gaze away from that arresting visage, and then, in a voice filled with awe, my brother said: "WHAT a face!"

I fled in embarrassment and cannot recall how those at the table recovered themselves, but I heard my Grandmother's explosive laughter as Jordie was hustled from their presence, and long afterwards she was still fond of telling that story of Jordie's moment of truth, imitating his tone when she repeated the line, "WHAT a face!" laughing until she cried.

There were parties everywhere during Chinese New Year and Grandpa would take us to visit his old friends during this holiday. We loved going with him to these unfamiliar places, getting an inside look at the private and palatial compounds of the rich Chinese whom Grandpa had known all his life. They would give us small red envelopes with money inside, and we'd hold our hands together and bow, saying, "Kung-shi fah zeh" which meant Happy New Year in the Shanghai dialect. It seemed to amuse everyone immensely to hear the little "foreigners" give this greeting, and Grandpa seemed proud that we spoke the language so well, looking approvingly as we engaged the host's children in polite conversation, and said: "Zyah-zyah-noong for thank you to our hosts."

We behaved ourselves properly when we accompanied our Grandfather, not that we feared being punished for rudeness but because we could not bear to do anything which might cause him the slightest humiliation. In Western cultures I think parents tend to control children by playing on their sense of guilt, whereas the Chinese place the emphasis on a sense of shame. In our case, we were raised with a combination of the two, thus having been treated to the worst of both possible worlds since Grandma followed the Western way of guilt in her attitude toward childish wrong-doing. Grandpa's method of discipline was effective and one hard look from his fiery eyes was enough to keep us in line. Grandma could shout and yell, cajole and threaten, to no avail, and have to resort to physical violence when all else had failed her in getting us to pay attention and do as she told us. Grandpa, on the other hand, needed only to turn his head toward the one of us behaving badly and, fixing a stern eye on the offender, could produce such a feeling of discomfort and shame that the antic performance would stop immediately. Grandpa did not tell us to "be good." He didn't say, "Behave yourselves." What he did say was: "Don't draw attention to yourselves." which is the very best admonition to give to children.

We did not have a tree at Christmastime, and I don't remember lots of gaily wrapped presents. Ida would see to it that we each got something new in the way of clothing, and perhaps there were a few gifts, but Christmas was not celebrated in traditional ways in our house. One season, when it was not possible to get a turkey or a goose, Grandpa ordered the cook to roast two chickens with stuffing and said we would have dinner when the family returned from Christmas Mass. My Grandparents must have had a serious disagreement that morning because Grandma huffed to church with the boys, leaving Annie and me to accompany Grandpa on a later tram. We did not see her at Mass, and she might have gone to another place for the service. When we arrived at home we found that Grandma had preceded us by some half an hour and had ordered the cook to serve her and the boys the dinner my Grandpa had so carefully planned. We came to the table to find her sitting over the remains of the two roast chickens, picking through the stuffing and belching discreetly.

My Grandpa was thoroughly annoyed, but seated himself with as much dignity as he could muster and we had our Christmas dinner, a sorry sight, at the other end of the table in complete silence and chagrin. The chestnut stuffing, which I loved, stuck in my craw from the rage I felt for my Grandmother's indefensible behavior, but I knew better by then than to criticize her in front of Grandpa. She watched us for a while and then rose lazily, saying in a barely audible voice dripping with disdain: "Silly old man." and languidly left the room sighing. Grandpa raised his chin, surveyed the wreckage of our forlorn festive table, cut a piece of chicken with quiet precision and chewed it thoughtfully, saying not a word. I never asked what that was all about.

Annie has a memory of riding with me to Hungjao Road on the back of my bike, and I was amazed at the accuracy of what she remembered. Nina and I sometimes rode out that far because I would tell her about the mansion we used to live in before the war, and we'd go to find it and see who occupied it then. We went there secretly with plans to recapture the Moorish style house and would spend an hour or two creeping around the fence and peeking in the gate. One hot summer day, with Annie as extra baggage, we cycled into the country and as we neared the old house we were stopped by a friendly English lady in front of her gate. She hailed us and invited us into her garden which abounded in snapdragons, roses, wisteria and hollyhocks. We had never seen such a magical place, with its bird bath, sun dial and a green platform swing in which we could all sit and sway back and forth. Bees busied themselves over the flower beds competing with an Artful Dodger of a hummingbird who darted from bloom to bloom, whirring and hovering. The English lady was delighted to have us for company and had her servants bring out a Dundee cake and tea biscuits with a great pitcher of ice cold lemonade for us. We made grateful little sounds and put on our best convent manners, giving no hint of our true purpose in that neighborhood, and had the loveliest afternoon of Annie's childhood.

Auntie Ida and a brawny friend named Barney Wall took us on a picnic. She packed a scrumptious lunch in a big basket and we drove to some bosky dell where the landscape was hilly, the rolling topography pleasing us greatly because Shanghai is built on flat reclaimed marshy land where a bump in the road was regarded as "scenery." We were told that the Chinese cicadas came out to chirp their stringy song once in every seventeen years, and this was their time. We lay under the trees on a blanket and listened to the insect concert, a thousand variations on the cicada theme blending into one strumming, throbbing roundelay. The sun was hot through the dappled branches as we watched the puffed cheeks and swollen bellies of clouds billowing across the blue dome of sky, trailing their feathery capes into ever changing costume and design, Annie and the boys rolled down the short inclines like human logs, laughing and tumbling; Barney held Ida's hand in his and they spoke quietly to one another; and everything in the world seemed peaceful, safe and right for a little while.

Grandma met a man who said he would teach her how to make vinegar. She was very interested in learning how to make things of that sort, and she came home to tell us excitedly that she had invited this person for tea tomorrow and that he had promised to bring his mother. The cook went to great pains to make little sandwiches, and Grandma sent me to the bakery to buy a box of "petit fours." The next day, she went to much trouble making sure that the fanciest table cloth we owned was properly ironed by the amah, and she set the table herself with the finest china she'd been able to salvage from the "good old days." She even tidied up the sitting room, shoving all her assorted books and papers into boxes which were then pushed under the beds in our room.

Grandma spent a lot of time in the bathroom arranging her hair over each ear, and after her knotted bun was pinned in place; she stuck in a false kiss-curl made from her own braid. She used little red paper leaves which came in a tiny booklet to rouge her cheeks and lips, and this she did just before the guests were due to arrive. I had not seen her make such a fuss over anyone before, and thought that the people paying us a visit that day must surely be very special.

The doorbell rang. I was told to answer it and show the lady and gentleman into the sitting room where Grandma made last minute preparations for the tea. I opened the door to find a handsome but shabbily dressed fellow standing there with his hat in one hand and a paper bag in the other. He had a pleasant expectant look on his face and smiled at me, bowing from the waist. In his German accent he said he wished to see Mrs. Vincent, and I ushered him into Grandma's strangely fluttery presence.

She looked up, smiling archly, a provocative expression which I had never seen before on her suddenly pretty face surprised me, and she said: "Oh, I am so sorry that your mother could not come for tea. I do hope she is not ill."

The young man looked puzzled and glanced about the room. Grandma said, by way of explanation: "You told me you would bring your mother when I invited you to come to my house that day we met."

"Ach, but I 'AVE brought my muzzer," said he, producing a Mason jar from the paper bag he carried, and holding it aloft he exhibited a hideously ugly amorphous mass the size of a pound of tripe, undulating sinuously in a brackish liquid.

I screamed, believing that he had indeed brought his mother pickled in a jar, and Grandma screamed because I had. The poor man jumped six inches off the floor thinking he had inadvertently wandered into a mad house, and the cook ran in to see if the visitor was attacking his employer and her granddaughter. In the confusion which followed, the beleaguered vinegarist managed to explain that his "mother" was really the culture for the vinegar. But I had seen enough and refused to sit at the table as they took their seats, preferring to watch this sinister fellow from behind the door as my Grandmother prettily offered him another sandwich or frosted cake, looking for all the world like a dyspeptic Queen of Hearts addressing a nervous White Rabbit as she poured tea into the clattering cup he was trying to hold in his shaking hand.

Grandma liked us best when we played together to the exclusion of other children. Whenever I showed a preference for Nina's company, leaving my sister and brothers to their own devices, she would look at me and say: "Blood is thicker than water."

I would go anyway, but the remark hung over me like a leaden veil, and I was too young to realize the tyranny of words or even to laugh at the over dramatization my grandmother gave to the simplest situation. Her infatuation with hyperbole extended into the remotest corner of the most mundane aspects of our lives, bestowing upon everything her fanciful exaggerations, embroidering the patchwork of our days with sequins and thread of gold, millions of multi-colored beads and the semi-precious stones of her rich imagination.

Chapter 16

Our life with our Grandmother was episodic, as is life anywhere. We learned to ride the roller-coaster of her many moods, entering into the spirit of fun when she was feeling whimsical, and staying well out of her way when we saw dark clouds forming on the horizon of the limitless seas of her emotion.

Early on, I realized that Grandma was frequently bored and that she battled her ennui, using us to drive away the sense of time hanging heavily upon her, and also for the simple amusement which we afforded her merely because we were children, and mainly because we were completely in her power and belonged to her for ill and for good.

Some days she would aid and abet us in our manic behavior, as when she played the marching numbers for our parades around the apartment; but at other times she seemed totally intolerant of the smallest sound we might make, when even our whispering to one another gave rise to her angry commands for silence. There was no consistency in our relationship with Grandma, and she proved herself to be a champion at unpredictability, surprising us at every turn, until her very caprice became what we expected in our daily lives.

To be sure, there were small cruelties which she visited upon us that go unnoticed in many families, but there were also many instances of what she considered to be "fun" which had an element of sadism in them, like a touch of fleabane in a spinach soufflé. Grandma did not busy herself with the marketing or the cooking since the cook, Dah-soo, was hired to do that job; she had two amahs in the apartment to clean and dust and do the laundry, which was done by hand in the bathtub; and all four of us could by then dress ourselves and tend to our private needs. My Grandpa was not a demanding man in that, like so many other husbands, he did not require constant fetching and carrying, and I never once saw Grandma dance attendance upon her husband. Once a week she did count the sheets and pillowcases which were sent to the laundry shop, making sure that the same numbers of pieces of linen which went out would be returned; and, once in a while, she discussed with the cook some special dish she wished him to fix for her that day. She did read a great deal, mostly newspapers, and got me in the habit of reading them as well. I am sure that I would be a lot better off if I never read the news, it all being so distressing these days, but I am constitutionally incapable of letting a twenty-four hour period go by without having a look at how the world is doing. Annie put on Grandma's spectacles and her house slippers and sat in her armchair with the Shanghai Times held out in her short arms, pretending to read. It was before she had started school and we had a good laugh at her since she held the paper upside down while looking as though she were reading the most interesting article. We were always a good audience for each other and the notice we paid Annie for being the clown of our family whetted her appetite for the addictive sound of applause.

Ida had thrown away a hat she'd tired of which sported a long pheasant feather, and Grandma retrieved it, saving the feather which she put to good use during hot summer nights when sleep evaded her. I'd wake to the sound of her suppressed giggling to see her perched on the edge of my brothers' bed, and she would motion for me to come and join the fun. The boys, sprawled together in sound sleep, their arms and legs thrown across each other in a tangle, were fair game, unprotected from that merry Andrew's insatiable need for amusement, and I would watch her tickle their nostrils with the fine tip of the feather and rock with laughter at the unconscious twitching's it would produce of their innocent faces as they slept. She'd touch the insides of their ears and go into spasms of glee to see them slap the sides of their heads, brushing away what felt like gnats or mosquitoes which often plagued us during the sticky summer nights. Once, Grandpa came into the room while she was having her fun in this manner. I heard him say: "Oh leave the poor things alone." I turned in my bed and said: "It keeps her quiet and happy, Grandpa." And he looked at me curiously and gave a little laugh, leaving her to her nocturnal trickery.

Sometimes Grandma would invite me to be in cahoots with her saying:

"Mary, you sit here and watch this."

She'd call the kids to sit at her feet and start to tell them a wild tale of bears in the woods chasing after lost girls and boys, and in the telling manage to make a lot of terrible faces showing alarm, fear, and the looks that appear when one hides or is threatened; and the children would be rapt, listening to her, and ape her every change of facial expression, opening their mouths if she did, or screwing up their noses, or gritting their teeth, or widening their eyes as the story unfolded. Of course, it was entertaining to all of us, to them listening to the tale of horror and to me, watching them unwittingly grimacing and mirroring her performance. They could never understand why it was so funny to Grandma and me, and wore an air of uncertain gaiety of their own during these times.

Grandma loved to see Jordie or Annie whirling around the rooms as children will do, making themselves dizzy so that they staggered when they stopped going round, and would laugh uproariously to see them trying to navigate the long hallway, their giddy bodies drifting against the walls, unable to walk a straight line. It was a completely successful ploy by virtue of which we could distract her at almost any time, and we would resort to this formula whenever we were in danger of being scolded or smacked for some mischief done earlier and discovered. If we could get her to laugh, all would be quickly forgotten, and we became very expert at this ruse, even though we might have realized that as official court jesters it was a cheap shot and unworthy of our talents.

At the top of the Wing On Company, or perhaps it was the Sun Company, which were large department stores downtown, there was a roller skating rink on the roof, and Grandma would take us there periodically for a go-round. None of us knew how to skate when we first went to this crowded place, and Grandma was faint from laughing so hard at our antics on the slippery floor in the unfamiliar skates the attendant had screwed onto our shoes. We took it all in fun, even though we ended up with terrible scrapes on our arms and elbows, skinned our knees and hurt out bottoms from all the falling down we did that day. We made valiant efforts to remain in an upright position, but kept skidding clumsily, our feet flying out from under us unexpectedly, crashing into other skaters, and grabbing total strangers, hanging onto them for dear life, while Grandma stood on the sidelines holding the guard-rail for support since she was helpless with laughter, roaring and shaking, tears streaming down her cheeks as she held one hand to her side and rocked back and forth hysterically on her heels.

When we became proficient at the sport and could glide gracefully around the rink without falling stupidly on top of one another, Grandma lost all interest in these excursions and stopped taking us until we made convincing pretense of more buffoonery, at which point her interest revived, and we discovered that we had a price to pay and could enjoy the skating rink as long as we included an occasional spectacular fall for our Grandmother's diversion.

It is obvious that she thrived on disaster and had no interest in life if all was, unfortunately, going well. The worse the news was in the papers, the better she liked it, and she not only spent several hours a day reading the many dailies and monthlies which flooded our apartment, but she also kept up a steady correspondence with several of them. She had an opinion on every subject and wrote lengthy letters to the editor on her views on religion, world affairs, customs and manners, and the behavior of anyone in the public eye. She had been forbidden by Grandpa to use her true name in signing these letters, and sent them off over the pseudonym of "A Roman Catholic" or "Servant of Christ the King" or "Student of the Bible" or "A Catholic Mother". Other readers would take issue with her views and excoriate the anonymous writer in the columns for her antediluvian attitudes and thought patterns, which only poured fuel on her fire, giving her yet another opportunity to shoot off a few more salvos, which was no trouble whatever since she had an inexhaustible supply of ammunition.

One of Grandma's paper opponents, a man who signed himself Charles Rankin, (an agent of the Devil, no doubt,) took her to task and wrote to a magazine called The Chinese Nation, accusing her of putting forth claims regarding the Catholic Church which were "untenable and insupportable." Mr. Rankin called the writer of the letter to which he had taken offense "...ignorant...superstitious...uinscriptural...unenlightened... dictatorial...arbitrary...interfering...ineffectual...and stupid..." making the mistake of thinking that "G. Vincent" as Grandma had signed herself then, was a man, and referred throughout his diatribe to Mr. G. Vincent. It gave my Grandfather quite a turn, and it was after this that he forbade Grandma to sign anything but a "*nom de plume*" to her inflammatory missives to the press from then on.

Apparently, her letters to the editor had begun many years before, and I have a collection of clippings she'd saved, some dating back to 1928 when she wrote in regard to the opening of Jessfield Park to the Chinese populace. This was the infamous park which bore the sign "No Dogs or Chinese Allowed" at its fabled gates, and when the ban was lifted to admit Chinese to Jessfield as well as to Luna Park, Grandma wrote an irate letter to the North China Daily News complaining that now that the doors were open to them, "...only fifteen Chinese people attended the municipal Orchestra concert in Jessfield Park, whereas ten thousand jammed into Luna Park to bet on the dog races held there." How human they were.

Besides writing regularly to warn Shanghailanders that the end of the world was at hand, she also took the time to publicly scold someone's servant whom she had caught in a breach of trust. A yellowed clipping showed excerpts from one of Grandma's letters:

> "While shopping on Avenue Haig, corner of Bubbling Well Road this morning I saw a baby in a very beautiful English pram chewing on two dirty coppers held in his dear little hand. I took them out of his mouth and drew the attention of the amah to the matter, saying she should be more careful and that I would report the matter to the child's mother. The amah is a tall, slender woman with hair cut in mannish style. Upon admonishing her, she said

to me, "You silly ass." The baby has lovely blond hair, with a face broken out with a heat rash. I hope the above description will call the child's mother's attention to reprove her amah, and I will gladly see her in person if she will communicate with me through the medium of this paper." This one was signed, "For More Watchful Amahs."

The letter was answered, also in print, by another person who wrote:

"Your correspondent 'For More Watchful Amahs' has done a public spirited action in writing to the Press thus bringing to public notice what I consider a most scandalous state of affairs. I, too, saw a small child on the corner of King Albert Street and Avenue Foch, not in an English pram but in a perfectly good one, though I could not say if it had been used previously in the same family. To my horror, Sir, that child, I think he was what I have heard described as an unspotted flaxen haired boy, was sucking the stub of a big black cigar. The Amah very smartly dressed wore one of those knitted hats, like a salmon net, over an Eton Crop. When I quietly reproached her with Fairbain's Riot Wagon or snatching the cigar from the child's mouth, what did she reply to me? 'Forget it,' she said, and strolled off toward the Canidrome. Now, Sir, my point in writing you at this length is to bring to the notice of the foreign public of Shanghai the necessity of organizing to prevent such demoralization of our children, for are they not, Sir, the hope of our various Empires?"

This, surely, is what started it all for Grandma and her letters to the editors. In those days, the targets of her ire were not exactly world shaking, but it was a good beginning, nonetheless, and if the sun has indeed set on the British Empire, part of the blame can be laid to the cheeky amahs of Shanghai who corrupted their tiny colonial masters, weakening the moral fiber of the rising generation of those who bore the "white man's burden" by allowing them, in their prams, Sir, to suck on filthy coins and vile cigars.

Recently, in leafing through the collection of disintegrating newsprint, I came across a page from the North China Daily News dated November 30, 1939, and I could not see why it had been saved. Turning it over, I saw nothing but advertisements and a partial column of the classified section, and I almost put it aside until my eye fell on an ad which jogged my memory, thrusting me back in time. I was eleven then, and already had developed the newspaper habit, reading everything I could and sometimes idling over the "Wanted" pages. I remember that Grandma, highly agitated and in righteous indignation, had informed me that some wicked girl was performing nightly in a disreputable cabaret in Frenchtown, and Grandma had heard that her act consisted of "having doings" with a horse.

"Imagine! Have you ever heard of such a disgusting thing?" she asked me.

Well, hardly. I was, of course, properly shocked. Some days later I happened to read an advertisement which read:

> "Lady wants to buy bright, smart pony. Must be sound cross-bred, have light mouth and jump well. Good home. Willing to pay reasonable price."

In horrified surprise at the brazenness of some people, I remembered saying: "Grandma, look at THIS!"

And she read the ad with intense interest, muttering that business must be doing so well at that evil place that now more of these shameless girls were imitating the act for the entertainment of other depraved audiences.

I had forgotten that episode of my young newspaper reading days and she must have kept the clipping only because I'd brought it to her attention and amused her for a moment or two, all those many years ago.

Grandma had a "lactarium fixation" and would visit dairies the way some folks went to beauty parlors or libraries. We'd trot around behind the Culty Dairy or the Model Dairies, this last one having a mechanized display of the entire dairy operation, from miniature cows grazing in the fields to a network of see-through pipes where the milk was pasteurized and put into tiny bottles which we could watch coming off a Lilliputian conveyor belt at the end of the display. The owners of this wonderful establishment were more than pleased to show people through the plant, and we loved the automatic milking machines, which were an innovation, and being given glasses of ice cold milk as it came off the refrigerated coils.

The dairies were not our only haunts, and we also accompanied Grandma to the various Russian creameries in the area where she would buy great hunks of pale yellow butter which the clerk spaded out of a big wooden barrel, slapping the beautiful mounds onto a piece of waxed paper on the scale. At our favorite Slavic buttery we could also sit at little round tables and have pots of yogurt with cinnamon-sugar sprinkled on top. Grandma believed very earnestly in the efficacy of yogurt and its health-giving properties.

There was something about Russians themselves which attracted her, although she spoke bitterly against the "Red" variety, reserving her approval for those she recognized as "White". She would whisper to me furtively, as we waited to be served, eyeing the proprietor and his helpers as they weighed and packaged those creamy wares for their countrymen customers, all chattering in that most foreign of languages to our ears.

Whispering, she'd say: "The Russians make love in ways that no one else knows about, and even when their women marry non-Russians you can be sure that they always have a Russian lover on the side since nobody else can do it their way, you know."

I would look around at these mysterious men and women, wondering what secrets were theirs, if only they could tell, while my Grandmother smiled and nodded, returning their friendly acknowledgment of our presence in their midst.

The most serious tragedy of the war was when a shortage of butter finally hit us, and we knew then that the world situation was grave and portentous. Grandma had managed to buy a pound of tinned Australian butter on the black market, and Grandpa cautioned us to eat sparingly of it. Grandma said that she would prefer to have her fill of it while she could, and eat dry bread when it was gone, rather than stint on butter when she had it before her. It was a perfect illustration of the differences in these two persons' entire approach to life. We watched Grandma plaster her piece of bread with thick pats of the scarce commodity, biting off each morsel defiantly as Grandpa motioned for us to leave it alone. She had devoured almost a quarter of the tin of butter when Grandpa made a move to wrap it up again and return it to its container to be enjoyed at a later time, but before he could fold the paper around the yellow lump, Grandma seized it in her hand and with a wild angry look started toward the window with the obvious intent of hurling the precious stuff into the street. We all jumped up to prevent her from committing this criminal act, holding her fast while Grandpa scraped the oily mass form her fingers as Vinnie held her arm firmly above his head. The butter, all squished and out of shape, was smoothed back into the tin, covered and put away carefully, as Grandma, quite overcome, went muttering to her bed where she sulked and sighed loudly for some time. Nothing more was said, and the incident was never mentioned again, and I think that was the very last piece of butter I saw until we got to prison camp.

To this day, I equate butter with wealth, and am happier to have several pounds of it in my freezer than I am in having money in the bank.

In the "old days", Grandma told me, she used to have a blind Chinese man come to the house to give her a massage. Being sightless, he was able to give her a complete treatment while she lay before him without a stitch on, and this made perfectly good sense to me. She was exceedingly fond of being "worked over" as she put it, and taught us the expert manipulation of tired muscles not only of the back, but also of the arms and hands, fingers especially, neck and head, and ending gloriously with the feet and toes. She said that as long as we happened to still be the "right size" we were to walk on her back whenever she felt a need for it, and we never minded running up and down from her well-upholstered gluteus maximus to her somewhat sharp deltoidal area, sometimes losing our balance and slipping off as another of us scrambled for the empty place on the ample expanse of her back. She loved it, our busy treatment putting her in an excellent mood, keeping the lot of us quiet and happy at once.

Whenever she'd call one of us, Grandma always ran all of our names together, shouting:

"MARYVINCENTJORDIEANNIE.
"MARYVINCENTJORDIEANNIE!"
before she could remember which one of us she actually meant to hail.

"Want to learn the Siamese national anthem?" Grandma would ask. The boys, always eager for some new nonsense, learned the song immediately, and not knowing what a trick she was playing on them would go around singing the following to the tune of "God Save the King."

Ah Wah Tah Nah, Siam
Ah Wah Tah Nah, Siam
Ah Wah Tah Nahss.

Grandma loved that. Vincent and Jordie were such willing victims.

Surprisingly, I did not object to being served boiled tongue at dinner, finding it rather delicious. One day, however, as I hungrily cut into a piece Grandpa had placed on my plate, Grandma, who hated it, looked at my portion and intoned piously: "That is the tongue that never told a lie."

My taste for it evaporated with the words, and Grandpa said, as she reached for the dish of ginger chicken and lily buds to put over the rice in her bowl, wrinkling her nose with a final glance at the slice of tongue in front of me.

My poor Grandfather, I sometimes thought, had five children to bring up in that apartment, and had all but lost control of the oldest one whose name was Georgina.

Grandpa rarely amused his wife purposely, but I remember her being quite taken one evening when to illustrate his constant exhortations about not wasting food, he had tied a knot in a corner of his linen handkerchief and put a finger into the knot to make it more like a head, with two other fingers creating the arms of his hand puppet. He wiggled this playfully at us, having it give us a bow and a few waves, and said:

"Here is a short sermon for you," and attempted to throw his voice into the hankie-puppet.

"Dearly Beloved,
Do you know it's a sin
To eat potatoes and throw 'way the skin?
The skin feeds the pigs and the pigs feed you.
Dearly Beloved, let us pray."

Perhaps it was the unexpectedness of my grandfather's try at whimsy we found so appealing, and Grandma, in spite of herself, was just as tickled with his performance as we were and said, without cruelty:"You silly old man."

Adolf Hitler had come to power in Germany, and great numbers of Jews fled for their lives, many finding their way to Shanghai where they did their best to make a living for their families who were forced to exist in reduced circumstances from what they had been accustomed to in their native land. Almost all of them were highly educated, belonging to the professional class, many chemists among them. Grandma befriended a man who sold her a formula for an excellent tooth powder, and she immediately ordered supplies of calcium carbonate, diatomaceous earth (no shortage of that in China), methyl salicylate, Kieselguhr, and other unpronounceable ingredients, mixing and measuring them on our dining room table, and creating havoc in the household for days on end. Grandma also ordered hundreds of little blue bottles with screw caps, and had bundles of labels printed. These labels bore the picture of Saint Therese of Lisieux, the Little Flower of Jesus, as a First Communicant with her saintly eyes raised to Heaven, and the contents of the bottles were dubbed by their manufacturer, (in the only cottage industry of its kind in the City of Shanghai) as "Little Flower Tooth Powder." When Auntie Ida questioned the propriety of commercializing poor Therese, Grandma quickly pointed to a supply of St. Joseph Aspirin she had, saying that what she proposed was not exactly unprecedented.

For weeks, we were kept busy sticking labels on bottles, funneling the sweet smelling powder into their narrow necks and screwing on the metal tops, after which we boxed them carefully to be ready for the vast demanding market which Grandma confidently expected to come thundering to our door, and which never materialized. There were many shortages in the days to come, but we never ran out of tooth powder, finding it useful for other purposes as well, such as foot powder and as a relief for prickly heat rash. We used to sprinkle the insides of our tennis shoes with the magic stuff and our feet would slip right into their gummy interiors, even without socks. Our friends could never understand why there was a faint aroma of chewing gum hanging over us long after chiclets had disappeared from the sweet shops during the war, and we'd say: "What smell? I don't smell anything," and look around sniffing the air suspiciously.

The amahs sewed two face cloths together, making a pocket, filled it with Little Flower Tooth Powder, and discovered yet another use for the cooling concoction. After our baths, they would pat us all over with the terry cloth powder filled puffs, and we smelled delicious and felt smooth and soft to the touch.

When the world didn't beat a path to Grandma's door in search of her astounding formula, she decided that as an extra attraction we would offer a free toothbrush with every bottle purchased. Another chemist had shown her how to make Bakelite toothbrushes in the kitchen, and one day we came home from school to be greeted by the amahs and cook fleeing the apartment with their aprons held over their faces and tears in their eyes. We could not imagine what was happening, but once inside the hallway we discovered the most chokingly putrid smell we had ever encountered, which made it impossible to remain on the premises for even a moment. Seeing us all routed by the terrible odor caused by the Bakelite brush handles which she was cooking in the oven like so many gingerbread boys, gave Grandma more excitement than she'd had since trying to cure Vincent of his tic, and she laughed and cried, pointing at us as we staggered around through the rooms, coughing and gagging and holding our noses.

We said that we ought to send Grandma over to Germany to wage chemical warfare on the Nazis and have it all over with in an afternoon. Her Bakelite gas was far worse than the mustard gas of the First World War, and if it didn't kill you, it drove you crazy enough so that you wished it had. Grandma loved that remark, and repeated what we'd said to Grandpa to take his mind off the smell when he came home, only by then it had dissipated somewhat and he was not treated to the full effect as we had been. Needless to say, we suffered no shortage of toothbrushes during the war either, and these items were surprisingly durable and well-made considering the "mad scientist" who had brought them forth like plastic cookies in her apartment kitchen.

Musical Beds. It might sound a bit risqué but there was nothing scandalous in the way in which we played this absorbing game. Every so often, I would wake in the middle of the night from a bad dream and being frightened would get up and creep into bed with Grandma, snuggling up to her for security and comfort, and making sure that the mosquito net was tucked closely under the mattress after I got in.

Then, Annie would wake, and finding me gone from her side would look over and see that I was with Grandma; so she'd get in with us, making a sandwich of Grandma. Our hot little bodies would be too much for her, and she'd quietly crawl out from between Annie and me and settle herself in our empty bed. Vincent would hear a hoot in the alley and wake up looking for a safer place to sleep, and seeing Grandma in our bed would slip under the netting with her. Jordie, like Annie with me, so accustomed to sleeping with his big brother, and feeling him gone, would follow Vincent to where Grandma was still trying to get a few hours of sleep.

When the boys had finally gone off to "The Land of Nod:" once more, Grandma would extricate herself and make a last ditch attempt at rest before the day broke, burrowing into the narrow bed the boys had vacated. In the morning, we'd all be in different beds and no one had a clear recollection of what happened during the night, and since Grandma would be snoring loudly there was no explanation from her about the puzzling switch. I would have completely forgotten my bad dream and spend the better part of the day wondering what strange amusement it afforded Grandma to shift us from bed to bed that way while we slept, and could not see why she insisted on this ridiculous practice, unless, of course, it was a ruse to confuse the Devil who would not know which one of us he had come torment that night. That being the case, it was quite an acceptable procedure, and I would try to remember to say what a good idea it was when I got home from school; only, I always forgot, until it happened again.

Chapter 17

I wrote a letter to Louise and told her how Mother Lewis, my teacher, would address us. That stalwart nun, in a breathless voice, would say,

"Come, my beloved, quickly now."

She used this expression when she wanted us to move in single file down the corridor, or when she wished us to close our history books and open our geography books, and for any other occasion which called for the class to act as one body. I loved that woman with all my heart and soul and would have followed her into the maw of hell had she needed a convoy. Mother Lewis was brisk, kind, strict and perfect, and evoked a response in her girls available to no other teacher in the Sacred Heart Convent. I had her for two years of my attendance there, and can remember no one else as an instructor, although I know there were others in previous years. That good lady made the history of England come alive for us, and breathed relevancy and immediacy into the "glory that was Greece and the grandeur that was Rome." She was a patrician in the true sense of the word and we were inordinately proud to be numbered among Mother Lewis' "beloved."

My Auntie Ida introduced me to a tall, blond Swedish woman whose husband was the Spanish Consul, and she soon asked if I might be allowed to go to her house once a week to help with her English pronunciation. The lady sent a liveried chauffer in their black limousine to bring me to her home, and I was utterly charmed by the round house in which she lived. Every room was pie-shaped, and the center of the house was an octagonal courtyard with a fountain in the middle, the light pouring in from the ceiling, the top of the structure being one enormous sun-room with garden furniture and potted plants in wild green profusion. We'd have tea together, she and I, as I drilled her in the correct pronunciation of the words "through" and "though" and other combinations of "th". I'd ask her to read to me from a child's version of the works of Shakespeare I brought along, and would correct her as she went haltingly down the page. She was vastly amused by my insistence on the constant repetition of words with which she had difficulty, not stopping until I was satisfied that she had said them properly.

The lady had no children of her own, and had not been in the company of youngsters very much in her life, and I imagine that she found me diverting as well as educational.

I told her about Mother Lewis and how particular she was with us in school, and patterned my teaching etiquette after my dear instructor, who might have been annoyed by my solemn tutorial technique had she been a witness to these sessions in the plushly carpeted room. I was filled with self-importance at having been requested to give the Swedish lady pointers in English, but I was even more impressed with her circular house, and it has since been my dearest wish to build a home exactly like it.

Several times a week I would ride my bicycle into the countryside to visit Bunny Barnes who lived across the railroad tracks in her Grandpa's house. He was very much like my own grandfather, they both having had the same upbringing and Eurasian background. Bunny's Grandpa operated the Columbia Dairy and was married to a comfortable Japanese lady who made the biggest cream puffs I had ever seen, and they'd be filled with the freshest, sweetest, thickest cream in China. We'd stuff ourselves with the beautiful pastries and do our homework together, talking about our lives and families and sharing little confidences.

On my way to Bunny's I'd ride past a beggar who lay on a straw mat on a small incline, and whenever I had an extra copper I'd toss it to him. We got to know one another and he'd nod at me as I pedaled by. One day, Annie was with me, sitting behind on the bicycle, and as we approached the familiar sight of the old fellow on his mat, I sensed that something was wrong. I told Annie not to look and she hid her face in my back as I saw that the man was dead. Rigor mortis had set in and his arms and legs had crooked and hardened in an upward position, his face staring at the open sky. Someone had stolen his ragged shoes and a couple of bony dogs were eating what they could of the pitiful corpse.

I turned back and headed for home, not wanting to pass that way again in the dusk, and watched people walking to and fro in front of where the dead beggar lay, hardly anyone bothering to cast a glance in his direction.

The last time I rode to Bunny's dairy home was during a time when the Japanese were blockading Shanghai, causing an upsurge in the smuggling of rice into the City. Smugglers would sew many pounds of rice into their clothing so that it looked like the usual heavy padding which Chinese peasants wore, and that day the sentinels who guarded the railroad tracks at the crossing I used had discovered two men trying to bring rice into Shanghai in this fashion.

There was a disturbance at the gate as I came through, but I didn't know what the trouble was. Two hours later, as I rode home again, I saw that the guards had done their work. They had decapitated the two Chinese rice smugglers and the severed heads had been impaled on the bamboo posts on either side of the crossing, while the naked bodies were left slumped at the base of the poles, their ripped clothing strewn about in tatters. I had no choice but to ride between this gory sight, which I did without speaking a word or changing the expression on my face, and although it frightened me, I was not sick at heart as I had been upon discovering the woodenly stiff beggar on the mound who had died all alone for no reason.

The cook bought rice in large sacks for our family, and the amah said that if I wished to strengthen my fingernails I should run my hands straight into the raw grains without bending my fingers as far in as I was able to go. It was not an easy thing to do, and I spent a great deal of time in this practice, remembering that someone might have paid with his life for the bag of rice being in our house.

Annie was prepared to receive her First Holy Communion when she was six, and I secretly envied the smoothness of the proceedings, remembering the farcical events of my own Greatest Day in Shameen. We had saved the lovely Indian lawn dress which I had worn, and it fitted Annie perfectly. Grandma was beside herself and made a tremendous fuss over my sister who relished every moment in the glare of the spotlight that day. Annie had her picture taken in color, and Grandma had it printed in the newspaper for all to see. Our little sister was an exceptionally beautiful child and she grew up to have a lovely, vibrant and rich singing voice, which she used mainly to sing lullabies to her four children who have inherited their mother's arresting good looks and sunny nature.

The new girl in school looked very disgruntled. Her name was Sheila Hutton and she had previously attended the English Cathedral School, but had been transferred to our convent by her mother as a disciplinary measure. Sheila resisted the change and everyone was aware of her displeasure. Mother Lewis urged me to befriend her, and I felt it my duty to show Sheila around and help her get acquainted. She was a stubborn person, very opinionated for an eleven year old, and charged about the place looking angry and determined not to accept her new classmates. But I grew very fond of her and learned to gauge her many moods and to understand her volatile nature. She was highly intelligent and read voraciously, and I was drawn to her imaginative outlook and fierce independence. Somehow, she took a fancy to me and we became fast friends. And, indeed, after thirty-five years are still as close to each other as we were then.

When the Americans and British were interned in prison camps in Shanghai in 1942 and 1943, Sheila went to the Lungwha camp, and I to the one in Chapei. Later, my brothers and Annie and I were repatriated to the United States in an exchange of prisoners while the war still raged; after the hostilities had ceased Sheila and her mother and sister went to England. Sheila and her mother, Gweneth Hutton, had both been born in Shanghai but were "full-blooded" English people. Before they left the Orient, Sheila tracked me down through a cousin of mine who was still in the City; she wrote to me in America, and we have kept in touch ever since. We saw each other in England a few years ago, and she and her son have since come for a summer holiday to my home in California.

When we are together, we are still thirteen years old, and convince one another that neither of us has changed in the least, a fantasy which delights and pleases us enormously.

Being able to observe the Hutton family at such close range was an eye-opening experience for me. Sheila's father, a tall gruff man, was a good bit older than her mother, and they lived in a penthouse apartment closer to downtown Shanghai than was the I.S.S. Building. It was a magnificently appointed place, to my mind, and had two floors, which I found an astonishing arrangement for an apartment. Sheila invited me home to the Hanray Mansions many times, and I would often have dinner with her family and stay the night. The meals were invariably superb, and for the first time I tasted Boeuf a' la Stroganoff and pilaf.

Sitting at their sumptuous table which was impeccably set with gleaming silver and sparkling glassware, fresh flowers in the centerpiece, and their Number One Boy serving the dinner in a white jacket, I felt so honored and elegant. Sheila's parents sat at opposite ends of the dining table and held conversations in good natured tones of voice.

One evening, during dinner, I happened to look at Mrs. Hutton and caught an expression on her face which I had not seen anywhere before. A knowing and intimate warmth showed in her eyes, and a small half-smile played on her generous mouth. I glanced towards the other end of the table and saw that Mr. Hutton was regarding his wife with the same quiet affection and secret understanding, and, caught in the cross-fire of that loving silent exchange, for the first time in my life I knew that men and women who truly wanted one another shared some marvelous mystery known only to them, and I lowered my gaze to stare at the serviette on my lap, feeling abysmally sad that I had never seen that look around our own dining room table between any of the men and women in my family.

I can recognize "that look" whenever I see it now, although I am sorry to report that I have not noticed it too often among others; as for myself, for a little while, there was Remo.

Sheila had a dog named Winnie, after Mr. Churchill, and when the war was in full swing in Europe we drew up a formal contract which Winnie made legal with her footprint, declaring that thenceforth she would no longer be a German dog, but a proper English dachshund, and renounced her canine connection with anything smacking of Deutschland. Winnie, brave little patriot that she was, is the only dog I have ever really liked, although dogs seem to be fond of me, for some odd reason which I have not understood.

Sheila and I would go to our respective rooftops, seven floors up, and wave tablecloths to one another across the lower buildings between us when we weren't allowed to waste time together or talk on the phone after school as adolescent girls are wont to do, and we were no exception. A few times she'd come to my building and, taking turns, we would practice walking down the corridor away from each other as one or the other of us checked closely to make dead certain that we walked in straight lines, and didn't wriggle our bottoms, which was considered by us to be "terribly common." Whomever in their right minds, would have paid the slightest attention to two gangling, owlish girls with wispy braids, whether they walked provocatively or not, never occurred to us, unaware as we were of our singular unattractiveness and plainness. We were Champion Dowdy Girls.

After Pearl Harbor was attacked and the Americans were full in the war, the Japanese issued a proclamation forcing all enemy nationals to wear red arm-bands. I wore one with an "A" for American, and my number was 1007. Sheila wore one with a "B" for British and I can't remember her number, but she still has the armband having hidden it before it was confiscated by the guards at camp as mine had been. She had a pin which showed her to be a member of the NOBS (Noble Order of British Spitfires) and I coveted it genially; but we were so proud just wearing the red arm-bands and it instilled in me a sense of patriotism I had not experienced before. Publicly stating my nationality in a hostile environment gave me a great feeling of bravery and pride, even though it meant I was then barred from going to the movies, or any park, or other place of entertainment; at my age it wasn't likely that I'd be wanting to sit at a bar or go to a cabaret, and I did not mind being excluded from anything as long as I could wear my red American band around my arm.

Leslie Hutton, Sheila's father, died suddenly. The family and I as well, were in shock and when it came time for the funeral Mrs. Hutton refused to attend the service. I had never heard of such a thing before, and did not understand it at the time, although now I realize that she had loved her husband well while he lived and, knowing that funerals are a barbaric custom, had wisely chosen to remain at home. Sheila and I rode our bicycles to the Anglican Cathedral and came in while the service was in progress, taking our seats at the rear of the church near the heavy oaken doors. No one saw us and we sat quietly, side by side, Sheila wearing an angry look on her face.

Dean Trivett gave the eulogy and when he came to the part "...dust into dust, ashes into ashes..." my friend and I, gazing at the small bronze urn which held her father's remains, were seized by an uncontrollable urge to laugh. I suppose she started first, and then I, remembering what a large man he had been, now to be reduced to the contents of that tiny container, and unable to stem the rising laugh born of grief and nervousness, we finally had to leave the church before the service ended and rode back to the penthouse, whizzing through the streets and saying nothing.

As soon as we were safely inside the apartment, Sheila rushed up to her room and wept bitterly as I had never seen her do before, and I tried vainly to comfort her with little pats and clucks, not finding one meaningful word to say to my dear bereft friend.

It was the first time I had watched people dealing with their grief at the loss of a beloved one in a way to which I could relate. Sheila's tears were understandable, but so was her mother's dignified calm acceptance of death, and it has remained with me that those who create scenes at the biers of the dead are suspect, making much of their grief for a great show, acting out of the guilt and shame which undoubtedly afflict them for the wrong they'd done the deceased during his lifetime. I am impressed with the validity of a silent grief far more than I ever will be with the tearing of hair, the rending of garments and the weeping and wailing of hypocritical survivors. If one loved deeply and well in life, then in death there can be no regret, save that the face of the person one loved is hidden forevermore.

Quite often, we'd see a Chinese funeral procession wending its way to the burial grounds, the paid mourners dressed in traditional Chinese funereal white with white bands tied around their heads, moaning and keening loudly, giving the deceased his money's worth in noisy grief. Following the coffin would be a group of people carrying loops of gold and silver paper "currency" and many things fashioned from slivers of bamboo and thin paper, looking like so many kites, but all destined for the funeral pyre where copies of earthly goods would be burned to insure the dead man's comforts in the hereafter. There were paper clothes, radios, rickshaws, chairs, beds, and replicas of whatever favorite objects the deceased may have left behind. Gongs and drums were beaten on the way to the place of interment, and the coffin was left on top of the ground to be mounded over with dirt, or to have a small brick house with a tile roof built around the casket.

Sheila's father's funeral was the only non-Chinese one I attended in those years we spent in Shanghai, and had he been buried in the Oriental style I doubt that anyone would have frowned on us for our odd behavior, and perhaps we needn't have relieved the heartbroken tension which had built up in us by giving in to that seemingly unnatural laughter.

We had a chubby amah that was new to our household. She came from the countryside, and told me that she had left her three small children behind in her husband's care, and had come to the city to earn more money because they were so poor, and her husband had a difficult time making a living from farming. She had a round pleasant face and a soft voice, and I became very attached to her. I noticed that she wore homemade shoes which she had fashioned herself from cloth and layers of newspaper stitched together for the soles.

Whenever I was kept at home for any illness, no matter how slight, See-yoh Amah stayed in the room with me and did not leave my side for a minute. She'd sit on the bed and rub my back and wipe me off with warm towels, and it gave us the chance to talk at some length about the life she lived in the country when she went home to visit her husband and children. One day she confessed to me that she was pregnant and that soon she would have to leave us to have her baby. I was terribly sad at the thought of losing her and promised to keep her secret until it became too noticeable to conceal from Grandma, who would immediately send her away.

I told her that years ago I had seen a baby being born behind the fence of the Hungjao Road house, and so I knew what it looked like; but I wanted to know what it felt like, and asked her to tell me what she had experienced in giving birth to a child. See-yoh Amah (the word meant "small", and that she was in height, although not in girth), had a most engaging way of expressing herself, and in her melodious voice she told me of the times when she had her babies and described in fine detail every step along the way. I was almost twelve at the time, and the mysteries of conception were not clear in my mind, although I was a vast storehouse of misinformation and garbled facts. This gentle little woman, in her quiet style, told me everything with such simplicity and unself-conscious tenderness that it is a pity and a great loss to everyone that she had not been engaged to tour the world informing every other twelve-year old girl on the brink of womanhood about the facts of life, the miracle of procreation and the marvelous experience of giving birth to a human being. (In the present-day world of over-population, however, she might have been stoned for making it all sound so attractive and appealing.)

See-yoh Amah told it all to me in the beautiful masculine dialect I knew so well, painting her picture in bold strokes of subtle hue, eliminating unnecessary adornment and avoiding the use of sensation or too many old wives' tales. She said that when the pains started and she knew her time had come, she would call the village midwife who had special medicine to give her if the pains became too severe. However, the amah said,

"That medicine is so expensive. It costs fifty cents, so I have never asked for it yet."

She assured me that when my turn came to have a baby I would experience pain, but that it was not so hard to bear, and as long as I did not become frightened, everything would be all right.

She told me that it would be the hardest work I would ever do in my life and that good babies were born to brave women. Years later, her words came back to me, and helped me to have three very good babies indeed.

After her baby arrived, the amah said that the midwife washed it and wrapped it up, and that she herself then stirred about the house to prepare her husband's dinner, and he was so pleased and surprised to find a new member of the family awaiting him upon his return from the fields. She smiled at me in sweet satisfaction remembering those times, obviously looking forward to the next happy occasion ahead.

Auntie Ida told me that when I became twelve or so I would start menstruating, but she explained that this was "bad blood" which had to be flushed out of the system, and See-yoh Amah did not dispute that information; and for many years I did not know the true nature of the menses. When it finally happed to me one day while I was at school, I had forgotten my aunt's instructions and thought that I was going to bleed to death in an ignominious fashion and received permission to go home, my green face a telling reason to the nuns, and leaving my bicycle behind, I rode the tram back to the apartment wondering how I was going to explain my condition. When Auntie Ida came home she took a look at me and decided that I ought not to be sharing a bed with Annie any longer, and arranged for me to sleep in her room in a bed of my own.

She cautioned me not to say anything to Grandma of what happened to me as it would only give her more to worry about, and she showed me what to do regarding my new "problem." I didn't want my brothers to learn of this turn of events, and I suppose I fretted unduly over an excuse to give at being moved from our big room to Ida's; but nothing was said, and I saw that they accepted the idea of my now being too old to share sleeping quarters with them, my having stepped up to a higher rung on the ladder of maturity.

Ida's room was tidy to a fault and smelled of perfume and a camphor chest, and although it was in the same apartment, I felt as though I had moved into another world entirely. It must have been a big sacrifice on her part to have shared her privacy with me, and I did appreciate her recognizing my need for a little privacy of my own, which was not an easy thing to come by in our closely crowded flat.

Having her eye on me more than she had in the past, my aunt took notice of my phobic behavior, and although she could not understand instances such as why I had become so upset when a shoe clerk had held my ankles in the store as he tried to fit me with a new pair of Mary Janes, she was very patient and tolerant of me, trying continually to assure me that all was well. I was a skittish child and excitable, over-reacting to life the way Grandma did; but I was not unhappy, although I continued to mourn over the loss of my mother and kept a diary filled with melancholy thoughts and desolate yearnings.

I daydreamed constantly and invented another life so that at times it was a wrench to be jarred into the reality of my brothers and sister, and I was remote, a million light years away whenever Grandpa or Grandma spoke to me during much of that time.

Pig Latin became the rage of the younger set in these days, and the four of us would rattle it off with ease to the consternation of our elders. We were rarely treated to the sight of Grandpa's temper, but one time he leaped up from the table and shaking his fists at us, said,

"There will be no more Pig Talk here!" and it stopped.

The only other time I can recall my Grandpa giving a show of anger was when, having been berated all day by Grandma, we saw him standing before her in his BVD's, with his arms folded across his chest, listening doggedly to the abuse she heaped on him. Ida came into the room and said,

"For God's sake, Mama, leave him alone."

My Grandfather clenched his hands above his head and jumping up and down like a furious troll, shouted,

"I will not allow cursing in my house." Ida turned and left the room chastened and frustrated, as her mother watched her leave in contemptuous triumph.

There were many such scenes, and almost every time there was a row it concerned money. The war came ever closer, inflation threatened constantly, many commodities were in short supply or non-existent, and I suppose everyone's temper was short and the whole world was anxious and worried about the future which loomed darkly in black headlines in the newspapers. Nonetheless, the family fighting caused sickening knots in the pit of my stomach, and I fled to the safety of my school, glad that I had somewhere to go for a brief respite from the constant conflict in our home.

It was bad form to discuss one's home life at school, but Mother Lewis used to look at me with her practiced eye and ask,

"What ails you, my beloved?" and I could never tell her because I didn't really know what it was myself.

In a most confidential tone, Grandma once gave me what amounted to the bulk of her advice on matters pertaining to sex. She said, "Never marry a man who cannot make a circle around your ankle with his thumb and middle finger. If you do, it will never work. Never."

I had a great deal to worry about while I was growing up in Shanghai.

Chapter 18

"Let us, therefore, brace ourselves…"
Mr. Churchill, June 1940

A year and more, before the bombing of Pearl Harbor, the Japanese Army marched into Shanghai. Hundreds of soldiers in full battle gear paraded down Avenue Joffre past our apartment building. We watched from a friend's flat which faced the street and saw crowds of Chinese lined on the sidewalks waving small flags with the red ball of the Rising Sun in their hands. (The "Fried Egg" as we called it.)

Shanghai was thick with rumors, and the ones which frightened my grandparents most were reports that the Japanese were building concentration camps for American and British nationals living in the City. They, themselves, were in no danger of being imprisoned since they were citizens of Spain and neutral, but they feared for the four children they sheltered, knowing that we would be regarded in another light by the occupying army of Japan.

We had lived with the trappings of war for some long time and the presence of Japanese soldiers in Shanghai was a familiar sight to us. In 1941 the vise tightened around our City and we came to expect having our mail censored, and being forced to show registration papers at a series of barricades thrown up everywhere without warning. There were air raid drills and blackouts, and the shortages of food and other necessities of life became ever more acute. Shortwave radios were banned, the news was censored, and Carroll Alcott, an outspoken American radio broadcaster, left Shanghai.

Letters from Louise were few and far between, and little or no money was sent for our upkeep. I continued to write to my mother, and urged my brothers and Annie to do likewise, nagging them until they'd sit down to laboriously scribble out a note to her on the backs of letters of my own. We wrote much the same sort of letter to our mother, filled with urgent pleas to send for us and lugubrious statements of our loneliness and longing for her. We made little complaint, however, about our life with Grandma, and for all of its complexities and unpredictability we must have felt loved and cherished, and physically safe in that household.

In February 1941 I wrote to Louise:

"Grandpa told me that we will have to renew our passports in April, and in March most of the Americans are leaving. It seems to me that everybody gets notice to leave except us. Why is that, I wonder? I hope that you will send for us soon. It's so lonesome without a mother, but my Auntie Ida makes up for that."

In March we all had the measles together and couldn't have made a trip anyway. I wrote my mother about it telling her how dreadful the illness had been, but that:

"Anyway we are company for each other and that is better than being sick alone without someone around who knows just how you feel."

In April 1941 another letter from me to Louise said:

"Grandpa took us to the American Consulate and I had to sign a lot of papers and swear an oath on the Bible that what was written on the paper was true. I don't know what it was though. Then I had to have my fingerprint taken and all these things made me feel quite grown up although I am only twelve years old. I'll never forget this day."

Easter came and Auntie Ida gave us porcelain eggs filled with candy. She'd had our pictures taken for the last time, as it happened, and from the way we looked, so sleek and well-cared for, few would have suspected that the war was gaining momentum.

On the 12th of May, 1941, I sent a letter to Louise complaining bitterly that the convent was "the hardest, most particular school I've ever been to," asking that if I failed could I transfer to another place, although I did admit that the Sacred Heart was the finest school in Shanghai. But then, school was over in June and we looked forward eagerly to the resumption of classes in the fall.

Jordie wrote his mother about Annie's First Communion and also apologized for having been "very very naughty and lazy." He said that he was sorry and would try to be "gwad." Good? Never!

On June 8, 1941 I asked my mother: "Mummy, why don't you write more often? We don't have you near to talk to, so the least we can have is your thoughts."

In July I wrote to tell her that I had passed class with two prizes, one in Reading and the other in Grammar. It was certainly good news to me since I had been so certain I'd fail to be promoted that year, and the notice of our results did not come out for several weeks after school closed for the summer holidays. The suspense had been torturous.

The last time I was able to write to Louise was in November 1941. After Pearl Harbor there was no further mail exchanged between us. I had become extremely religious in the past two years, and wrote what amounted to a tract on piety, worrying that if my mother did not practice her religion she would not go to Heaven when she died, and would be lost to us forever, and it is quite true that I often cried myself to sleep considering this possibility. I wrote:

"If I don't see you again in this world, I would like to see you in the next." I assured her that I was not being prompted by "Someone" and gave a graphic description of the eternal tortures of Hell for my fallen-away-Catholic mother to ponder.

People were still evacuating Shanghai, and I prayed feverishly and hoped desperately every day that we would soon be among their number; but Louise could not send for us and Grandpa seemed powerless to do anything in that regard, and the United States Cavalry did not ride up on horseback. The last boatload of Americans sailed from the Bund, and I knew that our fate was sealed.

When war was declared between America and Japan, the city of Shanghai was cut off from the rest of the world, or so it seemed to me, and much of the next year found me withdrawn and ill a great deal of the time. It is as though I went through the following months like a sleepwalker and remember little of what went on around me. I lived an almost isolated life, perking up from time to time in Sheila's company or when I was with Bunny, and going through the motions in school and at home with a minimum of effort and little enthusiasm. I turned the little box-room into a place where I could sleep, and stayed to myself as much as I was able, reading constantly and writing in a journal which was eventually confiscated from me in prison camp.

I had abandoned all hope of ever seeing my mother again during my childhood, realizing that when we were finally reunited I would most probably be grown up and not have the same urgent need for her, and the realization was heart-breaking to me. Then, too, with the mails being stopped, the slim thread of communication was broken and I grieved as much as if I had heard that Louise had died.

Many of the Chinese had been whipped into an anti-foreign-devil froth and, siding with the Japanese conquerors, went through the streets chanting slogans about the "Sino-Japanese Co-Prosperity Sphere" with banners declaring "Asia for the Asiatics" held on poles as they marched. It was a nervous time for anyone of non-Oriental parentage to be living in Shanghai, and those of us who later wore arm-bands felt all the more heroic for literally wearing our hearts on our sleeves. We saw several angry crowds, but no one I knew was ever mobbed or hurt in any way for being an enemy national, at least, not in our little group.

In the midst of the war, Grandpa and Auntie Ida went to their offices, and we attended school, did our homework, fought amongst ourselves (when I was up to it), dreamed our dreams, kept our secrets, got into mischief and grew out of our clothes with alarming regularity. Shoes were an expensive luxury, and we would be scolded harshly for scuffing them or wearing them in the house when it was not necessary to do so. We were constantly admonished not to waste hot water, and had to share the tub-full between the four of us. I, being the oldest and the cleanest, naturally- insisted that I have the bathroom to myself first; then it was Annie's turn, and lastly the boys got into the water together and finished it off. Every scrap of soap was saved and then melted down to be hardened into a new cake for future use. The smallest piece of writing paper was treasured and we were told to always write on both sides and to use it very sparingly. A lack of hot water and a scarcity of paper spell disaster to me, even today.

Grandma took Annie to visit her sister in Hongkew, a stronghold of the Japanese, and upon their return they ran into a barricade of rolls of concertina barbed wire strung across the Hongkew Bridge which was guarded by a small company of Japanese soldiers with helmets, swords and rifles. Grandma produced her neutral papers of registration to the sentries, but they paid no attention to her pleas. It was growing dark and Grandma was afraid to be on the streets after nightfall in those days, and they were a long way from home. Annie, who had turned seven on the 7th of December, 1941, Pearl Harbor Day, made eyes at the captain of the guards, and for some unknown reason he was moved to release the child and her agitated terrorized grandmother. Perhaps the man was won by Annie's apparent lack of fear and her pixyish expression, which has rescued her from several tight situations since then.

There is a snapshot of my sister during these days, showing her striding down a sidewalk in Shanghai, arms swinging freely, sturdy little legs marching along, a most determined look on her pretty face; she is dressed in a tweed coat made from one of Grandma's old suits, and she wears such a hopeful and cheery expression, such a dauntless air. Annie still has that little coat which Grandma had kept after we were taken away, and I envy her that precious relic of our childhood. Next to Louise, I loved Annie best in those days, and love her still.

Ominous things were happening, and we would be caught up in the war more seriously than we'd expected at first. The Japanese did have a prison camp in Pootung and all the single men in the City who were classified as enemy nationals were interned, Barney Wall among them. He'd been kind to the four of us, and I remember him giving us dollar bills at Easter and Christmas when money was worth something. Then, it was worthless, inflation having exploded in Shanghai, and if you gave a beggar a one hundred dollar bill he'd sniff at it, letting the wind blow it away with the dead leaves.

Vincent and Jordie were befriended by a Chinese boy of seventeen whose name was Hoo-Hwa. He had taken a fancy to my brothers and was welcomed into our house since his father, a wealthy comprador, was an old friend of our Grandfather's. Hoo-Hwa was accompanied everywhere by his private body servant, and they came one evening to take the two boys to a special dinner. Vincent came home to tell us of the fabulous feast they had enjoyed, and, goggle-eyed, informed us that the restaurant bill had come to Six Thousand Dollars in Chinese money. Years later, when Vincent and Jordie were at Boys' Town in Nebraska, Hoo-Hwa paid them a visit. He had come to America while our Grandparents still lived in Shanghai, learned where my brothers were from Grandma. Hoo-Hwa appeared with the same Chinese servant he had had all his life, and the boys were amazed and thoroughly delighted to see him, although a bit embarrassed by the fact that the fellow still wore short pants as he had in Shanghai days, causing Vincent to explain his old friend's strange clothing to their companions at the school. Vincent says that he never heard from Hoo-Hwa again and is still dumbfounded over that encounter.

My brothers used to play in the fields behind the I.S.S. Building, and one day they saw a peasant carrying two heavy buckets of water on the ends of a bamboo shaft slung over his shoulders. Out of mischief, they ran at him, spilling the water, and the man cracked them over their heads with his long pole for the trouble they'd caused him. They got into other scrapes during these times, and Vincent went down the servants' entrance staircase one afternoon to see Jordie having a noisy exchange with a young amah. The angry girl filled her mouth with thick mucus and spat at Jordie who dodged quickly, Vincent receiving the benefit of her ire full in his face. The terrible twosome created another major disturbance when Grandma discovered that they and other boys in the apartment had congregated in the underground garage to examine one another, and putting the blame on Miguel, she engaged Mrs. Campos in a bloody battle which raged on unabated for many days. Grandpa took no sides in this conflict, and ignored it completely, as did I.

Vincent came upon a man in the fields who had tried to strangle himself with a piece of cord, and was unconscious when my brother found him. Vincent called a gendarme (the policemen in the French Concession where we lived still dressed as they did in Paris, and called themselves *gendarmes*), who promptly went over to the would-be suicide, giving him a rough kick and sending him on his way. It was a desperate time for many, but still not so serious that people did not engage in pleasant pastimes, and Vincent went on a picnic with a group of Russian friends one Saturday afternoon. They rode a bus, and he remembers that the area looked so familiar to him. The bus turned into the drive-way of a deserted house which had its windows and doors boarded up with planks when Vincent realized that they were on the grounds of our Grandpa's last house on Hungjao Road, and he looked around incredulously saying to his friends,

"I used to live here! This was my Grandfather's house!" But no one believed him, and he came home to tell me about it, saying how sad he had been to have seen it again in such a state of disrepair and neglect.

One of the last letters from Louise to me, in response to my incessant pleading that she send for us, stated that, "He who travels alone, travels fastest." I had wondered where it was she wanted to go in such a hurry. I was in a hurry myself, impatient to grow up, eager to stay alive long enough to see her again, and desperate to get away from the war zone with its threats of concentration camps and other horrors, which were now present realities. Ida had been most considerate of my letters to my mother, and she always allowed me to seal my envelopes since I worried over anyone else reading what I said to Louise. Ida took me seriously, which was very important for a child, and now that there was no further mail, either coming in or going out, she would reassure me constantly, saying that she was sure Louise was all right, that the war would soon be over and that we would be reunited with our mother. It was kind of her to say those things, but I did not believe them too strongly.

The months dragged on and I heard Grandpa say that he was "just buying time." Grandma became even more nervous and tense, worrying aloud night and day. She fretted mightily about the rioting in the streets and the reports of violence done to foreigners in the city. The American Red Cross gave us food coupons for certain items which were not available on grocery counters, and our cook would take a tiered aluminum container and pick up rations at their distribution center. Everything we had was used up to the last drop, and we all learned to "make do" in a thousand ways. Grandma would say,

"We should have read the handwriting on the wall," and it was the most mystifying remark I'd heard because I had read the handwriting on the wall of the back staircase and could not understand what all those obscenities had to do with our predicament.

My brothers got into a fight in the fields behind the apartment and threw a tin can at a German woman on a bicycle who made a great fuss and reported them to the Japanese sentry nearby; and for many days we lived in fear and trembling, dreading every knock at our door, sure that it would be a coalition of the Nazi Party and His Imperial Majesty's Army come to take Vincent and Jordie to their torture chamber.

Not unlike the beggar children we had watched playing in the bank window, so now I watched my brothers and sister go about their childish business of trying to catch sparrows in the fields by sprinkling salt on their tails, and not having any success with that method Vincent filled the sugar bowl with salt, while the others sat back to watch Grandma put three spoonsful into her cup of tea, paying dearly for the pleasure of that sputtering sight.

In the fall of 1942, Grandpa was notified that he must take me to the Japanese authorities, in order that I be duly registered as an enemy alien, and I was issued the red armband at that time. I was now fourteen. I remember having to stand in a long line for most of the day, and we listened to the others talking and learned that this was the prelude to being interned.

My Grandfather was faced with a most difficult decision now. He had been informed that there was no way of avoiding the fact that I was fourteen years of age, and since I was now considered an enemy national I would not be exempt from the "civilian assembly center," as the Japanese officials euphemistically referred to the camps which were being readied. Vincent, Jordie and Annie would be allowed to remain in the City with Grandpa and Grandma since they were twelve, ten and eight, respectively. However, in the event an exchange ship was negotiated, only prisoners of war would be eligible to leave China, which meant that I might be sent to America while the boys and Annie remained in Shanghai.

Grandpa discussed this with me, and I suddenly came alive after months of listless and dispirited malaise. I begged him not to separate us, saying that I was sure we'd be just as safe in a camp as out in the City, things being what they were. I promised him that I was fully capable of taking care of my brothers and sister, and he knew that I was. The family, and the servants, recognized that the other three children obeyed me far more readily than they did our Grandmother, and I was certain that somehow we would find a way to get along on our own, even in a prison camp.

For some reason, which I find difficult to explain, the thought of going into such a place did not frighten me in the least. It never once occurred to me that we would be killed or tortured and I had no fear of the Japanese, even though I had seen at first-hand what some of their soldiers had been capable of doing to the Chinese. But then, no child believes in his own death, nor can it even be imagined, convinced as we are of our immortality and invincibility. Secretly, I rejoiced at this turn of events in our lives, and sometimes considered the entire war as the modus operandi for accomplishing my dearest wish, which was to be reunited with Louise. I realize that it sounds insane, and perhaps it was, but I did not approach the very real probability of our incarceration with fear and dread, which may have made it that much easier to live through, to say nothing of the fact that it developed into the choicest adventure of our lives, up to that time.

The weeks during which my Grandpa agonized over whether to let me enter the camp alone or to allow the three younger children to accompany me were devastating, and there were endless discussions of the subject between him and Grandma and Auntie Ida. Listening to them talking about the various possibilities, the uncertainties of our being repatriated, the unknown length of the war, and what might face us in a prison camp, gave me many sleepless nights, and whenever I could I vaulted into their conversations, inveighing against the decision to separate us, regardless of the outcome.

Alone with Vincent, I asked my brother,
"Are you afraid?"
"No," he said.
"Do you think we can stay alive?"
"Sure we will."
"You'd want to go in together, wouldn't you?"
"If you go, we'll go. We'll go together."
"And you're not afraid?"
"Why should I be? You'll be there with us."

More than I had ever done before I now looked closely at my brothers and sister. Threatened by separation, they had taken on a deeper meaning for me and I scrutinized them each carefully, realizing that in spite of all the fighting we had done amongst ourselves, the awful nuisance those boys were, and the innumerable times I had wished I'd never seen any of them, in my heart of hearts I knew that there were only four "real" people in the world for me, and felt that without one another life would lose its piquancy and flavor and come to pitiful end. The thought of being separated galvanized us and it is as though we four became one with a single-minded determination to remain as a solid unit, our four hearts beating an intrepid rhythm as we locked together in our new-found esprit de corps.

I would wake early in the morning while everyone still slept, and go into the room where Vincent and Jordie lay entwined and study their faces intently. They looked so innocent and vulnerable with their damp dark hair and long eyelashes sweeping across their downy cheeks; and I vowed that as long as I was alive no one would dare to harm them, my precious little brothers. Looking at Annie curled into a ball on her pillow, a fierce surge of protectiveness welled within me, and I knew that I would be bereft to leave her behind, to see her no more. Torn between the ambivalence of wanting them to be safe, which meant having them remain in the City with our Grandparents, and wanting them to stay with me, which might mean danger and death in a Japanese prison camp, I chose the latter, convinced that we'd be happier dying alongside one another (although I knew it would never come to that,) than living apart, and I was certain the other three shared that conviction. Fourteen-year olds are notoriously given to dramatizing themselves. I was no exception.

Grandpa finally told me that, in his view, it was the wiser of the two choices to let us go together into the camp, since then we would all have an equal chance of being chosen in an exchange of prisoners in the event a ship came for that purpose. We were enormously relieved by his decision not to separate us, and I threw my arms around his neck, thanking him over and over again, and that hurdle was cleared, making way for the plans which would now have to be considered, the prospect of facing imprisonment having become a reality.

In mid-January of 1943 we were ordered by the Japanese authorities to report on February 25th to enter the compound at Chapei, a suburb of Shanghai. The weeks prior to our leaving home had a dream-like quality for me, and although I was genuinely sorry that we were to be taken from our Grandparents and Auntie Ida, the anticipation of being on our own, free (in an odd sense), and independent, was such heady stuff, making it most difficult to put on a sad face whenever Grandma brought up the subject of the imminent danger in which she was certain we four children were; and I sheepishly felt like Brer Rabbit crying out, "Don't throw me into the briar patch!" Children of that age invariably yearn to be free from parental control, and many fantasize about running away from home. I did not have to do that. It was going to happen through the exigencies of war, and it was not that we wished to be rid of any iron rule of our Grandparents in order to "turn wild" (or, "wilder", some might say), but simply to be on our own. As it developed, not surprisingly to me, we were a highly disciplined little group, and our esprit de corps served us well during the months we lived as prisoners of war.

Grandma's demeanor became much gentler and she ceased to shout and rail at us. The atmosphere around our apartment was reminiscent of that which prevails during the time of a fatal illness in some families, but we did not take advantage of the new order of our remaining days and behaved as well as we possibly could. Both Grandpa and Grandma would look at us sadly, shaking their heads and sighing, and our impending departure seemed to draw them closer to one another, sharing the loss of the noisy brood they had taken under their wing for so many years. Grandma would say: "I'm so terribly worried about you, Mary darling. You will watch over them, won't you? And pray all the time? And write me as often as you can?"

"Don't worry, Grandma. We'll be okay. We'll take care of one another, and I'll go to Mass every morning if they have church in camp, and I'll write whenever they allow me."

She'd cry and hold me close in her arms, and sigh: "I didn't think it would come to this. It's all been so strange, but I never dreamed that the end would be like this."

For me, it was no end...only a beginning, and I felt a twinge of disloyalty in looking forward to going to camp with such inexplicable eagerness and anticipation.

That last month at home in the apartment in the I.S.S. Building seemed to pass so slowly. Vincent and Jordie played raucous games with their friends on the roof garden, and watched Chinese lads playing shuttle-cock with their feet. The boys learned how to spin big humming tops and got into mischief of lesser gravity than before. I spent more time with Grandma shuffling through her old steamer trunks and listening to the familiar stories of our past. I came across a set of photographs of Smith which I had not seen before, taken at the Yu Yuen Road house. The pictures showed him with a full beard, in a series of frightening facial expressions which made him look positively diabolical, if not raving mad. I asked what the horrible photos meant, and Grandma tried to cover them up, saying,

"Your poor Papa was not himself in those days and we had a lot of trouble with him for a long time. He grew that beard and had pictures taken of it, and made those ugly faces for a joke, I suppose. I didn't want you to see these, and maybe I ought to throw them away."

I wish I hadn't seen them either, for that is the face I now remember whenever I think of him. Grandma must have discarded them as I did not find them among her things, later on.

Our Family of Seven before we went to Chapei 1942

Above: The Four Of Us

Left: Grandpa and Grandma

Right: Ida, Grandpa and Grandma

豫防注射接種濟證明書

氏名 M.L.G.スミス

性別 女　年齢 十四

右者「コレラ」「チフス」ニ對スル豫防注射並ニ接種ヲ完了セルコトヲ證明ス

昭和十八年九月十六日

在上海日本帝國總領事館

CERTIFICATE

This is to certify that

Miss M.L.G.Smith

Sex F Age 14

has been duly inoculated against chorela and typhus and vaccinated against small-pox.

H.I.J.M. CONSULATE-GENERAL
SHANGHAI.

September 14th 1943.

Below: Red Cross receipt for One food package 1943

C Form 1629A
Sept. 1943

AMERICAN RED CROSS

RECEIPT FOR PRISONER OF WAR PACKAGE

SMITH MARY LOUISE
(Last Name) (First and Middle Names) (Rank)

1007 CHAPEL CIVIL ASSEMBLY CENTRE AMERI
(Number) (Prison Camp) (Country)

I have received today one food package from THE AMERICAN NATIONAL RED CROSS through the International Red Cross Committee.

(Signed) Mary Smith

Nationality AMERICAN Date SEPT. 2, 1943

Below: Our passport photos taken before we were sent to prison camp. Mary 14, Vincent 12, Jordie 10, and Anne 8 years old.

Chapter 19

I made careful disposition of my most precious possessions, giving my favorite, Rae Doll, to Nee-Doo Amah, and a beloved stuffed Koala bear to Nina Pagani to remember me by, and suddenly, gripped by the fear that I would never see my Grandma or Grandpa or Auntie Ida again, I took special care to notice every little thing about them, burning the details into my memory of the smallest gesture, the faintest smile, the lightest inflection of their voices. I began to treasure every movement I could watch them make; the way Grandpa held his chopsticks and that familiar stance of his when he wound his old pendulum clock. (I have that clock now and wind it thinking of that sweet old man.) And, too, the way Grandma stirred her tea and the habit she had of putting her hand to her forehead as she lay in bed. The little dents Auntie Ida made in the material of her clothing between her thumb and middle finger, snapping the cloth out with her forefinger, making a small popping sound which intrigued me. It was an unconscious action on her part, and she would do this as she listened closely to whatever was being said, and I knew that if she were doing that as I spoke, my Aunt was truly listening. She did not drift away whenever I talked to her as Grandma often did, and as Louise had done frequently when she had been with us. Auntie Ida paid strict attention, fixing her bright brown eyes on mine, and I felt that whatever I said to her was accepted as valid and given its measure of importance. She had the gift of making the most insignificant person feel recognized, worthwhile and appreciated, and I am so grateful for the time I spent circling in her beneficent orbit.

Georgina was fifty-seven years old that year. She had become somewhat stout, but her legs were still shapely, and her hair was as black and glossy as it had ever been. Grandma's skin was smooth and unwrinkled and her hands were soft and flecked with brown spots. The outer corners of her brown eyes turned down slightly, and she smiled in a manner so as to conceal her faintly protruding teeth which were even, white and sound. She wore her long hair in a bun at the nape of her lovely neck, and I watched her braid it every day, weaving the three strands quickly with little flicks of the ends, holding it all together with large tortoise shell pins. She had discovered a style of dress which suited her because it hid her thickening torso, and she had ordered many dresses cut in this identical pattern, wearing no other kind for as long as I can remember. The costume consisted of a long-sleeved jacket, buttoned down the front to the waist at which point a short flounce flared out, coming past the upper part of her hips. This was worn over a matching skirt which had a slight flare, coming well below her knees, and she had sets of this outfit in at least two dozen kinds of fabric from poplin to silk jersey to bombazine. Grandma rarely left the house without putting on her hat, and she had a wide selection of headgear, favoring flowers and short veils.

My Grandmother was a very expressive woman, and when she talked she made wide sweeping gestures and employed her graceful hands constantly, using them to illustrate the many points she would be making to her listeners. But it was more than just the use of her hands one noticed; as she spoke she used her shoulders and elbows to denote disdain or surprise; she thrust her chin forward, or drew her neck back, stiffening her spine in relating some story showing chagrin or disgust. She'd whip her head around and say: "What was that? It gave me such a fright!"

If a car backfired in the street, she'd put her hands up to her chest with the palms facing outward and the fingers curling forward. Her "body English" might have been copied from the silent movies, when all they had were faces and gestures. Without giving Shakespeare credit for the line, Grandma often said that the world was a stage and the people on it only players. Her "play" ran for eighty-three years and she made a grand entrance every day of the run.

Grandpa did not change toward us during the days we waited to be sent to the camp. He always treated us with respect and affection, and continued to do so until the last day I saw him. Even though I had grown up considerably since the days I had sat in his lap every evening, so it began again to become a need in the both of us, and I would squeeze myself into his chair with him and, burying my face in his neck, I'd breathe in his essence so as never to forget that crisp, clean smell of his tobacco and ironed linen. Vincent Vizenzinovich had reached the age of seventy-seven by that time, but still could not be described as an "old man." He stood erect, carrying himself gracefully, his bearing almost military, his clothes neatly pressed and his shoes worn but shined and polished. The economy of his movements was not due to any infirmity but to the fact that he was a rather formal gentleman, not given to expansive behavior and florid language. His hair was completely white then, and he had as much of it as he'd ever had. His habits remained unchanged, and he was living testimony that a temperate, moderate life was indeed the best. In all of his adult years I think he maintained the same weight, but may have become thinner during those last troubled days. He was about five feet eight inches in height, and must have weighed about one hundred and sixty pounds. He moved deliberately and did not flap around or hurry in an unbecoming fashion. His life was as long as Grandma's was, and at eighty-four, he died as neatly as he had lived, quietly, in his sleep, in 1950.

We were in the middle of our school year in January 1943 and I worried about the loss of time in my studies, wondering when and how I would ever make it up some day. I went to the convent for the last day late in February, and Mother Lewis took me aside for a private talk and a final, tearful goodbye. I refused to believe that we might not see each other again, she and I, saying that the war would be over soon and I would return to school and catch up on my work. Mother Lewis revealed a side of herself I had not seen before; she, who was always so proper and correct, held my hands in hers, tears shining in her eyes and her voice quavering, said,

"You will be in my mind and heart every moment until I hear that you are safe again. Be brave, my beloved."

I cried going home on the tram, standing on the outer platform so no one would notice the tears I couldn't prevent.

The week before we left for prison camp, I went through the rooms of our apartment like one in a trance, touching every piece of furniture, running my hands over the religious statues atop the piano and on every table as though I were blind. I traced that pattern in the flowery cretonne slip-covers with my finger, and opened Grandpa's bureau drawers burying my face in his fragrant linen. I stood in the closet and filled my arms with Ida's clothes as they hung on their padded hangers, reveling in her special scent which broke my heart when I thought that I would smell it no more. The forks and knives we used every day, the plates with fruit painted on them, the designs in the tablecloth, the clocks and lamps- all were subjects for the camera my eyes became, and the memory of that last home of mine in Shanghai can still reassemble itself, allowing me to return in an instant to that far-off time that never seems so distant to Vincent, Jordie, Annie and me.

Vincent and I went into the street and hailed a rickshaw asking him to take us for a slow ride just around the block. It's the last time, we told each other, and confided in the rickshaw man that tomorrow we were going to a Japanese prison camp. He clucked his tongue and said, "Maskee, maskee," which meant "Never mind," in Pidgin English, and trundled us off down the road, shaking his head sadly.

That night, I crept into my Grandpa's bed and stayed until morning. We held each other and wept silently while he patted me and kissed my forehead.

"You be a brave girl, my little Mary," he said, "and know that I shall be praying for you every moment so that no harm comes to you and the other children. God will give you strength and watch over you. I know."

There have been many goodbyes said in my lifetime, and only one was more difficult than this farewell. Yet, we took our leave of one another without regret, which changes everything, going away with hearts filled with love and hope that someday we would see each other again. They had done their very best for The Four of Us, and no one has the right to expect more in life.

Chapter 20

Shanghai can be bitterly cold, and the morning of February 25, 1943 began with a frosty mist that made a somber day even gloomier. We gathered at the Columbia Country Club with our baggage and beds, looking with interest at the crowd of strangers with whom we would soon be sharing our lives. Grandma had packed us a hamper of goodies to tide us over until we got settled in the camp, and in a wicker suitcase which we guarded carefully there were tins of devilled ham, soda crackers, hard boiled eggs, cheese and salami, a jar of strawberry jam and several tins of English tea biscuits. It took several hours of waiting while everyone was processed, and our belongings were tagged and put on Lorries which went ahead of the group destined for camp.

Grandma, Grandpa and Auntie Ida hugged and kissed us for the last time as we boarded a bus for the Chapei Civilian Assembly Center. We waved from the windows until they were out of sight, and that feeling of exhilaration and excitement swept over me once again. We were on our own.

About five hundred Americans and Britishers made up the first wave of prisoners to be interned at Chapei, and among them were Carl Mydans, a photographer for Life Magazine, and his attractive wife, Shelley Smith, who was a writer. I had noticed a handsome couple during the processing at the Country Club, learning later that their names were Billy and Cheetah Carroll. She was a stunning Anglo-Indian beauty who wore a leopard skin coat, and they were a dance team who had entertained in most of the large cities of the Orient. Another couple, also performers, was Jimmy and Topsy Brown, who were the only Black Americans in camp with us. Jimmy played the trumpet just like Louis Armstrong, and Topsy was a dancer who did a wicked imitation of Shirley Temple in a polka dot dress and a curly blond wig. These show people eventually offered two productions to the inmates of Chapei which were the most entertaining stage events I have ever seen, all the more fun because they managed to draw a variety of people into the skits in the camp who turned out to be enormously amusing, even though they had never had any theatrical experience.

Upon our arrival, we were handed the following instructions, which I have from Sheila Hutton's collection of wartime memorabilia, and it is reprinted here exactly as given.

Regulations of the Civil Assembly Centre.

ARTICLE I. The provisions prescribed hereunder shall be Observed by those ordered to live in the Civil Assembly Centres.

Clause 1.

The Civil Assembly Centre being the best Home for those who live in it, must be loved and Cherished by all of them. All persons shall take care of their health and live in harmony with one another. There shall be no disputing, quarreling, disturbing or any other improper demeanors.

Clause 2.

In the daily routine enforced by the Civil Assembly Authorities, the turn-out, the roll-calls and the lights-Out shall especially be observed with precision.

Clause 3.

Food and other allowances being fixed by the Government, no alteration in them shall be allowed. Complaints or manifestations of discontent against the food provided or against its quantity, or any complaint against living conditions or equipments of the Civil Assembly Centre shall not be made.

Clause 4.

The orders given by the Japanese officials and police guards shall be strictly obeyed and there shall be no act of defiance.

Clause 5.
No going out of the Civil Assembly Centre is allowed except with permission granted by the Commandant of the Civil Assembly Centre. Such permission may be given only in the case of illness or in case of other unavoidable circumstances.

Clause 6.
For the time being, one letter a month, subject to censor by the Japanese officials, will be permitted to each person. Such letters must be typed or written in clear and legible handwriting; letters hard to read shall not be accepted.

Clause 7.
Those living in the Civil Assembly Centre shall be divided into a number of sections each composing of about twenty members which shall have its own chief responsible for the section members therein.

Clause 8.
The sections shall be formed into groups each of which shall have its own Captain. Orders and notifications by the Commandant or officials in charge of the Civil Assembly Centre shall be given to the Captains and they shall be transmitted through Captains to the Chiefs of Sections who in turn shall convey them to their respective members. The Captains and the Chiefs of Sections shall act as intermediaries in communicating the wishes of their members to the officials in charge.

Clause 9.
In order to facilitate self-administration in the Centre, there shall be divisions in charge of general affairs, accounts, food supplying, health, equipments, education and discipline. The personnel of these divisions shall be selected by those living in the Civil Assembly Centre.

Clause 10.
The instructions of the Captains, Chiefs of Sections and Divisions shall be obeyed and no act of defiance or complaint shall be made of them.

Clause 11.
As all members of each section shall be held responsible and punished for run-away of its member, caution should be taken by each of them to prevent such an occurrence.

Clause 12. No argument shall be made nor any rumor shall be circulated concerning the world situation nor any criticism against Japan shall be allowed.

Clause 13.
A fire would result in the greatest misery for all who live in the Centre; caution must strictly be taken by all members for its prevention. The Chief of Section before going to bed shall go on the round of each chamber and inspect ash-trays and others which might be the cause of a fire.

Clause 14.
Cooking and dish-washing, cleaning of the lavatory, bath, dining room, kitchen, playground, and others shall be done by those living in the Centre by turn. Each person shall serve his or her own meal.

Clause 15. The room shall be cleaned and put to order, bed made, and laundries done by each person.

Clause 16. In case when the dining room cannot accommodate all the members, a meal may be served in three or four turns. In such case each person shall take his or her meal in less than twenty-minutes.

Clause 17.
The lights-out of each chamber shall be done under the supervision of the Chiefs of Sections.

Article II. Violation of the above shall be dealt with disciplinary measures of short allowances, detention, etc., and in certain cases with severe punishments.

Article III. These regulations shall be enforced from the day of assembly at the Centre.

Article IV. When necessary, orders other than stipulated above will be given by the Commandant.

The Chapei camp had previously been a school, situated a few miles from the City of Shanghai, and I remember hearing that Grandpa used to go on shooting expeditions in Chapei in the 'olden days' which at one time had thousands of game birds in the area. There are snapshots of Grandpa and his hunting cronies, all carrying guns and wearing topees, at a pheasant shoot, taken not far from where we were imprisoned.

There were two main structures, the East Building and the West Building, and we were assigned to a room in the former. It was empty when we arrived, a long, narrow room with a door at either end and shelves across three walls. The fourth wall had four windows which looked over the double rolls of barbed wire which surrounded the entire compound, with a 'no-man's land' between, and a wide country road beyond where we often saw trucks and an occasional bicycle, with the usual number of Chinese wheelbarrows every day. There were open fields all around the north end of the camp, and a creek ran by the south end.

Being the first ones in the dormitory-like room, we took the corner which afforded us an entire window and a shelf to ourselves. The space allotted us was approximately eight feet wide and ten feet long, leaving space at the narrow end for a common pathway which our other camp-mates would use, and when the room was finally filled we numbered seventeen in all, two families of four persons and three families of three. We measured off the space allowed us and unfolded the boys' camp cots under the shelf so that Vincent's head pointed toward the window and Jordie's head lay directly in a line with Vin's feet. We piled our suitcases one atop the other, making a sort of table surface under the window, and set up the good bed Grandma had insisted we take for Annie and me to sleep in together. Vincent found a couple of nails and some twine and we immediately strung up a partition which we made from one of our sheets, giving ourselves a bit of privacy from whoever came to be our neighbors. There seems to be an innate desire in most living being to mark off their territory in any way possible to them, and our sheet-partition made it clear where our line was drawn.

As the weeks went on, we felt like the Three Bears (plus One) in their cottage in the woods. I made a pair of curtains for our window, and Vincent scrounged some wood from which I fashioned a crude and rickety table, which became our most prized possession, to replace the trunk-table we'd been using. Grandma had given each of us a small folding canvas stool and these served as chairs. We tacked pictures on the wall over our beds and kept our luggage underneath the boys' cots. The wood floors were cold and somewhere I found a piece of carpet which we placed in the center of our cubbyhole and would stand on this ragged object to get dressed on freezing mornings. I usually rose first and made the other three keep their heads turned away because it was the only real privacy I could get as I dressed myself.

Privacy was practically non-existent in camp. There were no curtains to the showers in the cement bath house, and no way to secure the flimsy doors in the toilets. I think there were two bathrooms on the floor of our building, each having three wash basins and three water closets, and most of the time one had to wait in line to use the facilities, unless, of course, one had dysentery, which was quite common, in which case everyone made room quickly.

I remember the first time I took Annie to the communal shower, holding our soap in a dish, our towels around our necks, and clattering in wearing our clumsy Chinese clogs. No one had told me that I would walk into a roomful of naked women, shouting and splashing, and never having seen such a sight before, I was quite taken aback and immediately walked outside again, wondering how I was going to avail myself of the hot water (which was only turned on during certain hours of the day), without anyone being able to see me. I had never in my life stood naked in a crowd of people, not even members of my own sex, and it had been some long time since even Nee-Doo Amah had seen me without my clothes. I thought of the first time I had locked her out of the bathroom in the I.S.S. Building, much to her vociferous annoyance, when I discovered that my body was taking on a new and different shape, two years before, and smiled at the irony of it all.

At the time I entered the camp, I had grown to five feet, two inches, and did not grow any taller; my weight was approximately one hundred and ten pounds which, by the time I left, seven months later, had dropped to eighty-seven pounds. Anyone wishing to lose weight should become afflicted with amoebic dysentery as that will do the trick in short order. I soon realized that no one was in the least way interested in what I looked like without my clothes on, but eased myself into this new and alarming situation by having Annie stand in front of me while we showered together, wearing our rubber bathing caps, and she kept her eyes averted all those months, knowing that I never really got over being shy. I found it grimly humorous that at eight I had been forced to wear a mu-mu in the bath in Manila, and here at fourteen I had to stand before God and everybody without a stitch on.

Our immediate neighbors in the room we occupied were a Welsh family named Jones. They were a scrappy, friendly lot and their two small sons were surprisingly pleasant. They had arranged their beds so that Mr. Jones slept next to Annie and me on the other side of the thin curtain which divided our section of the room from theirs. Annie slept on the inside of our bed so that she wouldn't fall out onto the floor as she sometimes did, but Mr. Jones woke everyone up several times during the night cursing my sister and complaining that she was kicking him through the curtain. Trying to keep the peace, I switched with Annie and apologized to Mr. Jones for the discomfort she had caused him. I cannot be sure, but during the next night I thought I felt a hand groping around on the other side of the cloth partition and came to the decision that Mr. Jones would have to become accustomed to being kicked to sleep. I think the upshot of it was that Mrs. Jones changed beds with her husband without further ado, and I moved back to the inside of our bed, leaving Annie to kick the air in peace and to fall out if she would.

Every morning we lined up in the corridors for roll call and the Japanese guards would march through the buildings listening to us count off our numbers and marking the results in their Doomsday Book. One time, Vincent, who had been very ill, could not get up and the guard went into the room to have a look at the "missing person." He felt Vinnie's head and behaved in a most solicitous manner, telling me to take good care of the boy and to have him to the infirmary as soon as the count had been taken. Another time, when Annie stayed in bed with a cold, the guard came in and poked his sword into her blanket, raising it slightly so he could see her properly. It gave me a bit of a turn, and I wished he had used his hand to draw the covers back, but he meant no harm, smiled in a friendly way and strode out.

I did our laundry in the large troughs by the bath house and hung out the wash with the other women several times a week. It was a good experience, and I know how it must have felt in primitive times when women got together at a river and scrubbed and chatted. We were ordered to remove the clotheslines each evening because there'd been complaints from the guards who patrolled the grounds at night about their getting tangled in the ropes strung across the area, and I think it robbed a few of us the small pleasure it gave to see the guards stumbling about in the dark when they'd walked into the lines unawares.

The Japanese guards had other complaints about their prisoners and we were cautioned against lying about in the tall grass at the south end of the camp where the soldiers of the Imperial Army had, to their horror and disgust, found several couples making love in absolute abandon. The offenders simply converted their outdoor sport to an indoor sport, ingeniously finding all sorts of cozy spots to pursue this particular activity, and we would discover the less fastidious among us blithely copulating on the stair, one inventive twosome managing to accomplish their purpose in the Tuppenny Upright position standing against a corridor wall, all of which goes to prove that love will find a way.

Once a month, we were allowed to receive a parcel from home, and after inspection of the packages by the Japanese commandant's office, at which time the sentries would help themselves first to whatever they fancied in the boxes that arrived, we would dig through the edible treasures from Auntie Ida and Grandma, rationing the candy and other treats they'd sent. In each parcel there was always a box of sanitary napkins for me, but something happened to my system during those months in prison camp and I had no need of them. It disturbed me, but I learned that oftentimes during war and other stressful occasions women were thrown off their natural cycles; so I ceased to worry about my temporary dislocation from the moon and the tides, and saved each allotment until I had a huge collection of the gauze and paper items carefully stashed in a trunk. I don't know why I saved them, except that nothing was ever to be thrown away, and they did come in handy when Vincent or Jordie needed a bandage for a skinned knee.

The food at Chapei was dreary, as one might expect, and not always edible. Our kitchen crews worked hard to make the meals as wholesome as possible, but there is not much the most imaginative cook can do with cabbage and rice, cracked wheat and tea. Bread was baked in the camp ovens, but it was dark, coarse and soggy, and rumor had it that the flour had been missed with sawdust, along with a generous helping of saltpeter which was supposed to depress the libidinous tendencies of the more sexually aggressive folk among us. However, judging from the number of pregnant women we were to see in the months ahead, both married and single, this treatment did not produce the desired effect.

Each prisoner received one egg per month, and we could stand in line and wait for the cooks to scramble them for us, or, as many did, prepare the egg privately on a makeshift stove behind the building, the Japanese Army's Clause 13 notwithstanding. Vincent built a small stove from a tin can which he packed around with mud, and he would squat, Chinese peasant style, in front of this primitive device, fanning his tiny flame until a good fire took hold, and he'd proudly cook our eggs on that. Actually, he usually used only three eggs (or less); in this fashion because Annie insisted on having hers cracked on her teeth over her open mouth, swallowing the raw egg in one happy gulp. It made us rather sick to watch her enjoying it that way, especially since one of the four eggs we received would invariably be rotten; but she had great faith that the bad egg would not fall to her. When the eggs arrived, we would spend considerable time switching them around before we decided whose egg was whose, and no matter how many times we traded them, my sister never once had a rotten egg slip down her gullet.

There was a small commissary where we could buy certain items if we had money, and peanut butter was a great favorite. It had a strange consistency, but it looked all right and tasted passably well, but when the jar had been emptied, I washed it and noticed that the brown color rinsed away, leaving a greyish paste clinging to the inside of the glass. We discovered that the peanut butter had been mixed with flour to stretch its bulk, and it was years before I could eat that brown spread again without becoming slightly ill.

Vincent read his first full-length book in camp. It was an adventure story about one Captain Slocum and he pored over it for days on end, surprising me with the unfamiliar sight of my brother totally absorbed in a book. I would have to tear him away from the exciting tale and force him to get in the "chow line" at mealtime. The kitchen crew posted the daily menu on a bulletin board, and one day it read, "Spare ribs." Not having seen meat in some time, we were elated, and I sent Vincent and Jordie down with our plates while Annie and I set the table. At first, we had all eaten in the mess hall, but as the camp filled up the room was assigned as sleeping quarters and prisoners then took their meals in their own rooms.

The boys came back with the dishes laden with an indefinable mélange of rice, cabbage and bits of meat and we sat down to dinner. Vincent hit something hard with his knife while cutting through the food on his plate, and pushing aside the watery rice and overcooked cabbage he came upon a piece of bone with three teeth protruding from it. He screamed and flung the bit of broken jaw with its pointed teeth out of the window, while the rest of us hurriedly ran off to the garbage cans and tossed the lot away. We made another dinner from our tiny stores, opening a precious tin of potted meat and a packet of soda crackers. For dessert, I cut one candy bar into four equal pieces, and we tried not to think about what sort of animal it was that we had almost eaten that evening.

Jordie came, with his innocent face, and asked me if he could use our can opener for a toy pistol as he wanted to get into a game of Bobbies and Thieves with some other boys and didn't have a gun. Unwittingly, I let him take it, and for days after that I noticed that his appetite had fallen off, although he seemed none the worse for the small amount of food he was ingesting. I inquired about his state of health, wondering how a sick boy could look so rosy and hale, but Jordie said he just didn't feel very well and couldn't eat. Soon after, an irate and corpulent English lady stormed into our room to tell me that my brother had pried open her cache of tinned fruit and meats and was helping himself, thank you very much. I was shocked and promised her that the wicked boy would be severely punished for his appalling thievery. Jordie confessed all, employing his super-tearful act, when confronted with the accusation, and the whipping he received from Vincent (who was carrying out my stern orders), was all the more vigorous for his not having shared the find with us, I am sure.

The Red Cross managed to get a few deliveries in to our camp, and the one I remember the best is the shipment of Sun Maid Raisins we were given one day. The Sun Bonnet Girl had come to the rescue again, just as she had on Vinnie's fourth birthday in Kowloon, but the boxes must have been held up at the dock for many weeks because the sweet, dark, sticky raisins were alive with worms. However, we poured boiling water over the dried fruit, skimmed off whatever rose to the top and finished off the contribution anyway.

Somehow, we found out through a friend who had returned to camp from a trip to the hospital in Shanghai that our Auntie Ida was planning to ride her bicycle past our compound on a given date. We knew that we would be in great danger if we waved at her or tried to yell across the barbed wire, but we wanted to see her so desperately and also needed her to see that we were alive and well. All day we waited outside our building where we had a long view of anyone riding by on the road which skirted the camp, and sometime that afternoon Ida pedaled slowly down the wide country lane. A Japanese guard patrolled constantly in the no-man's land area which ran between the double rolls of barbed wire, and we would have been imperiled, as well as placing Auntie Ida in jeopardy, had he seen us making any sign to her. So, we stood as near as we could to the barricade and talked very loudly to each other, yelling things we wanted our aunt to hear, but acting as though we were just shouting at one another. I told the younger children to jump around and skip, and to do somersaults, which they did, while I stood sideways as though I were not really looking in my aunt's direction, and I tried to think of things to say which would give her an idea that all went well with us. She came close enough so that we were able to look into each other's eyes, and it was terribly difficult not to cry and wave to her. It was wonderful to see her dear face, and I was overcome with an inexorable homesickness and a longing to see Grandma and Grandpa. As she passed, we clenched our fists and stuck our thumbs up, turning our backs as we did this, hoping no guard would catch on to what we were doing, and I know Ida got the message and a close look at The Four of Us besides. She had been very brave to ride all the way to Chapei and I could almost see Grandma laughing to hear Ida tell her how Annie and Jordie were still behaving like little monkeys, jumping and somersaulting around behind the barbed wire, like chimpanzees at the zoo; and Grandma did laugh through her tears.

Vincent fell in love with a twenty-year old, but as he was only twelve she hardly knew he was alive. She was a beautiful young woman, whose name I can't remember, and my brother mooned around the room, and lurked in the hallways hoping for a glance from her smouldering eyes. In the evenings we were allowed to walk in a large circle around the compound in front of the West Building and he would walk round and round, hoping to brush against his lady love and have her smile upon him. Most of us took advantage of these evening constitutionals, but since the area was so spread out there was lots of room for everyone, and ample time for private conversation.

Some of Grandma's relatives were also in camp with us, and I would stroll with one or more of these distant cousins, listening to their funny stories and enjoying the recognition they gave me. The oldest daughter of one of these families, my cousin Mamie Bell, was particularly kind to me and was sympathetic about teaching name to braid my own hair, which was fairly long and something of a nuisance to me since I had never learned to take care of it properly, the amah having done it up each day while I was still at home.

Two Franciscan priests were interned with us and said Mass every morning in a shed at a roughly constructed altar. The younger one was a tall, incredibly handsome Irishman with curly iron-grey hair. His name was Leon Sullivan and he came from Ann Arbor, Michigan, and I, even more hopelessly than Vincent, fell in love with this man of God, swooning to catch a glimpse of him striding gracefully across the grounds in his brown religious habit with its cowl and his knotted rope tied about his waist. He came to notice me because I attended the six o'clock Mass every morning which found me in good health, and often in the balmy spring evening Father Sullivan would gather a small group of us for a walk in that charmed circle. At first, I walked behind him with another girl, but gradually became friendlier so that sometimes I actually walked by his side and could look right up into his marvelous face as we strolled, listening to him tell us of the days when he ministered to a band of Chinese guerrillas he found fighting the Japanese in the mountains to the north.

When the gentle spring days melted into the scorching summer and black clouds of mosquitoes filled the camp making it miserable to sleep indoors, we often sat on the front steps of the West Building and fanned ourselves, slapping at the noisome insects and listening to that beautiful man speak of his home and mother in America. In private, I would indulge in a well-worn fantasy that Father Sullivan was only masquerading as a priest for his own protection, and that he was neither consecrated to the Lord nor pledged to any woman, and that after the war, when I grew up, we would find one another and I would be his forever. I think he knew that I loved him with all my fierce little heart, and although he never said one word to purposely fan the flames of the violent crush I had on him, nor was he in any way demonstrative toward me, that man's dark brown, deep-set eyes looking into mine drove me to a fine madness, filling my head with romantic notions of love which could never be requited. When we left Chapei as exchange prisoners, Father Sullivan was among those who stayed on in camp until the end of the war, and when I said my heart-broken goodbyes to him, I feared it would be forever, and it has been that.

It did not take me long in life to learn that almost no relationship is everlasting, and that we attach ourselves to people we love, only to have them die, or leave us, or be lost to us in a thousand ways; and yet, we never seem to despair, and allow our love to happen over and over, showing all of its many faces, renewing our faith in still another stranger, investing our time and selves, trusting once more to the unknown, and giving our hearts here to a child, there to a friend, now to a lover, and then to a husband in a sphere that contracts and expands with the years; and for all its pain I would neither be nor have it otherwise.

Sitting on the steps of the West Building one evening before we left the camp, I told Father Sullivan something of my phobias, and asked him how I could overcome them and simplify my life. He said perhaps I could think of all the things I disliked so intensely as being in one room in the same time frame, and that this reconstruction might cause me to remember an incident in the past which had been shut out on purpose. (I did not know the word "repression" then,which might have given rise to the phobic behavior of which I was so keenly aware and distressed.) It was not until many years later that I was finally able to do this; looking back, looking inward, I remembered what Leon Sullivan had said, and it was like gazing deep into a fathomless well, seeing there the reflection of a bright, full moon come sailing across a cloudless sky.

There is no palpable answer to the question, "What three days?", but I am content to leave it be and to wonder no more, because the hour grows late and, as it is, almost everything "turned out all right" in the end.

Chapter 21

The months in the camp came and went, and there were constant rumors of an exchange of prisoners in the offing. The garbage piled up and suddenly there was a mountain of discarded tin cans heaped in a corner of the compound. The boys used to play in the dump with other kids, climbing the great mound as though it were Everest itself. They'd sit on the top and look out into the neighboring fields, watching Chinese peasant children afar flying their brightly colored paper kites and remembering how they used to do the same when they lived at home in Shanghai during the windy season.

In passing, I would like to note that for all the dreary conditions of prison camp life, I never once saw a rat in the camp. Actually, I can't remember seeing a rat at any time while I lived in the Orient, although we heard about them a great deal. I used to ask the amah if it were true that Chinese people ate rats as the foreigners said they did, and she would scoff and laughingly deny it. She told me that the only time she herself ever saw a rat was when someone in her village caught one and nailed it to a board while it was still alive. She went on to say that in times of famine hungry people will eat anything, including rats, and in dire necessity she knew of peasants who ate their own babies. In light of that, the Chapei Civilian Assembly Centre was not such a bad place to be, after all.

Our volunteer camp patrol went on their rounds ahead of the Japanese guards in the morning, and they would greet the booted sentries as they passed each other with great ceremony. Our raffish fellows would stop and bow courteously, giving what the guard took to be the proper Japanese salutation which was "Ashi-mas", when what they were actually saying was, "Kiss my ass" and the sentry would smile and bow in return. We laughed about that and hoped that the patrol would not meet a guard who understood English and might be moved to decapitate us on the spot.

There was a young Japanese guard who spoke English in a halting fashion, and he befriended Jordie, letting my younger brother play with his sword. Once, he said to Jordie:

"Maybe you will leave here soon and go to America and come back to shoot me when you are bigger."

"Maybe I will," Jordie said, and the guard laughed.

I knew Jordie could ingratiate himself with King Kong if the occasion ever arose, but I was alarmed when I discovered that he had become a sort of mascot at the sentries' guard house, and one evening he didn't show up at dinner time which worried me greatly. I sent Vincent around to look for him, but Jordie was nowhere to be found. Finally, just before the night roll-call which our section chief took at bedtime, here came Jordie, strolling nonchalantly towards the East Building with a look of smug satisfaction on his face. The little bugger was picking his teeth! He'd been to dinner in the guard house where the sentries had stuffed him with hot white rice, crispy tempura and delicious sukiyaki, all of which was tantalizingly evident to us every time he belched, and we looked upon him in awe for managing to live so sumptuously under the present conditions.

Jordie's guard friend told the kids he was going on a short leave to the City and asked if there was anything they'd like him to bring back for them. Vincent asked him to bring them some balloons, and when he returned he seemed quite upset at having to disappoint his little friends, saying that he had searched all of Shanghai and could not find one balloon anywhere.

"Rubber is scarce, and there is a war on, you know," he said.

At Mass, one early morning, I saw a Chinese loitering around the shed. He was a great surprise to us and no one could understand how he had found his way into our camp which was so closely guarded. When the Japanese discovered the man, who looked and acted in a decidedly demented manner, they dragged him over every inch of the stockade trying to find out where it was that he had come in. They thought that if it were simple enough for this man to get into the compound, it would be just as easy for any of us to get out; but the man, being confused and distressed, could make no sense of their questioning and babbled continuously. I had been one of the first to see him, and when I saw him again the next day, his features had become indistinguishable from the beating he had sustained; his eyes had all but disappeared and the blood which had flowed from his head had dried as it ran down his cheeks and neck. The sight of him scrabbling on the ground horrified me, and a strange quiet fell over the camp while he was being interrogated by the Japanese captain of the guards. That next night, we heard his screams from the guard house, and the patrol told our camp chairman that they had smelled burning flesh when they'd gone past the building where the sentries were stationed. We never saw the man again, and no one, to my knowledge, ever tried to escape from Chapei.

A man named Mr. Ball attempted to slip a letter to a passing Chinese peasant on the creek side of the compound, hoping to have it delivered to someone in Shanghai; but he was discovered and put under arrest. Everyone in camp was worried about what would happen, and after several anxious hours the sirens went off, alerting us to gather in front of the West Building. We assembled, fifteen hundred of us, men, women and children, and stood silently in the hot sun waiting to hear what the punishment would be. The commandant mounted a box and read the charges against Ball who stood at attention by his side, and many of us were sure that our letter-smuggler was to be shot in front of our eyes.

The ending to all the excitement was anti-climactic, to say the least, because the disciplinary measures taken were that Mr. Ball was to be confined to his room for one month, and the hot water was to be turned off for one day. The crowd let out a whooping roar and Mr. Ball was carried into the West Building on the shoulders of his mates, and for thirty days there was a continuous party held in the dormitory Mr. Ball occupied. No one really minded the lack of hot water for the one twenty-four period as it only meant a respite from doing the laundry for some of us, and we could still boil water for tea.

Toward the end of our confinement even we ran out of toothpaste, having used the Little Flower Tooth Powder for so many other purposes, including trading it for various and sundry foodstuffs. Someone convinced us that a mixture of cigar ashes and salt made an excellent cleaning agent for the teeth, and, since there did not seem to be a shortage of cigars, a few of us would sit patiently with anyone smoking the evil smelling things and collect their ashes in a small tin which we would then mix with salt and use quite effectively.

No one died of starvation in the camp, but some of the children could often be seen standing by the steps of the buildings licking the stones in the construction. None of the four of us had a need to do that, but others had found this practice filled a lack in their systems, and it continued all the while we were in that place.

An inventive chap made me a laundry plunger from a stick with a tin can nailed to one end. He had punched holes in the can and said that if I soaked my wash for a bit, and then pounded it in the soapy water with this device it would save me from having to scrub it as I usually did, giving me a cleaner end-product in the bargain. I used my home-made washing machine for several months and although it was a mite hard on the fabrics, it lightened the load considerably and was not so damaging to my hands.

Dysentery was ever present in our camp and I learned my way around the infirmary very quickly. Frequently, I would become so dehydrated that the camp doctor kept me there overnight under observation. The medical staff was made up of other prisoners and it was a very efficient and knowledgeable group. I came to know a young woman from Tasmania who had served with her husband as a missionary for the China Inland Missions when the war caught up with them, and she spent the whole time in a bed in the camp hospital, dying of beri-beri. I can't recall her name, but she was the most cheerful and courageous person I met in camp and we would lie awake at night and speak of home, she telling me of that green and lovely land so far away that she was never to see again. I couldn't believe it when she died and took it very hard when she was moved to a clinic in the City and never returned.

The nights when I stayed in the hospital room in camp did not cause me much worry over my brothers and Annie because the infirmary was just down the hall from our own room, and I could even hear their voices, which was a great comfort to me. They behaved themselves rather well, all things considered, and I found that the worst punishment I could mete out to them was to ignore them completely, (the worst punishment is not to be punished at all, I think), in an icy silence, my wordless disapproval being far more effective than a good clout on their heads, although if the truth be known, I was generally too weak to administer a heavy-handed swat to any of them. They learned to keep their eyes on me and if I thought that some behavior or other was to cease at once, they knew quite well what a certain look would mean, and mended their ways immediately. I used to marvel at the control they allowed me to exercise over them, and somehow I managed to keep the upper hand with my brothers and sister, although they could have easily overpowered me had they chosen to do so, the "Chapei Trots" having weakened me so drastically. At least I had stopped wheezing, I told myself, grateful for the fact that I was able to draw a deep breath without choking. Vincent and I became very close during those months in camp and he was my good right arm on whom I could always depend.

Annie and I have always been very affectionate with one another and I was terribly glad to have her to hug and cuddle; but the thing I missed most was having someone to hug and cuddle me as Grandpa had done so often, and I longed to feel the warmth of my Grandma's hand on my head, or Auntie Ida's arm around my shoulders, and there was no one in camp who could acceptably make an outward show of affection toward me without it seeming misplaced or peculiar. One needs others to truly feel where one's own physical boundaries begin and end, and fourteen-year old girls are awkward in so many ways as it is; but there were times when even a prim, independent and guarded young woman such as I needed a reassuring embrace and not knowing how to manage this requirement, I would make do by holding my warm, sweet little sister who knew just how to curve her delicious self against my body, and we would fall asleep as we had done all our lives, safe with one another.

Sheila Hutton wrote to me on a form letter and I scribbled a message back on the reverse side of the paper. We were each allowed to send one letter a month, so I wrote to Grandpa as Mary, to Auntie Ida as Vincent, to Grandma as Jordie, and sometimes to Sheila as Annie. Sheila wrote me twice one month by signing her own name to one letter and her sister's name to another. There is always some way to beat the system if one tries hard enough.

Sheila kept many things from our war-time adventures and has shared them with me to put in this book. I had also saved every memento of camp life that I could, but at the end it was all confiscated from me during the baggage inspections before we left Chapei.

Sheila stayed on in Lungwha Camp until the war ended and then was liberated, which enabled her to retain possession of all the bits and pieces of her days as a prisoner of war, and I am thankful that my friend had such squirrely tendencies because these scraps of paper are precious to us still.

When the Hutton family went to the prison camp at Lungwha, they had left their beautiful penthouse apartment just as it was, and were forbidden by the Japanese to take anything with them. During the time they were imprisoned, the Japanese authorities used the flat to house visiting officials and military personnel in the upper echelons. Three years later, when the war ended and those in camps were liberated; Mrs. Hutton hitched a ride and went straight to the Hanray Mansions, where the same elevator man greeted her in surprise.

She was admitted to her old apartment by the Japanese housekeeper in attendance with a lot of "walla-walla" (which means commotion in Pidgin English), and much bowing, and she discovered that everything, down to the last detail, was exactly as she had left it three years before. Her pot plants were thriving (they had put crushed egg-shells in the soil), and even the note pad by the telephone still had the last notations Mrs. Hutton had made on it before she left for Lungwha. Her old servants had been retained by the Japanese and had kept everything just as she had had them do when she lived there. It is possible that one Mrs. Nagami, who had been an executive in the Japanese Gendarmerie, had taken special care of the Hutton penthouse because Mr. Hutton, before his death, had always treated that formidable woman with respect and courtesy, and she was now repaying his family for the civility he had shown her.

It was a most astonishing fact that the Hutton apartment had not been looted as so many of the homes of enemy nationals had, and the looting had been done not by the Japanese, but by the Chinese who'd been treated so viciously and starved.

A school was organized in the camp and those who had been teachers on the outside held classes for the children, trying to help them keep up with the studies they were missing. My brothers and Annie attended every day until the school was abandoned for lack of materials. I went as often as I could when not occupied with the laundry or the ailment which held me in its grip. The boys and Annie had only a rare bout with dysentery and enjoyed good health most of the time we spent at Chapei. I worried over being held back in school when we would finally be released, but as it turned out I was put into the tenth grade when we arrived in California that next year. Camp school kept the kids busy for a while, and there was also a meager library of old and well-thumbed books available to us.

A little girl in our section liked to play a game with us, scrambling to the top of the trunks in the hallway and then saying in a teasing voice, "Catch me" as she fell forward, never fearing that we would fail to do so. Sometimes, when I least expected it, I would hear her calling, "Catch me," and I'd rush over and find her in mid-air, saving her in the nick of time. What faith in humanity that child must have been developing.

Jordie engaged another small boy in a rock fight and found himself in a great deal of trouble. He had a formal hearing in the Commandant's office, and that Japanese worthy sentenced Jordie to the punishment of emptying the spittoons in his office twice a day. By the time the sentence had been carried out over the period of one week, Jordie had become a fixture in the Commandant's office and a favorite of his staff. One day, Jordie asked if he could look at the heavy Samurai swords hanging on the wall, and to his delight he was handed an armful of swords and allowed to play with them in the compound. Several other boys gathered around and they had a marvelous time thrusting and parrying with the menacing weapons the rest of the day.

A platoon of Japanese soldiers were billeted in the nearby fields, and for days we heard them practicing their battle cries as they surged forward against an imaginary enemy battalion, bayonets fixed, screaming their bloodcurdling "Bonzai" and stabbing the air with their weapons. The performance caused some anxiety among the prisoners, but it only lasted for a few days, and then I suppose the Imperial Army dispatched the group to try out the maneuvers on genuine U.S. Marines in the Pacific Theater of War.

Gambling was very popular in prison camp and one could find a card game in any room at almost any time of the night or day. People gambled for food mainly, and sometimes I'd see some of them wagering on how many seeds there might be in an orange, the one coming closes to the correct number winning the orange as a prize, which was an old Chinese pastime.

We dreamed constantly of rich, delicious food, and talked to one another about what we'd order as soon as we were free. There was powdered milk available in small quantities, and a canned variety from Japan whose label advertised it as "My Mother's Milk" causing it to be scorned by the majority of queasy folk; but whatever milk there was the children were given first priority. The meals in camp were most unsatisfactory in the beginning of our confinement, and then seemed to improve slightly. Perhaps it was because we got used to it and it filled our bellies, but did not do much for our palates or souls, and its beneficial effects were negligible as far as I was concerned. I would fall asleep thinking of Bunny Barnes and the beautiful cream puffs we'd had at the Columbia Dairy, and all the tasty street chow we used to buy on the way home from school. One day, Grandma sent us six salamis and a friend named Jeannie Zentner showed me how to trade them off in inches for other commodities for me and the kids. For two inches we got a half cup of sugar, for four inches, a can of soup, and at the end we had a nice collection of tea and crackers, jam and a tin of butter which turned out to be rancid, but we ate it anyway, and several other kinds of food we preferred over the salami.

Jeannie Zentner had been a friend of my mother's and we used to be fascinated watching that lady smoke cigarettes. She could inhale the smoke and then have it curl up into her nostrils in a most amazing way, and I have not seen anyone do that since.

Cheetah and Billy Carroll spent weeks preparing the camp shows, and we watched so many of the rehearsals that by the time the show opened we knew every word of all the songs, and each skit was so familiar that any one of us could have stepped in and done a turn or two. The Carrolls specialized in dramatic dances and one of their numbers showed Billy as Count Dracula with Cheetah as his victim. She was spectacular in a long white diaphanous gown, and she wore her black hair hanging down her back and a passionate expression on her mysterious face. We loved it when Billy recoiled in horror at the sight of the silver cross Cheetah held up to him at the end, and then I think she killed him with a spike through his heart for a grand finale. The musicians in camp provided an excellent accompaniment to all this merriment and some clever person wrote parodies to popular songs for the chorus to come out and sing. They did "Thanks for the Memory" to these words:

Thanks for the memory
Of standing in a queue,
Being served with Chapei stew,
The meat was hard
There was no lard
So bean oil had to do,
Oh, thank you so much

The Japanese guards were invited to the opening night and they sat in the front row as guests of honor, applauding and smiling broadly, even when the skits and songs were about them, none of which were complimentary, but not understanding English that well a great deal was lost on our keepers, most fortunately for us.

A tall, thin and angular gentleman named Crenshaw Holt had been persuaded to come onstage dressed as the Queen of the Nile to do a hootchy-kootchy number, and it brought down the house. His nickname was Cumshaw which in Pidgin English meant graft or gratuity, depending upon whether one was the giver or the taker. Ordinarily, Mr. Holt was a taciturn, grumpy sort of fellow, so his appearance was a real coup for the show's producers. A group of the burliest, hairiest men in camp was coerced into dressing up in ballerina costumes made from mosquito netting, and they did a hilarious dance reminiscent of the hippopotami in Disney's "Fantasia." Topsy Brown did her Shirley Temple impersonation to wild applause, and we had a magician, a juggler and assorted theatrical delights. In the seven months we were imprisoned, there were only two camp shows, but these productions kept dozens of people busy night and day, and I daresay that the time flew by for them. We treated our "stars" with the greatest deference and they soon became Very Important Persons in the compound.

Years later, I happened to meet Cheetah Carroll on a street in Fresno, California, and we had an exciting reunion, chirping about what a small world it truly was.

In early August of 1943 rumors of a ship coming to take exchange prisoners buzzed through the camp like a swarm of hornets. Every day we heard some new story of the negotiations between the Allied Nations and Japan regarding how this momentous trade would take place. Six weeks went by and suddenly we learned that a ship would be coming. For several days we waited for the list of names to come out, informing us of who was to be allowed to leave the camp, and since our initial "S" was toward the end of the alphabet, we did not know until less than a week before departure that we four had been chosen. Annie remembers standing in front of the moveable bulletin board with me while I read off the names, and the morning that I found ours on the list she says she could feel the tension as I silently gripped her hand. It would have been unseemly to show the glorious excitement I felt in the presence of my fellow camp mates who also read the lists with hope, only to be left in shocked despair knowing they'd have to stay behind. The method of choosing us was not far from having the Japanese officials sweep through the camp pointing at us at random, saying, "You, you, you and you." But the pattern they appeared to follow was to designate those men who were sick, disabled or not of military age, and then whatever women and children there were to meet the balance of the quota. Many families were separated in the arbitrary system, as it was, causing much anguish and many tears.

The Fates and the Japanese were kind, and The Four of Us remained together as a set, and I was relieved and grateful.

We started packing immediately, trying not to seem too elated in the face of so many who were compelled to stay on for God knew how long, and soberly offered our stores of food to our neighbors and other items of which we had to divest ourselves, almost sorrowfully parting with our rickety table.

Everyone was trying to be happy for those who had been singled out for the trip, but we knew what was in their hearts, and for many of them freedom was a long way off. There didn't seem to be anything appropriate to say to those who had not been tabbed.

The word "repatriation" meant "going home" and we spoke of it in this manner, even though America had never been home to any of the four of us. I wondered if my mother knew that we were coming, and all the old dreams and hopes revived themselves in me. We talked excitedly about how it was going to be and what we would say and do when we were reunited. I didn't even know then that my mother and her second husband had moved to California, and thought that we would be living in New York State where they had been before we were sent to prison camp. California was not the only surprise in store for us, and we could think only of how marvelous it was going to be once we set foot in The Promised Land and were with our mother once again.

Father Sullivan took me aside and made me promise that if things did not go well for us I promised I would get in touch with his mother in Ann Arbor. I gave him my word that I would, but I assured him that nothing could go wrong and that a wonderful life awaited my brothers and Annie and me. He smiled, and insisted that I take his mother's address anyway. I wrote it down in my precious journal and was so pleased that at least we would keep in touch with one another after the war when he could return home to Michigan.

But then we submitted to the first baggage inspection, and the guard assigned to our section confiscated a pair of brand new shoes in pink leather which Grandma had sent me and which I'd been saving to wear in case we left camp. The crowning blow came when he took away my journal with several important addresses in it, all our photographs, our birth, baptism, school and other certificates. Medicine of any kind was forbidden to be taken out of camp, and no written material whatsoever was allowed us, except for one book: The Bible. I had my mother's Long Island address down by heart, luckily I thought, so I marked the Good Book letter by letter, and number by number, knowing what a big country America was and afraid we might be lost or stranded when we arrived in the States in the event that my mother did not know we were being "sent home." She did receive notification of the ship's arrival via a telegram from Cordell Hull, who was Secretary of State at the time, but I learned this later.

During times of privation, people save the silliest things, and in packing our belongings I had left the many dozens of sani-naps in the bottom of our one big trunk. At a second inspection, those of us who were being searched again had gathered in the exercise area in alphabetical order, and Vincent was helping me show the guard what else we had to declare. A new guard whom I did not know came up to rout through our luggage and when he discovered the aforementioned items neatly kept in their original wrappings, he said I could not take them because of the printing on the covering paper. He picked up one of the packages and bounced it on the palm of his hand, and with a knowing smirk, said: "What is this? What is inside?"

I was furious that this arrogant little martinet thought he could humiliate me in front of my fellow camp mates, and I answered frostily that if he did not know what they were what difference did it make? His face darkened with anger and he slapped his hand on the hilt of his long clanking sword. Then suddenly he ripped open all seven packages (there were twenty naps in each), and flung them into the air so that it rained Kotex while the guard vented his fury. Everyone turned to see what the matter was, and I coolly went about the business of tidying up the other suitcases and trunks while Vincent scurried around the area retrieving all one hundred and forty of the damned things, stuffing them into the big trunk and then sitting on top of it as though nothing had happened. We never discussed it, but I was so grateful to Vincent for coming to my rescue and being so dignified about it all when I had been mortified beyond endurance. The guard cursed me and stamped away. I refused to look at him.

There was no time after that first inspection to see Father Sullivan again and mark my Bible with his mother's address, as all we were able to do was to say a hurried and sorrowful goodbye to one another on the steps, and I dearly wanted to throw my arms around him, but we just shook hands and he smiled with tears in his eyes and turned away. I came to wish, in the days that followed, that I could write to Mrs. Sullivan in Ann Arbor, Michigan, but there was no way.

Our grandparents were informed of the impending trip from Shanghai and the Japanese allowed them to come to the camp for a last look at us. They stood in a long line with other relatives and friends from the outside waiting to see their own people who'd be leaving, and when our turn came we were given a scant five minutes for that last visit. After not having seen them for seven months it was a pitifully short time and all we could do was cry and hug each other. It was the craziest five minutes I'd spent in my life and we were devastated. We clung to Grandma and Grandpa, kissing them and crying, and I found it excruciating and nightmarish. Auntie Ida had not been allowed to come, and I wept and grieved not to see her one last time. Still, it was better than not having seen them at all, and I'd have been comforted had I known that I would indeed see them all again after the war. The Japanese guards were not rough when they pulled us apart to herd us out of the small visiting room, and not a few of them looked with great compassion on the scene of emotional carnage they were witnessing. They were human too and far from home themselves, and no doubt missed their own loved ones who many of them, not as lucky as we, were never to see again

Chapter 22

On September 14, 1943 we were inoculated against cholera and typhus, and vaccinated against small-pox, receiving certificates to that effect from His Imperial Japanese Majesty's Consulate-General in Shanghai. These cards were one of the few things I was able to save and they have been kept in a scrap book all these years. I had to sign many legal papers prior to leaving the camp and discovered later, when we'd been in the United States for some time, that I had pledged myself to paying the American Government the sum of five hundred dollars for each of us for the trip on the M. S. "Gripsholm." The sum of $2000 was my sole responsibility, and the United States Treasury Department kept after me for the next fifteen years for this money; and as the interest accrued, it became an impossible sum to raise. The case was finally settled in 1957 when our Government agreed to accept $500 from me, and waived the interest altogether. The debt had loomed over me for many years, and I had been most concerned at my inability to pay it, especially since it was the only debt I ever incurred which was beyond my capacity to discharge.

My fifteenth birthday fell on the day we left the prison camp at Chapei, and on the 18th of September, 1943, we boarded the bus which took us to the customs house. The Japanese had blocked off the roads around the Bund. and our Grandparents and Auntie Ida came down to see us off, but were obliged to remain behind the barriers. We saw them immediately as we drove into the area because Grandma had her old, familiar umbrella which she brandished above the heads of the crowd, and we waved frantically to one another, blowing kisses and giving the thumbs-up sign. We couldn't do much more because of the heavy guard around us on the Bund, but we were ecstatic at seeing their faces in all the attendant excitement. Inside the customs house, there was one final inspection, and then we were put on the tender for the "Teia Maru."

I took a long last look at dear old Shanghai, our home for so many years, and thought of the friends and loved ones I'd be leaving, of all the sad and wonderful times we'd had, and I knew I would have to come back one day, perhaps not to live, but just to look at everything I had loved.

The "Teia Maru" had been the former French steamship "Aramis" and had originally been built to carry five hundred passengers; but when the full complement of prisoners was finally assembled from the other stops we made, our number reached fifteen hundred repatriates. We were to sail to Goa, India, where we would meet the "Gripsholm" and be exchanged for Japanese prisoners who had been held by the United States.

The sick and the elderly, and the women with small children were given cabins. Vincent and Jordie were sent below decks where they were crowded in with a large group of males, and eventually there were six hundred men and boys stacked like cord wood in the various holds. Annie and I found ourselves in the company of two hundred and eighty women and girls who were assigned sleeping quarters on an enclosed deck, and many more slept in the former social halls on board. The conditions were far worse than they had ever been in the prison camps, and my brothers, who said the hold was like the Black Hole of Calcutta, took their blankets topside at night and slept together in some canvas tarps because they were afraid of the rough men with whom they were supposed to share quarters. Vincent said the place below decks was choking with cigarette smoke and the din created by the men playing incessant games of cards kept them awake all night.

On our closed-in decks, and in the halls, double-decker platforms, all of a piece, had been built, and on their surfaces straw pallets, covered in rough muslin, were laid side by side. We tried to make jokes about the beds, saying that when we retired we literally "hit the hay." No linen was issued to anyone except for a wool blanket each, and I can't remember having a pillow. The pallets were two feet wide, just enough room to lie on motionless with our arms at our sides, and when the ship rolled and pitched, those on the end would tumble out onto the deck, as the rest of us found ourselves on someone else's pad, and we rarely woke up in the same slot where we'd gone to sleep the night before. It was hot and humid in that part of the world in September and October, and sometimes a few of us would try to sleep on the open deck. One night, when we thought we'd try this arrangement, we were almost trampled to death by a boisterous band of prisoners from the Pootung camp, which had held Allied military personnel caught in Shanghai after Pearl Harbor, and filled with cheap Japanese wine they staggered around the ship celebrating their release from the worst camp in the City, terrorizing everyone with their brawling and swearing accompanied by loud, lascivious singing. We thought we'd be safe on the women's deck, but drunken sailors are not widely acclaimed for their princely deportment and gentle manners.

It was not an easy task keeping the boys and Annie within the scope of my vision at all times, and I was beset by the constant fear that they would fall overboard, knowing that no one would stop the ship to rescue them if it happened. Annie, of course, spent every sleeping and waking moment with me, and I insisted that Vincent and Jordie report to me immediately each morning, and kept them as close as possible during the day. At bedtime, I would anxiously watch them disappear down the steps into the "Black Hole", not knowing that they'd be creeping back on deck later at night.

Apparently, our shipmates came to know the identity of my brothers and Annie, and, as it had happened in Chapei, the three kids said they could not easily get into trouble because people would invariably say,

"Just you wait until your Big Sister finds out about this," striking terror into their hearts with the words.

There were several sittings in the dining rooms, and bells were constantly being rung to announce the serving of the next group. Everything we ate seemed to be curried, and I grew to hate the sight and smell of it. For breakfast we were served "congee", which is thin rice gruel, and after we'd picked out the maggots, arranging them neatly on the rim of the soup plate, we'd try to eat what was left. Maggots have an eerie resemblance to grains of rice when they are cooked, and I was glad that my eyesight was so sharp in those years.

Before leaving Chapei, I had unwittingly signed for an advance of money from the American authorities which was part of the ultimate bill I received; at my age and in my eagerness to be reunited with my mother, I am afraid that I neglected to read the fine print in all the papers I signed. However, I am sure I would have signed them in any event, even if I had been fully aware of the debt I was saddling myself with at that time. I remember that I had $3000 in Chinese paper money which was worth approximately $40 in U.S. gold, and most of this was spent on the prison ship to buy pieces of sponge cake, a tiny square of it going for five dollars, which I bought to augment the two dreadful meals we got each day in the "Teia Maru" dining room. The Japanese cooks on board took unfair advantage of their "captive audience" and unloaded vast amounts of poisonous wine and papery cake on us at exorbitant prices.

Each passenger was given a "travel kit" upon boarding the ship, compliments of His Imperial Majesty, and the packet contained a lifetime supply of Japanese propaganda, including a booklet entitled "The Coming American Revolution", a tin of something labeled "Fruit Sarad", a bar of salt-water soap and a roll of toilet tissue with the words "Crape Paper" printed on the wrapping. The "Fruit Sarad" provided an urgent and compelling reason for most of us to go through the "Crape Paper" in short order, and when the supply was exhausted, as were we, we switched over to the sheets of Japanese propaganda. It was unfortunate that the salt-water soap was not edible since there were no baths available to any of us, drinking water itself was at a premium, and the soap was little used. The men on board were lucky as they were hosed off with salt water on one of the lower decks about once a week; but the women had no facilities whatever for keeping themselves clean, and the total result was most appallingly unpleasant, to say the very least.

Not one emergency drill was ever held on the "Teia Mara", and when we had a good look at the life boats, we knew why. They were filled with debris, and most of them had gaping holes in their undersides, and wouldn't have done anyone a bit of good if an emergency had arisen. We were told that we were in constant danger of being torpedoed, and this information did little for the peace of mind aboard ship, especially when we became aware of the condition of the life boats. There were some life jackets around, hanging on the bulkheads, but there were more of us than there were of them, and I often wondered who would be saved in case the ship sank.

When we docked in Hong Kong, our first stop, to pick up prisoners from the camp at Fort Stanley, those of us from Shanghai hung over the railings to see who would be coming aboard to join us, and I saw a heavy-set woman in a flowery dress with large, beautiful eyes making her way up the gangplank. She held a little girl, about two years old, on one hip, and had a Chinese basket by the handle in the crook of one elbow. In her mouth was a huge cigar which she was puffing mightily, and we gawked at the sight, wondering who she was. I learned later that this was the fabled Emily Hahn, an American who wrote several books after the war, and I had heard of her when she lived in Shanghai because she had a pet monkey which she led around on a leash, and the animal wore a diaper held together with a big gold safety pin, as myth would have it. I never saw the lady again after the trip was over, but I read a few of her books, and wonder what her daughter Carola looks like now. Carola Boxer had been an exquisite child and I minded her for her mother a few times during that voyage, although we could not understand one another since the little girl had been taught to speak only Mandarin, as I recall.

The "Teia Maru" then docked in Manila, and we took on another group from the ill-famed Santo Tomas prison camp, (where Vincent and Jordie had attended school in 1938), and the people who came aboard there looked much worse than any of us, bedraggled as we were, many of them being in the most dire physical shape. Only a handful of newcomers joined us in Saigon and Singapore, and we stayed on the ship, which always docked far out from the wharves of these places, never seeing very much from where we were anchored in the bay.

In Manila harbor, dozens of small dug-outs were paddled alongside the "Teia Maru", the Filipino natives bringing fruit to sell the passengers as they had been used to doing in peace-time;

but this exchange was forbidden by the Japanese, and we stood on the decks, our mouths watering at the sight of the little boats overflowing with bananas and coconuts and other tropical fruits. One enterprising Filipino managed to clamber up the side of our ship on a line, but before he reached the railing, a Japanese guard caught sight of him and leaped into the rigging to kick him away when he boarded; but the guard lost his footing and fell into the water, while hundreds of us, who witnessed the scene, cheered and shouted, whistled and hooted, clapping our hand s and stomping our feet on the deck. Before the day ended, someone from a dug-out took careful aim and threw a pummel up to Annie which she caught to resounding cheers, and she remembers how she peeled that sweet grapefruit-like delight and stuffed it into her mouth.

We whiled away the hours on the "Teia Maru" watching the flying fish and hoping not to sight any bombers bearing either American or Japanese insignia. The only book I had to read was the Bible I'd brought with me, and for the first time in my life became fairly well acquainted with The Word. There were some Maryknoll nuns on board ship, and Sister Mary Gemma, Sister Mary Peters and Sister Mary Corita held informal classes for the children. I took advantage of their presence and set about to learn algebra under their tutelage and when I had completed certain aspects of it on the Gripsholm, they presented me with a "certificate" which was accepted by the John Marshall High School in Los Angeles where I was soon to be a student.

We spent thirty days exactly on the "Teia Maru", and our condition was indescribably wretched. My long hair had not been washed since the last week we spent in the prison camp and I had kept it tightly braided all those weeks so that it resembled nothing less than a bird's nest after the season was long over and the birds had flown south for the winter. Annie's hair was not quite so bad because, although it was filthy, I had managed to brush it every day and she might have passed a casual inspection. We'd tried to wash our hands and faces in the weak trickle of water that dripped from a basin in the one toilet we shared with some hundreds of other women on our deck, and I'd even wiped my hands and neck with the hot tea I didn't drink at mealtimes. It is amazing how accustomed one can become to one's own smell, even when the acculturation process has left a deep mark, and one is fully and alarmingly aware of the disgusting effects of the unsanitary conditions which might prevail.

A few days before we reached Goa, India, to meet the "Gripsholm," I was determined to have some sort of bath. Drinking water, during the trip, had been very scarce and water for bathing was out of the question, but I, then still a firm believer in "cumshaw", went hunting for a steward, (they were practically non-existent), and found someone who agreed to sell Annie and me a bath for $40. We followed him furtively to a lower deck where he showed us into a dank closet which contained a small, gritty, grimy bath-tub. He put in the plug and turned on the water after doing something to the pipes with a wrench, and let a few inches of greenish brown water sputter into the tub. Then, he worked the wrench on the pipes again and left, and I suppose what he gave us was whatever water had remained in the pipes from the time before. We locked the door and got into that awful tub, and using the Royal salt-water soap had the most marvelous ten minutes of that hellish trip. We got as clean as we possibly could, which is not to say that we go any too clean, but Annie and I could not have been happier had we been Claudette Colbert soaking herself in a vat of the scented milk of a hundred asses.

We sailed into Goa, Portuguese India, on October the 18th and remained aboard ship the first day, waiting for the "Gripsholm" to join us. The next morning, the Motor Ship "Gripsholm", a Swedish liner with a big red cross painted on its sides, sailed into the harbor, a grand contrast to the shabby hulk of the "Teia Maru". We stood on the decks of the prison ship, craning our necks and straining our eyes to have a look at our deliverance and its cargo of Japanese from America for whom we were being traded, shouting friendly greetings to one another. The crew of the "Gripsholm" hurled oranges at us from their stern to our bow, but most of the fruit fell into the water between the ships. The beautiful Swedish vessel was truly an enchanting sight to behold that night, glittering with thousands of lights in the darkened harbor, and we quivered in anticipation.

The next morning the formal exchange of prisoners got under way. We filed off the "Teia Maru" as the Japanese from America filed off the "Gripsholm" in a sort of Noah's Ark procession, and we were counted, one for one, and checked with careful precision. When it came my turn to stand in front of the American officials at tables they had set up, a man, who told me his name was also Smith, looked quizzically at me, and asked if I were the "Mary Smith" who was travelling with my two brothers, Vincent and Jordie, and a sister, Annie, and when I nodded, he said he'd been in correspondence with our mother and that he would send her a cable at once to tell her we were on the ship. I had some difficulty holding back my tears at the sound of Louise's name, but I went on down the line, herding the boys and Annie in front of me, answering the rest of the questions and showing the other officials our small-pox and cholera certificates.

I was infinitely relieved to learn that Louise would know we were on our way, and the yearning for her increased in a renewed surge of intensity. I longed to have my own mother in charge of all of us, not that I resented the responsibility which had been thrust upon me, but there was that small part of me needing to still be dependent, which craved having "Mummy" tuck me in bed at night and to assure me that everything was going to be fine, just fine. I loved Vincent and Jordie and Annie, but I couldn't remember a time when I'd not been all they had, and I ached to share the burden I shouldered, although I did so willingly. This Mr. Smith had suddenly made my mother a reality to me once again, and I counted the days and hours until I could see her and surrender my precious charges to her care and safe-keeping.

With the formalities of the exchange completed, we were allowed to move freely about for the next day or so, but Goa is a tiny place and there was not much we could actually do there. However, it was where Saint Francis Xavier was buried, and we visited his grave in a small stone hut to view his mummified arm reposing in a glass casket. Many years later, this same arm was trundled throughout the United States on exhibition, and I saw it presented to the faithful after a Mass I had attended in San

Francisco. I would not have kissed the arm in Goa, and I had no wish to do so then, either.

Annie tugged excitedly at my sleeve to tell me that an Indian porter with flashing teeth in his teak-colored face had smiled at her, and the amazing thing was that he had the bluest flue eyes my sister had ever seen.

I looked around me, and although I was enjoying the first real taste of freedom in many a month, I could not help but be revolted by the loathsome stench of that place, which was alive with flies and other insects, and many of the people were covered with sores. There were street peddlers, just as there had been in Shanghai, but their offerings for sale did not look wholesome and I forbade the boys to buy any from the sticky trays held out by children our own ages.

The memory of Goa becomes most vivid when I think of the prisoners who came from America to change places with us. These Japanese people, who, in truth, were more American than we were, mingled with us asking hundreds of questions. We spoke to many of them and they all exhibited a kind of terror at what lay in store for them, whereas we felt that Heaven had just opened its gates for us. Remembering the manner in which we had been chosen for the exchange – for example the elderly, the sick, the preponderance of children and women among us - we marveled at how unfair a trade it was because those who disembarked from the "Gripsholm" were healthy and bright-eyed, alert and well dressed. They had many luxuries in their possession, many of them having brought expensive furnishings from America, and, since the "Teia Maru" was so much smaller a vessel than the "Gripsholm", all these crated treasures were dumped over the side by the Japanese authorities, to be salvaged later by the people of Goa, and there was much weeping and wailing from our counterparts.

The first thing that had happened to them was that when they boarded the "Teia Maru" their men were assigned to the enclosed decks where Annie and I had been, and their women were stuffed into the holds as Vincent and Jordie had been, reversing the situation, which doubtless caused the new passengers of the old "Aramis" to all but drown in waves of sickening shock.

When we talked to the Japanese from America, (they were a mixed lot of those born in Japan who were being sent back, and their American-born sons and daughters), many among their great numbers of men being of military age, and most of them having been educated as engineers and chemists and the like, we were intrigued by their American accents, and loved to listen to their slangy speech, especially since my brothers and Annie and I spoke with a decidedly British accent and were not in the least like these "Americans" who chattered nervously about how they would all "go home" as soon as the war was over.

I heard folks in our own group from Shanghai wondering out loud what the United States Government had been thinking of to send to Japan such a superior intellectual and physical force, only to have it turned back against America once this boatload was absorbed into the Japanese war machine. I must confess that I felt a great pity for those who took our places, however, thinking that they faced greater horrors and dangers than we would ever know, never dreaming then that the day would soon come when I'd wish we were all back, safe, in the Chapei prison camp in war-torn Shanghai.

Chapter 23

For the first time in over two years we saw the American flag flying from the mast of the "Gripsholm", and those glorious stars and stripes fluttering above us infused me with a sense of "home and country" I'd never quite felt before, and, other than the months when I wore my red armband, I don't think I ever really identified with America prior to being part of that exchange of prisoners. We knew little of American history, had never celebrated the Fourth of July, and for most of my life I'd been aware only of English history and holidays such as Guy Fawkes Day, and actually felt more English than American. But Old Glory changed that, and I was proud to be a citizen of the United States, a strange new sense of nationalism rising in my breast. Well, I thought, we ARE "going home" they tell us, so "home" it shall be. We learned to say the Pledge of Allegiance, which sounded as though it had been composed by the same person who'd done so much for the King James' version of The Bible, and shyly tried to keep up with all the verses in the "Star Spangled Banner." Listening to "America the Beautiful" brought a great lump to my throat and I wept unabashedly, longing to see those "amber waves of grain."

More than freedom, more than safety, more than comfort, the "Gripsholm" meant FOOD, and the abundance of fresh fruit and vegetables, rafts of delectable pastries, pitcher upon pitcher of sweet, foamy milk, crusty rolls and delicate buns, (one wanted to kiss them!) in great profusion, enormous trays of baked hams and turkeys, platters of whole salmon garnished with lemon peel roses and parsley, great haunches of rare roast beef, mounds of golden butter, shimmering towers of jeweled gelatin creations, and countless tiers of gorgeous Swedish hors d'oeuvres dazzled our eyes and overwhelmed even the strongest among us so that many wept as they gazed upon the tables groaning under the weight of the welcoming buffet the ship's cooks had prepared for us. While we waited in the long lines that circled the top deck to reach the tables, stewards moved up and down distributing the large economy sized bars of Hershey's and Nestlé's milk chocolate and brought us flagons of ice water which we drank out of clean paper cups as we stood patiently in the brilliant Indian sun. Those who'd been fed would come out of the dining rooms and tell us in wide-eyed amazement of the wonders we would soon see and taste and the excitement on board far exceeded anything I had experienced before.

When we finally reached the tables laden with their marvelous spread, I saw the centerpiece which was a cornucopia spilling over with pineapples and pears, tangerines and apples, grapes and bananas, and that beautiful still life remains in my mind's eye as the one true symbol of the rewards of survival and endurance for all time. The chefs, wearing their tall puffed hats and stiffly starched white aprons, beamed broadly at their ragged guests and with expansive gestures urged us to take whatever we fancied, and to be sure to be back for seconds and thirds if we wished. I can't remember what I piled on my plate, or even what I did, but Annie says that she recalls watching me take my eyes off her and the boys for the first time in over a year and, oblivious to everything and everyone, I went outside on the deck and sat on the steps of a gangway to feast in silent and secretive satisfaction, and she saw me with my guard down for once, which, for her, was a rare sight, and for a moment I seemed like a stranger to her, as indeed I must have been.

Several of those among us, too long in the war, fearful that the food would run out, stuffed their pockets with whatever they could, only to find that the initial feast was just the beginning of a six-week banquet that seemed to get more sumptuous every day. We were told later that the crew on the "Gripsholm" had been warned not to present us with too rich a welcoming feed because we had been accustomed to such meager fare for so long that we might all get sick if we stuffed ourselves that first day, (which some of us did), and ever after I have thought affectionately of Scandinavian understatement and reticence, and will never quite believe that those people are as somber as rumor will have it.

Annie and I were given a cabin to share with an elderly missionary lady and her fussy daughter. They disapproved of almost everything we said, did or were, and we tip-toed around them so as not to incur their further disfavor, having as little to do with them as possible. They were not from our prison camp and had not known us before we became room-mates, and perhaps because of our English accents there was an unspoken suspicion on their part toward Annie and me that left us with the distinct impression that these ladies were not entirely certain that we belonged on the ship at all. It would have mattered little to them, I am sure, if I had troubled to explain our circumstances, pointing out that children of United States citizens can claim America as their own regardless of where they happen to have been born.

Vincent and Jordie had a cabin on another deck with two gentlemen who were kind and non-committal and they got on famously together. I felt a lot easier on the "Gripsholm" and was not as reluctant to let the boys out of my sight on that spacious ship. There were two swimming pools on board and the three kids were in it, splashing and diving, almost all day. Annie, who did not know how to swim, tried to keep pace with her brothers and jumped in the deep end on her first try. She sank like a stone to the bottom and Jordie gallantly dove in to rescue her, and she wore a life-belt the rest of the journey.

We had crisp, clean sheets and fluffy pillows on our single bunks and I reveled in the luxury of them. Baths and showers, with no shortage of hot water, scented soap and fresh thick towels were ours for the asking, and I washed my hair several times a week on board. Any time of the day there were frosty cokes on ice for whoever had a thirst, and the food staggered the imagination. Sometimes, we'd stand at the stern and watch in horror the crew dumping barrels of garbage into the foam, and it was the only sight on the "Gripsholm" that caused me any degree of real pain. I grieved to see the many baskets of vegetables and fruit thrown away, thinking of how we'd have used it all in Chapei, and how happy our fellow campmates would have been to eat what was only refuse here. It is still very difficult for me to waste food in any way and I've never been able to take abundance for granted.

Hollywood movies were shown several times every day and the bill changed frequently. We saw "Yankee Doodle Dandy" many times, and choked up, right on cue, at all the patriotic scenes. James Cagney, how we loved him! There was a movie on Stephen Foster, starring Don Ameche, which introduced us to a whole raft of American songs, and then Rita Hayworth charmed us in "Cover Girl", becoming a favorite of every movie fan on board.

I did not know how these two movie stars would figure in our lives at the time, but when we arrived in New York, my mother had sold our story to be used on the "What's New" N.B.C. program on radio, and Don Ameche was the host of that show, interviewing Louise in Hollywood, while his brother, Jim Ameche, questioned the four of us in New York on a coast-to-coast hook-up. As for Miss Hayworth, Louise was working at the Columbia Studios in Los Angeles then and had her picture taken with the red-headed film queen showing them both looking at a photograph of us children taken before the war.

Still, in the midst of all the high-powered entertainment available, the most touching performance was the sound of an occasional lone sailor playing a harmonica in the night air, and the strains of "There's a Long Long Trail A-Winding" made me homesick for Shanghai and all those left behind whom I thought I'd never see again.

We'd not been on the "Gripsholm" long before Jordie got into trouble. There had been two convicted criminals put on the "Teia Maru" in Shanghai whom the Japanese had allowed to roam at large; but upon boarding the "Gripsholm" the American authorities had immediately incarcerated these "bad guys" in the brig. Somehow, they had Jordie smuggling cigarettes to them, the details of this endeavor never were made clear to me, or I've blocked them out, but his actions caused a great flap and the only thing that saved my naughty brother from further misfortune was that very soon after this he became deathly sea-sick and remained so for many days. Being sea-sick is a most humbling experience and Jordie was sufficiently chastened from his bout of "mal-de-mer", and there was no need on my part to add any further to his suffering.

The first stop the "Gripsholm" made was Port Elizabeth, South Africa, where we docked for three days. We were allowed to go ashore there and the people greeted our ship by flying Old Glory alongside the Union Jack, and we had a sense of our freedom again just to look at the flags whipping in the breeze.

We went into the shops, not believing our eyes, and would have bought out the stores if we'd had any money to spend. We visited the famous Snake Farm and watched the keeper carry his reptile charges around draped over his neck and shoulders, and we shivered in disbelief at his bravery.

I had never heard of apartheid and was amazed to see signs, in Africa, that read "White Only", forgetting that the same thing was done in Chinese in their own country as well. It never ceases to astonish me that vast numbers of peoples will allow themselves to be so ill-used by a handful of "masters", but I am neither an economist nor a historian, and am baffled still by many things such as this.

Twelve more days out to sea and then, Rio! We sailed into Rio de Janeiro harbor very early in the morning of the 15th of November, 1943, and the city looked as though it were made of pale, pink sugar blocks in the rosy light of the new day which was breaking. The Red Cross came aboard and invited us to their headquarters where we were shown racks and racks of used clothing to choose what we wanted. We were sorely in need of things to wear since every one of us was shabby and ragged, and I suppose a few kind souls had banded together determined to help us arrive in New York looking fairly presentable. However, the Red Cross grab-bag clothes, which were clean enough, were incredibly dowdy and we took a few things so as not to hurt the good people's feelings, and I hope they never realized how patronizing we were; but we never wore any of them, preferring our own old duds with their certain panache, except for new flannel nightgowns given to Annie and me, and the warm pajamas the boys received.

A children's party was organized among the American community in Rio and Jordie and Annie were carted off to wear paper hats and eat cake and ice cream. Vincent and I, too old to be regarded as "kiddies" roamed about not far from the dock, poking our noses into cafes and shops. We heard a great roar of strange music coming from a place that had a sign which read "U.S.O." and peered in the doors to see dozens of U.S. sailors in white suits gyrating with girls in flowery dresses. Vincent said, after a few moments: "Is it all right for us to watch this?"

But I wasn't sure, and was almost surprised to learn that these revelers were dancing something called the "Boogie-Woogie" and were not performing the devilish rites of a frenzied coven.

The next day we were told that the Americans in Rio were dividing us up among them, and we four had received an invitation to spend the afternoon with a couple called Mr. and Mrs. Rhoads. She was a sweet, little woman who came brightly to fetch us in her car, taking us to their spectacular apartment overlooking the Copacabana Beach, and we gazed down on the wavy patterns in the broad sidewalk, pointing out the "Gripsholm" to one another, laughing to see it looking so tiny from where we were, high above the beach.

Mrs. Rhoads had no children of her own and her husband, whom she called "Dusty," came home before dinner and was most affable and friendly. He was an airline pilot, as I recall. They had a wall in their living room which was one huge aquarium, and their collection of tropical fish and underwater flora was the most fantastic décor I've seen yet. They were both extremely kind and didn't bombard us with questions, answering our own instead, and we were full of them.

When they returned us to the ship that evening, Mrs. Rhoads put out her hand to me as we were crossing the street, just as though I were a child, and I, who had been so long holding and guarding my brothers and sister, gave the American lady my little paw with a mixture of shyness, wonder and gratitude, and my heart leapt within me because, this, I told myself, was how it was going to be in just a few days when I'd be with my own mother again. She'll take my hand, just like this, and all will be well because I shall be safe with Louise in California.

Mary's Report Card from Gripsholm 1943

MOTORSHIP GRIPSHOLM

November 30, 1943

To Whom It May Concern:

During the two and a half months Repatriation trip Mary Smith covered the following in Algebra attaining a 90% grade.

Addition, subtraction, multiplication, division, enclosing in and removing parentheses, factoring, simple and complex fractions, simplifying radicals, linear and quadratic equations, and substituting in formulas.

As we had no text book a very limited amount of work was done in problems.

Mary has been a very industrious pupil, the request for work coming from herself, besides being a very busy mother to her two younger brothe and sister. Her solicitude and mature judgment in caring for them has won the admiration of all.

Sister Mary Corita

Maryknoll Motherhouse
Maryknoll, Ossining, N. Y.

Chapter 24

The Statue of Liberty came into view and the entire ship erupted into cheers and tears. The City of New York loomed in front of us. New York! Where I was born. Home at last!

The customs house was packed and everyone was excited and busily preparing their belongings, saying goodbye to one another, shouting to friends and relatives who had come to take them home. I had no idea of what was to become of us. I searched the throng for my mother's face, but did not find it, and I worried about how we would get in touch with her. It was two o'clock in the afternoon when we disembarked from the "Gripsholm": and I kept the boys and Annie by my side so no one would get lost at the last minute, and hoped that soon someone would come for us. No one came. We sat and waited until ten o'clock that night, and everyone had been processed and had departed. There were still some baggage attendants around the place and a few clerks behind counters, but the rush was over and everyone had been sorted out except The Four of Us.

We waited.

It was hard to keep our spirits up, and hope was beginning to fade as it occurred to me that I no longer had control over our destiny, the long wait presaging the disaster which lurked in the deepening gloom. Some workers with luggage dollies moved about languidly, and my brothers and Annie said how hungry they were. We had nothing to eat, and we had no funds even if there had been a sandwich bar open at that hour. No one cried, and I must say they were brave little kids even if they did get restive and squirmy. We kept looking around, and someone said we'd be called for soon.

But no one came.

A dark young man scurried in and had no trouble finding us in that great, empty hall. He introduced himself, saying his name was Robert Cenadella. "You won't forget me because it's like Cinderella," he said cheerily, and told me he was a Public Relations man for the J. Walter Thompson Advertising Company. I had no idea of what he was talking about, and had never heard of a "public relations man." He said he was in charge of us, and hailed a taxi, taking us to the Belmont Plaza Hotel. I kept asking where my mother was, and he seemed surprised that I was so baffled by it all, and told me Louise was in Hollywood. I asked if she would telephone us. He said, no, she wouldn't be calling us before the broadcast.

"What broadcast?" I asked.

We were exhausted, hungry, frightened and my nerves were completely fraught, but he fed us when we arrived at the hotel, and the children felt a little better for the sandwiches and milk brought up to the room. I could not understand what was happening and Mr. Cenadella was under the impression that I had been informed and was just somewhat thick and stupid, which I had begun to suspect I was.

The next day, a Miss Pauline Reynard came to see us, and she had a photographer with her. Her name fitted her like her skin; she was a brittle, nervous woman with hard dark eyes and she pummeled me with questions about prison camp and the trip from Japanese occupied Shanghai, wanting to know, in a clinical manner, if we had been beaten or tortured or starved, and she wrote down every word I said to her on a little pad.

We'd gotten up early and I had the boys and Annie dress themselves before anyone came into our rooms, but Miss Reynard insisted that we change back into our nightgowns and pajamas while the breakfast they'd ordered for us congealed and hardened, and when we were suitably attired in our bed clothes again, which we'd put on over our street clothes, she had the photographer take dozens of pictures of us "enjoying the first big breakfast in the Promised Land."

These people were only doing their jobs, and it was finally explained to me that their purpose was to build a story on us from which they would then write a radio script using the material they gleaned from our conversations, and to get things going Miss Reynard and Mr. Cenadella, together with the constantly darting photographer, took us around the great city to get our first impressions of New York. We went to the Automat, to the Five and Dime stores, to the top of the Empire State Building, and they scribbled everything we said in their notebooks. There was little difficulty in getting Jordie to perform, but the rest of us were not too readily accessible.

One of my Grandma's sisters who was living on the East Coast came to see us in the hotel, but it was all so terribly confusing that I can remember nothing of her visit except that she, poor creature, only added to the emotional disarray. She did, however, introduce Annie to the sheer delight of eating Blue Point Oysters, and in the week we stayed in New York my sister must surely have consumed a bucketful of them. She was quite able to do this as we were allowed to order anything we wished, having been told that the "expense account" held no restrictions when it came to our food preferences, and my sister developed some very expensive tastes in an extremely short period of time.

The next afternoon, Miss Reynard took me alone to see an artist by the name of John Groth, and we spent several hours in his studio apartment while he made sketches of scenes I tried to describe to him of our life in camp. He was a most kindly person, and I liked him almost immediately, showing little reluctance in talking to him about our "adventures", especially when he made a quick drawing of our room at Chapei and it came out exactly as it had actually been. The Groth sketches, plus a number of pictures of us, and the lengthy interviews done over the days, appeared in a four-page spread a week or so later.

After the hours with Mr. Groth, we picked up the boys and Annie and were taken to the Chrysler Building where we were made to pose in front of a huge, brick wall in the basement. They brought some of our threadbare bags along and had us stand against this wall for the effect it created, which was stark and prison-like. There was no need for anyone to tell us to look forlorn and anxious.

"Why are we doing this?" I asked Mr. Cenadella.

"Oh, it's just ballyhoo," he answered.

"Ballyhoo?"

"Yes, this is all going to be in the Sunday supplement of a daily newspaper here," he told me.

"Why can't we talk to our mother?"

"Well, we want to hold off on that until you are all actually on the air so that it will sound authentic," he said.

"Why is it all happening in the first place?" I asked.

"Well, there's a lot of moola in this," he said.

"Moola?" I muttered wonderingly.

As we came out of the elevator, a cluster of curious sightseers crowded around and asked for our autographs.

"Are these the Quiz Kids?" someone asked, pointing at us.

"What's 'quizkidz'? I said, leaden-hearted at the spectacle we seemed to be making of ourselves without even trying.

After four days of this utterly baffling nonsense I had begun to despair of ever seeing my mother again and was completely put off by the treatment we had been subjected to, feeling not unlike a monkey on display. We were taken to a studio and given a script which we were told we would read on the air when the broadcast was made, and as I read it I was appalled at the inane drivel I would be expected to say as my own words. I made several energetic objections, but no one paid the slightest attention, and we were in effect, told to read it and shut up. We ran through the puerile script a few times, and I wish I'd had the nerve to take my two brothers and Annie and walked out on the entire project. But I had nowhere to go, we knew no one in that great frightening city, so I swallowed my pride, thinking that it would soon be over and we'd be free to leave. It was a terrible compromise of my self, and I despised having to "sell out" as it were, but under the circumstances, we had no choice, so we "read it and shut up."

Louise was in Hollywood with Don Ameche, and there we were with his brother, Jim. Don opened the program with the following words:

"On Wednesday the "Gripsholm" docked in New York, bringing to America 1500 citizens who had been interned by the Japanese. Four of these repatriates were American children coming from Shanghai who had never seen America before. They are Mary 15, Vincent 13, Jordie 11 and Annie who will be 9 next Tuesday. Their mother, Louise, left Shanghai in 1939 on a business trip that took her to Manila and later to California. She has not seen the children since because the Japanese occupation of Shanghai made it impossible for her to send for them. Their mother is here in Hollywood with me now, while the four children are in a New York studio with my brother, Jim. We're going to have the children and their mother speak to each other for the first time in five years. Come in, Jim."

Jim came in, and I almost went out of my head to hear my mother's voice over the air waves! We talked to one another, all of us in turn, following the stilted, phony script, and the words turned to ashes in my mouth. It was a high price to pay, and we paid it as willingly as we could.

Louise: "Annie, you were only four when I left you. Can you remember me, Annie?"
Annie: "I think so. I remember a nice looking lady and I think it's you."
Louise: "I hope I can live up to that, Annie."

Jim Ameche closed the show saying: "The children will see you next week in Hollywood and I certainly wish I could be there at that reunion." His brother Don said, "Thank you for being with us. We know your reunion with the children will be a very joyous one."

Later, we learned that people cried when they heard this broadcast and the studio received dozens of letters about our "heart-rending story." I have often wondered how the media would have handled a follow-up report on "The Four Little Smiths and How They Grew."

We travelled across the country on the Pennsylvania Trailblazer which was crowded with soldiers going to the war we'd recently left behind, and it took us a week to make the journey. I spent the time writing brief descriptions of Vincent, Jordie and Annie for our mother, and I suppose something of myself emerged from these vignettes. I also wrote short accounts of our time in Chapei and of the trips on the "Teia Maru" and the "Gripsholm" which my mother saved.

I watched the countryside rushing by as we hurtled toward Los Angeles and perhaps the reason I busied myself with writing introductions of my brothers and sister was because I felt the four little corners we'd made into a very special world would not be standing in quite the same way ever again. The week in New York had dulled the keen edge of my yearning. The days of waiting before we were allowed to speak to Louise, and then only on the radio with no private moment between us, augured ill in my mind, and my heart was heavy with foreboding and uneasiness.

Train rides, I thought, give one too much time to think.

Louise showing Rita Hayworth our photograph. Columbia Studios, Hollywood, 1'

Louise above with Rita Hayworth in Hollywood showing a picture of The Four Of Us before she saw us for the first time in five years.

EPILOGUE

What actually happens to one is of very little significance compared to what one does in a given set of circumstances. The only relevant aspect of any human adventure is how one behaves during whatever it is that occurs; how one deals with the vicissitudes of life; and how one plays the hand that is dealt. Nothing else really matters.

It was as if Louise had come to fetch us in a canoe, and I, overburdened with five years' accumulation of totally unrealistic expectations, was unwilling and unable to come aboard without this excess baggage to which I clung so desperately. Not surprisingly, the unseaworthy little craft foundered and capsized in the first storm, and I learned that happy endings came true mostly in books.

We came apart as a unit, The Four Of Us, but we remained close to one another, and are still loving and delighted in each other's company. We grew up and found our own way in the world, working and raising families of beautiful children who will do the same in their time.

We did what we knew best how to do.

We got on with our lives

Mary Vincent Anne George
1972

This picture was taken in my living room in Fresno, California in early September, 1972, when the four of us were together for the first time in several years.

A bird's-eye view of the Bund and waterfront in Shanghai, as it appeared in 1949.

MARCH 20, 2005, SAN FRANCISCO CHRONICLE MAGAZINE

www.ingramcontent.com/pod-product-compliance
Lightning Source LLC
Chambersburg PA
CBHW071424150426
43191CB00008B/1037

* 9 7 8 0 7 8 8 4 5 3 4 7 2 *